CYCLE ZOO
STEPHEN NURSE

BIKES FOR THE 21ST CENTURY

Published by Silverbird Publishing

First published in Australia in 2021 by Stephen Nurse
© 2021 Stephen Nurse

ISBN: 978-0-6489252-4-8

Contact: modularbikes.com.au
instagram@stevenurseau

This work is copyright. All rights reserved. Apart from any fair dealing for the purposes of study, research or review, as permitted under Australian copyright law, no part of this publication may be reproduced, distributed, or transmitted in any other form or by any means, including photocopying, recording, or other electronic or mechanical methods, without the prior written permission of the publisher.

 A catalogue record for this book is available from the National Library of Australia

Cover images by Stephen Nurse

Table of Contents

Acknowledgements		iv
Foreword		v
Introduction		vii
1	Cycling Principles	1
2	Bicycles and Components	22
3	Cycle Commuting	42
4	Electric Cycles and Vehicles	47
5	Cycling for a Cause with Gayle Potts	55
6	City Cycling with Nell Sudano	66
7	Recumbent Bikes	78
8	Speedbikes with Adam Hari	99
9	Recumbent Trikes, Velomobiles and Quads	111
10	Tandems	134
11	Carrying Loads and Passengers	150
12	Crate Bikes by Steve Nurse	171
13	Kids' Bikes	181
14	Modular Cycles	189
15	Cycle Stability	199
16	Tilting Trikes	208
17	Some Long-wheelbase Front-wheel Drives	229
18	Tools	255
19	Digital and Design Tools	262
20	Materials for Cycle Building	277
21	A Boardgame with Alyson McDonald	286
Appendix: Rise of rear pivot in Vuong Trikes		300
Glossary		301
Picture credits		307

Acknowledgements

Thanks to everyone concerned with making this book.
It couldn't have been done without:

My family Christine and Ewan Nurse and Phoebe Venables

Contributors Gayle Potts, Nell Sudano, Alyson McDonald, Adam Hari and Daniel Oakman

Blogger and photographer Jun Nogami, https://jnyyz.wordpress.com/

Photographer Kim Aagaard, https://www.instagram.com/bicycles_only/

John Hagan and Jeremy Lawrence, back cover photos

Encouragement from Carole Wilkinson

Editor Neil Conning and designer Luke Harris

And lastly technical editor and contributor George Durbridge.

Foreword

My mind fizzed with a heady mix of nervous excitement and something close to fear. 'Just lie back and relax', was the only instruction offered to me, as I lay back onto the seat, lifted my feet to the pedals and started to roll down the hill. As my speed increased, so too did my anxiety. At any moment I expected to lose control and crash, but I didn't. As my momentum dissipated, I wobbled to a stop. I walked the bike back up the hill and made another descent, then another, and another, my confidence growing with every ride. I was now riding a recumbent bicycle, a machine I had only gazed at from afar, unsure how it was even physically possible for the rider to remain upright from their reclined position. I tried many different bikes that day. Once I found the right one for me, I soon became proficient at pedalling while lying comfortably on my back. It would take time for the strangeness of that sensation to fade, and to feel like I wasn't riding in violation of the laws of physics.

Mastering that wondrous contraption was a revelation. It renewed my passion for long-distance riding and introduced me to a wider network of cyclists. I was now a member of the cycling zoo, to use Steve's inclusive phrase for the diverse community of cycle designers, makers and riders that he examines in his new book, *Cycle Zoo*.

I hasten to add that *Cycle Zoo* is not a history of recumbentry. It is much more than that. The diversity of people, machines and ideas explored in this book is extraordinary and inspiring. Steve examines all manner of cycles, from tandems and tilting trikes to cargo bikes, recumbents and speedbikes. He speaks with cycle designers and volunteer groups such as Wecycle, a social enterprise group that refurbishes and rehomes used bicycles. There is a fascinating section on reusing existing material to create one's own cycles, being Steve's field of expertise. Steve treats all members of the zoo with generosity and respect, honouring their creativity and ingenuity.

There is quiet rebelliousness in the stories told in the *Cycle Zoo*. Corporate interests have long shaped the kind of bikes and clothes that Australian riders have been able to buy. The largest commercial manufacturers have forced riders to bend and adapt their bodies to the machines they produce, based on the erroneous assumption that everyday riders aspire to dress and ride like professional cyclists. Steve's book rejects the constraints imposed by the manufacturing giants. Instead, he rejoices in the agency and creativity that each of us possesses. He writes about how to rethink the way we ride in ways that respond to individual needs as well as the needs of the environment. If Australian cycling culture is to evolve into a more sophisticated and responsive force, the inclusivity celebrated here is an important way forward.

In Steve's words, '*Cycling is ... a rolling together of science, history, art, society, engineering but most of all human tenacity.*' He might have added one more theme: joy. Steve's book is the story of the human powered vehicle, in all its richness and variety. It is about the satisfaction that comes with designing and making things for ourselves. Above all, it is a celebration of riding and exploring the world by human power (or perhaps with just a little electrical assistance). At this point in history, a time of environmental uncertainty and virus-enforced isolation, I cannot think of a more timely and relevant publication.

So, lie back, relax, and enjoy Steve's grand tour of the cycle zoo.

Daniel Oakman, November 2020

Daniel is the author of *Wild Ride: Epic Cycling Journeys through the Heart of Australia* (Melbourne Books, 2020) and *Oppy: The Life of Sir Hubert Opperman* (Melbourne Books, 2018).

Introduction

For many, degradation of the environment due to climate change, overuse of cars, and reliance on non-renewable resources are serious issues. It may seem impossible for us to help, but it isn't. At least on a personal level we can change to improve the environment for ourselves and our kids. An example is using human powered or low-pollution transport when we can. This is healthy, worthy and fun.

In the early 1900s, engineers and scientists moved away from designing bicycles to motorcycles, cars and aircraft. The big challenges of this century are to do with the environment, and I hope that engineers and scientists will again take up cycle design. Designing, working on and building cycles is a small-scale, enjoyable process. It satisfies, and helps our personal and collective environments.

This book is about cycling in a broad sense — 'human powered land transport' — and starts where many bike books leave off. As well as bicycles, it discusses tandems, recumbent bikes and trikes, family cycling, load cycles and prototypes. There are many hundreds of machines available as human powered land transport and the introduction diagrams show cycles with their speed, load carrying capacity and cost. They are an attempt at 'the big picture of cycling' and should help you work out what sort of cycle you might want. Of course there are other criteria for human powered vehicles, such as size, what we are used to, what our friends like, off-road ability, passenger carrying, weight, appearance and colour, and these are important too. Most of all, have fun!

Although this book is divided into chapters, information is spread throughout. For example, tandems are discussed in the modular bikes chapter, trikes in the tandems chapter, and there is information on all cycles in the materials chapter. If a word or acronym looks difficult or unusual, I have included a glossary, and you might find it there. To simplify, I have mostly used inch wheel sizes: 16", 20", 24", 28". This is because a 20" wheel is usually 20" (508mm) outside diameter. Metric wheel sizes (say 700C) don't define diameter because they depend on tyre size.

0.1   Cycling jobs by speed and load.

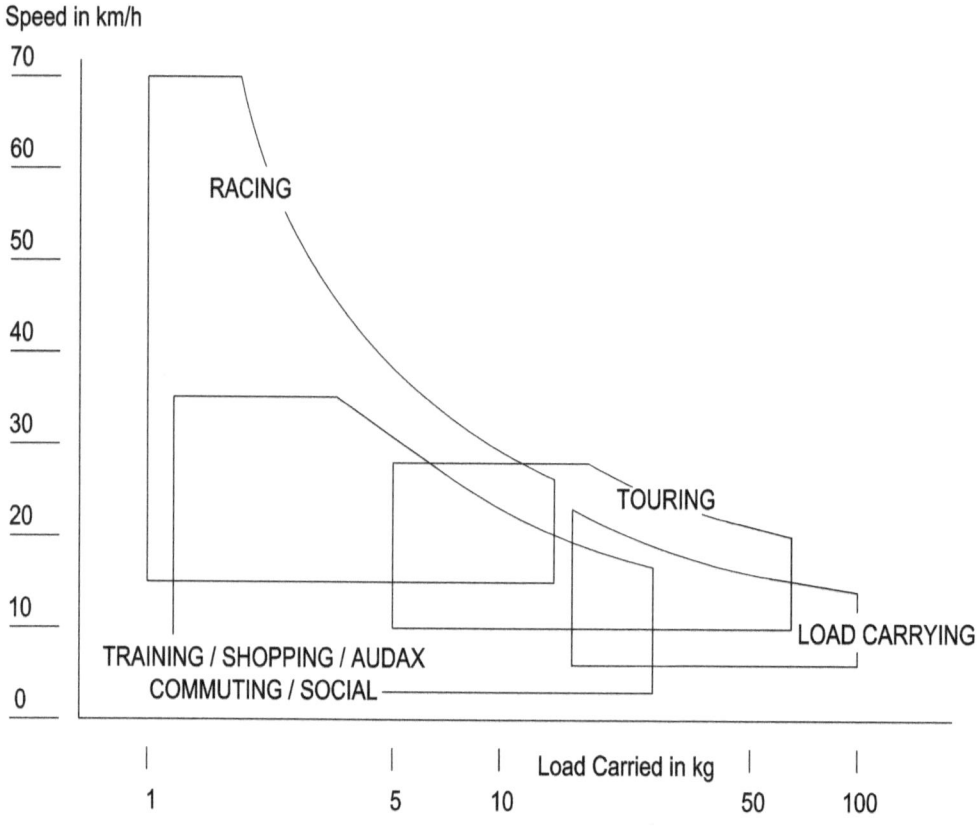

0.2 Cycle types by maximum speed and load capacity.

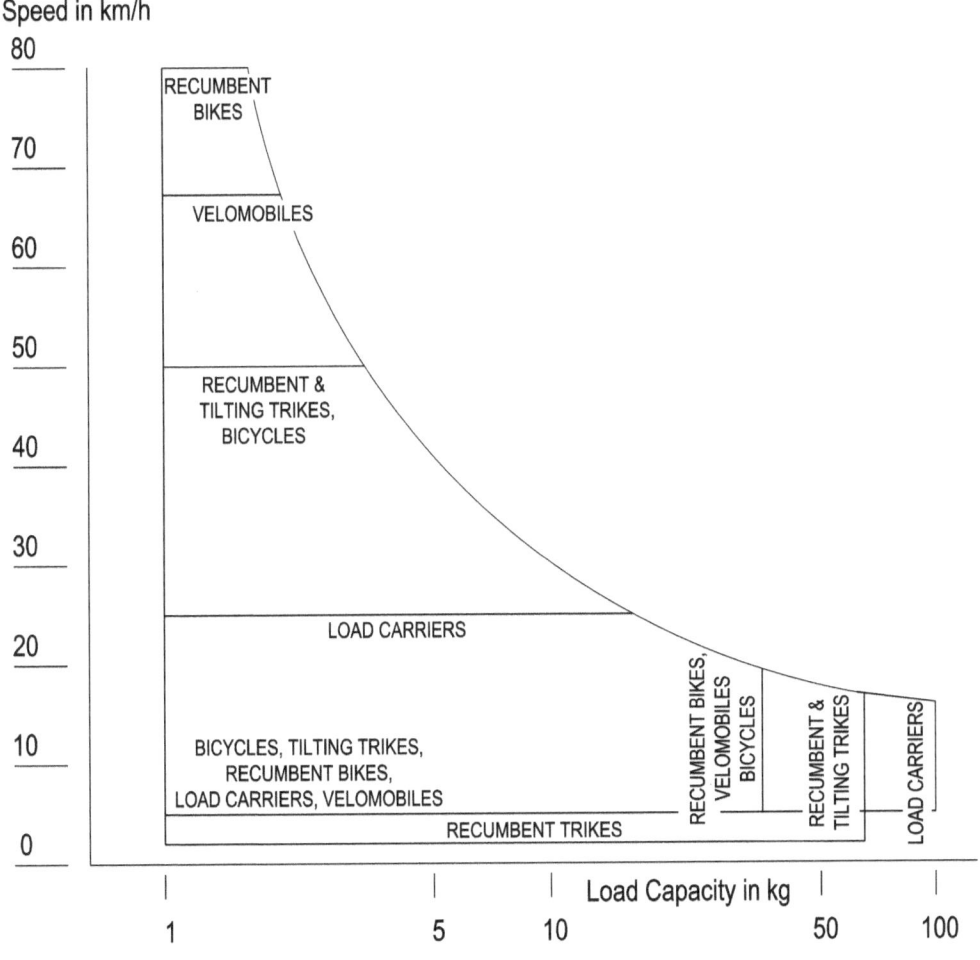

CYCLE ZOO

0.3 Cycle types and costs in Australian dollars.

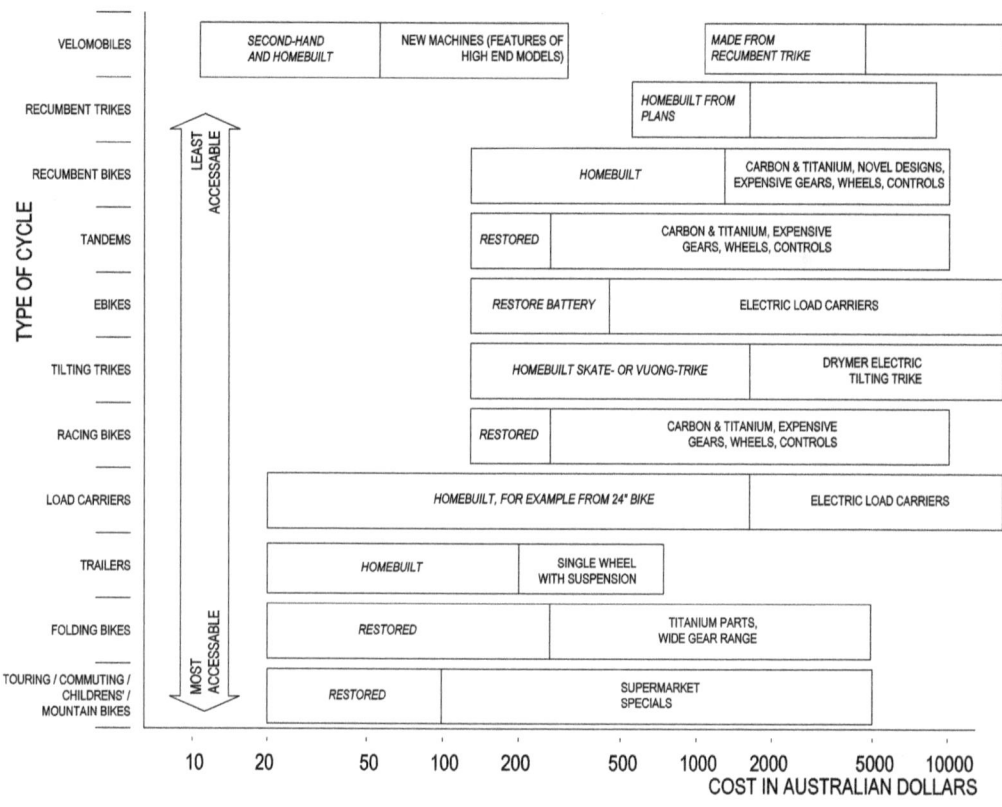

1 Cycling Principles

Cycles depend on inventions and concepts including structural tubes, roller bearings, pneumatic tyres, levers, cables, symmetry and suspension. Laws of physics relating to mass and acceleration, pressure and area, wind and rolling resistance govern cyclists' performances. Most of this cycling engineering was described in Archibald Sharp's book *Bicycles and Tricycles* in 1896, and I am re-presenting some of it here.

This chapter also includes industrial design elements, because how people promote and perceive designs is vital to how bikes are made and sold. As Wiebe Bijker says, 'A successful engineer is not purely a technical wizard but an economical, political, and social one as well.'

Mass, acceleration and gravity

The mass of a laden cycle (cycle, rider and luggage) is important because:
- Stopping or starting needs force proportional to mass. This means that, for the same effort, a light laden cycle will start and stop faster than a heavy one.
- Climbing needs force proportional to the laden mass and related to the slope. A combination of rider and cycle will have a slope angle that's too steep and can't be climbed. With all else equal, a heavier cycle will always stop on a shallower slope and be slower uphill.
- The mass of the cycle itself is only critically important when racing, or when picking it up to load into a car or onto public transport. Down hills, mass helps cycles go faster, but unfortunately we can't have downhills all the time!

Structural elements

So cycles need to be light for acceleration and to be driven uphill without overexertion, and this needs sensible use of materials. For example, a bike made of solid steel bars would not use material efficiently, and would cost and weigh a lot. Hollowing out a 25mm round steel bar to 1 or 2mm wall thickness keeps much of its strength while reducing weight (1.1). The same principles apply to aluminium/titanium/glass and carbon-fibre-reinforced plastic tubes and square/oval/other shaped tubes. Tubular structures that have high strength-to-weight ratios don't just occur in manufactured parts; they are in nature-engineered materials like bones and bamboo as well.

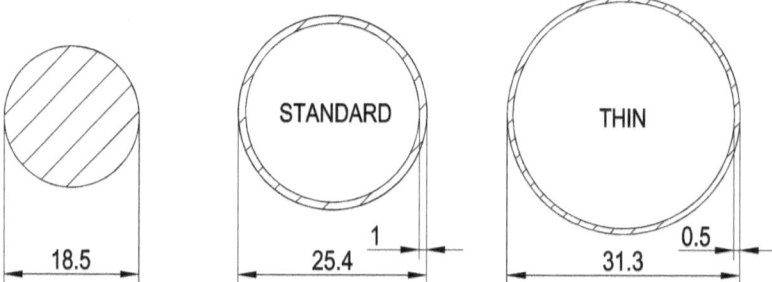

1.1 Beam profiles which twist equally under the same force. The solid weighs 3.5 times the standard tube and the thin tube weighs 0.63 times the standard.

When a tubular beam is loaded to support weight, the depth of section affects performance and efficiency (1.2). Non-tubular beams such as 'I' beams (rotated 'H' beams) are often used in buildings and other structures that make sensible, sparing use of material.

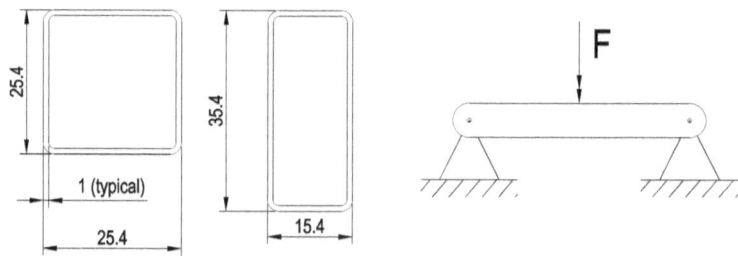

1.2 Depth of Section: The rectangular beam resists bending 1.6 times as well as the square, although they weigh the same.

Beams including triangle shapes (roof or bridge trusses) make strong and efficient structures. So conventional bike frames from tubes arranged in triangles are strong for their weight.

As well as structural principles to follow, there are ones to avoid. Sudden diameter changes and holes in tubes cause stress concentrations and eventual cracking. Workarounds include radiusing, tapering and reinforcing tubes as shown in 1.3.

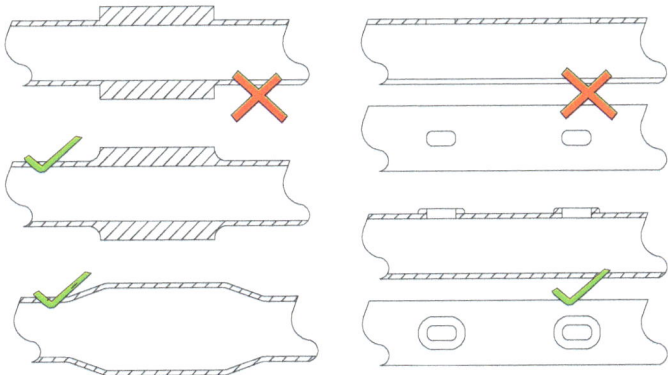

1.3   Structural dos and don'ts. Left: Sharp corners concentrate stress leading to cracks. Right: Holes concentrate stress.

Levers

A lever is a machine: it transforms motion by decreasing movement while increasing force or increasing movement while decreasing force (1.4). Torque (force × distance) remains equal. On cycles, levers wrangle power from what we can produce (pedal rotation by leg power at appropriate speeds) to what we want (forward motion for transport).

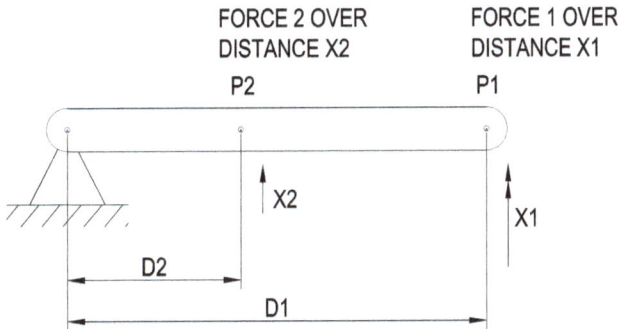

1.4   Levers increase force while decreasing motion, i.e. at P2, F2 = F1 × (D1/D2) and X2 = X1 × (D2/D1). Force at P2 acts oppositely, decreasing force and increasing motion at P1.

Levers can act with a central static point or fulcrum (1.5), and act through rods or chains (1.6). Cycle drives use both principles. A bike chain on sprockets is a continually acting lever, creating a higher angular velocity in the driven wheel than in the driving wheel.

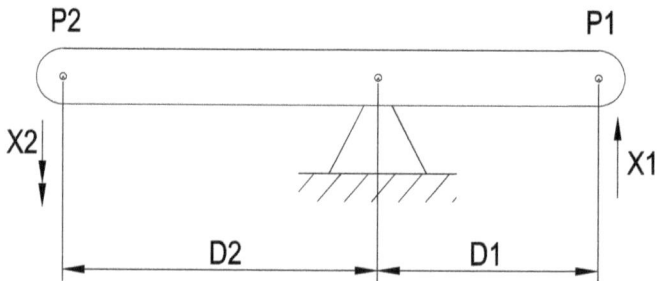

1.5 Lever acts through fulcrum decreases force and increase motion, i.e. at P2, Force F2 = F1 * (D1/D2) and distance X2 = X1 * (D2/D1)

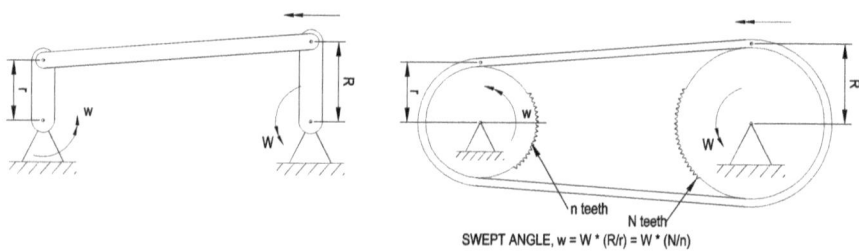

1.6 Rod lever and its chain drive equivalent.

A rod pressing on a second rod acts as a lever. The force and velocity at the contact point is the same on each rod, but the longer rod moves with less angular velocity but more torque due to length ratios (1.7). The continuously acting machine based on these levers is the meshed gear (1.7). These are used in hub (rear wheel centre) gearboxes using epicyclic geartrains and providing 2-14 gear ratios.

Some cycles have two chain drives, or a gear hub combining hub and derailleur gears such as the Sturmey Archer CS-RF3. The gear element ratios are multiplied to establish an overall ratio.

1 Cycling Principles

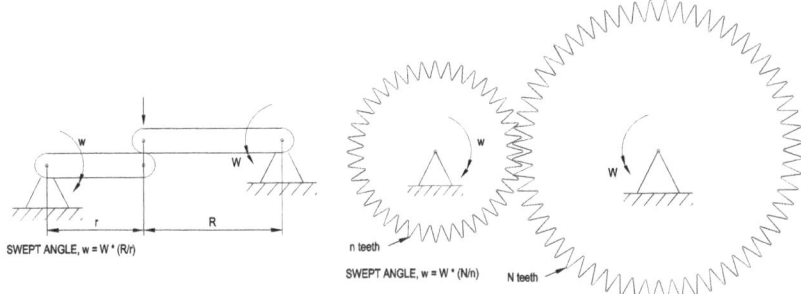

1.7   Pressure lever and its gear drive equivalent.

Pedalling, chains and gearboxes operate continuously. However, gearchanges and braking occur only intermittently, and are actuated through cables and levers. As cable inners are pulled, brakes and gears are actuated through tension, and a reacting compression is carried by cable outers and the bike frame. Cable inners can't work in compression, and return to rest position is done by springs, stops and friction mechanisms (1.8).

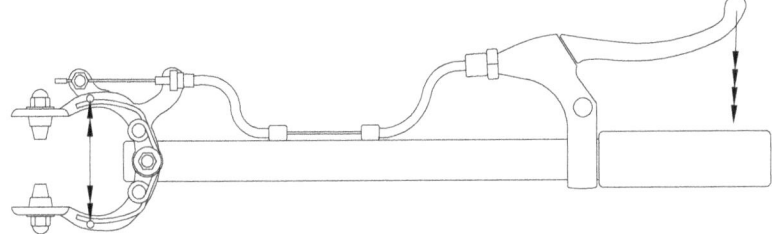

1.8   Brake systems include cable inners in tension. Cable outers and the frame are compressed, and lever force overcomes spring force to actuate.

The chain, and brake and gear control are the cycle's push-and-pull components. They transmit power and control from the rider to the cycle.

Push and pull

Literal push-and-pull cycle components are described above, but in making cycles there is also figurative push-and-pull relating to demand.

If you are a bike maker, and a customer wants your product by a given date, there is motivation to complete on time and do a good job. A customer is 'someone wanting it', and it could be yourself preparing a bike for a race, making a bike for a friend's birthday present, or a client paying money. Even if nobody wants the bike, creating a schedule or artificial 'pull' motivation makes sense. We all want to achieve things, and having completion dates helps.

A method of creating 'pull' for a product is patronage. This is where sponsors commission work or employ an artist or craftsperson for special works. This still exists, but in the world of unusual bikes there are now alternatives such as internet crowdsourcing to create pull.

Crowdsourcing is a method of empowerment, but the artist or craftsperson needs to sell their ideas and their ability to reproduce them to a selective audience. Bell Cycles make a very short front-wheel-drive cycle that was successfully crowdfunded (http://bellcycles.com).

So far this topic has only mentioned pull, but sometimes push production is necessary. 'Push production' means making for stock based on anticipated demand, not actual demand. This can be unavoidable in small-scale bike production. The aluminium section for my bike frames comes in 6m lengths. I can't buy or obtain shorter lengths, so have no choice but to buy three frames worth for anticipated demand. Similarly, for me laser cutting involves design, obtaining quotes, obtaining material, delivering material and finally picking up products. The time and effort spent on parts make it worth buying extra parts for a small extra cost even if demand is low.

Suspension

Suspension is a cycle's handling of bumps, and good suspension isolates riders from bumps and minimises energy loss and deceleration. Almost every cycle has variable suspension in the form of pneumatic tyres. Here are suspension options for comfort and less energy loss:
- Larger cycle wheels rise slower over bumps and are passive suspension (1.9).
- Isolating cycle parts gives reduced unsprung masses. Some mountain and folding bikes have full suspension; that is both wheels on small suspended sub-frames (1.10).
- Town bikes can have suspended seats, isolating just the rider (1.10).
- Riders who stand on the pedals turn their legs into springs over bumps. Arms have this sort of resilience most of the time (1.11).
- Isolation can be achieved by having long distances between wheels and the rider. Some recumbents with small front wheels use this suspension type. However, a lightly laden front wheel puts more weight on the back, so back-wheel suspension then needs consideration.

On recumbents, mesh seats and padded seats are part of suspension (1.12). Flexible frame elements give small but important amounts of suspension. Flexible frame elements include carbon fibre forks, seat and chainstays, and a titanium crossbeam in the Azub Ti-Fly trike (1.13).

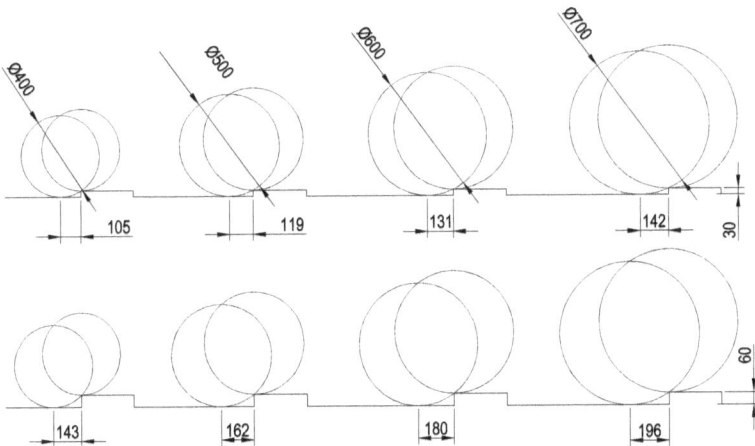

1.9   Distances for rise over 30 and 60mm bumps for various wheel sizes.

1.10   Full suspension and seat suspension isolate riders from harsh terrain (unsprung masses hatched).

1.11   Suspension by standing on pedals (unsprung masses hatched).

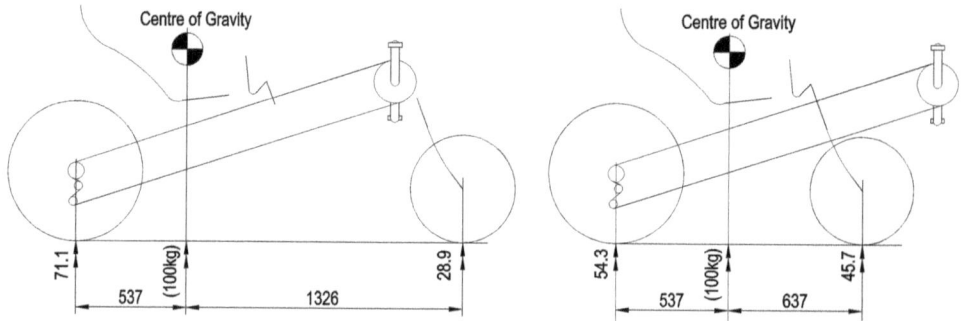

1.12 Wheel loads of recumbents weighing 100kg with the rider. The longer bike has passive front-wheel suspension at the cost of more weight at the back.

1.13 Giant OCR1 road bike: carbon front forks, chainstays and seatstays (hatched) for suspension.

In all suspension design, care must be taken to avoid bobbing, which is flexing of suspension elements during pedalling. It wastes energy and reduces speed.

Pressure and area

The pressure on a surface is the force acting on it divided by its area. Pressure and area help explain the comfort of a bike and how well it rolls.

Seating: Humans are a fragile collection of mostly liquid supported by bone and surrounded by skin. Rapid acceleration or deceleration or too much pressure causes pain — nature's way of saying 'stop the wounding'. For comfort, you need to reduce pressure by sitting or lying on something large and/or soft

(1.14, 1.15). Soft surfaces change shape to better support the body and absorb acceleration or gravity force, and include gels, mesh seats, foams, chamois, cloths, leather and sheepskin.

1.14   Timber and artificial turf on crates increase area and softness (large area bike seat in background).

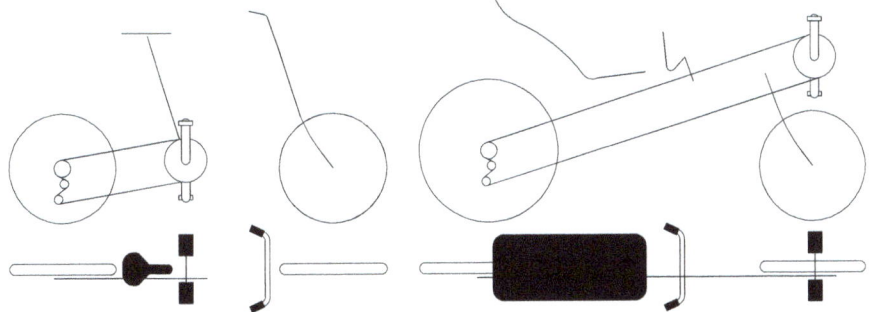

1.15   Bicycle and recumbent bicycle showing areas supporting the body.

On bicycles, the body is supported on the bottom, feet and hands by the saddle, handlebars and pedals. The percentage of body weight borne by bottom, feet and hands depends on the rider's posture.

Upright riding on a roadster can cause the least body stress because weight is concentrated on seat and pedals, and the seat is a generous size and often suspended. Roadsters are usually ridden in street clothing.

A bent-over racing bike set-up is more likely to be painful because the saddle area is often small and hard, and there is increased neck stress and wrist pressure. Racing bikes are rarely ridden without padded shorts, and the bike has to be set up well to avoid pain when riding long distances.

On recumbents with reclined backrests, body weight is taken by the backrest and seat. The hands rest on the steerer but don't bear much weight. Feet are usually clipped in to pedals, so legs hang from pedals rather than rest on them. Because the seat is large and pressures on the body are correspondingly low, the seat does not have to be particularly soft to be comfortable, but the rider's back can get sweaty. Sitting on an open-weave mesh seat or using open cushion material such as Ventisit/ACS10 allows air to reach the back, and can help with this ventilation problem. A comparison of seat sizes on recumbent, and uprights is shown in 1.15.

Tyres: As tyres roll, they deform, leading to energy loss and deceleration. This loss is a large part of rolling resistance; and the higher the tyre air pressure, the lower the deformation and rolling resistance.

Bumps waste energy and speed, and hard tyres won't absorb large bumps. Tyre types and pressures for best speed depend on road surface. On firm ground, tyre pressure is a compromise between high pressure/good rolling resistance and low pressure/suspension. Softer ground demands wider, lower pressure tyres. They have a large contact area and deform more but won't waste energy ploughing the ground.

On hard surfaces, almost all cycle tyre tread wastes energy. It is best avoided for city and town cycling on bitumen roads. The heavy tread on inexpensive mountain bike tyres is particularly bad.

Wind resistance: Tyres plough tracks through soft ground. This work done by the bike on the ground slows it down. Less obvious but just as present is work done on the air by cyclists. Just as correct tyre size and pressure minimise ground disturbance, certain cycle shapes and profiles minimise air disturbance.

Cycles that cut through air easily give the rider/cyclist combination a low frontal surface area and a smooth, sleek shape/low drag coefficient. These properties are especially important at high speeds, so it should come as no surprise that the speed-record-breaking cycles of this world are enclosed recumbent speedbikes whose design emphasises aerodynamics at the expense of everything else.

Good aerodynamic shapes have rounded front edges, gradually tapering trailing edges, and are 'clean' without extra protrusions. Good aerodynamic shapes (sometimes described as 'teardrop') help a cycle travel fast whether small (frame tube, spoke, tyre rim) or large scale (overall cycle shape) Good aerodynamic shapes are 'rounded in three dimensions' and the ideal shape is something like an airship balloon, i.e. long and cylindrical, rounded at one end and tapering to a point at the other.

Symmetry

Mostly our bodies look the same right and left, so our mirror-image is almost the same thing other people see. But we know that inside, our heart is on the left, our liver on the right, the two sides of our brain are different, and we may be left- or right-handed, so are not symmetrical inside. Why is that? Symmetry is a way of saving energy, of improving aesthetics, of design simplification, and of reducing the number of systems occurring in a body or in a machine. So things are made as symmetrical as possible, but this has limits, and we notice when symmetry is unconventionally dispensed with or followed slavishly.

Cycle wheels have rotational symmetry. There are many other good examples of symmetry in cycling, and here are a few:

Bike lanes on hilly, busy Lennox Street near us break symmetry for sensible reasons. The street has dedicated bike lanes for hill ascents but no dedicated lane for descents. Looked at from above, it makes no sense, but on the downhills, cyclists can achieve car-comparable speeds, and not hold up cars when mingling with them. On the opposite side, uphill forces dominate cyclists' motion, and they can't travel without holding up cars, so the bike lane is provided.

1.16   Asymmetric road layout, Lennox Street, Abbotsford.

1.17   Quick links have rotational symmetry when assembled. The two halves click into each other to form a chain link.

In cycle bottom brackets and pedals, symmetry is followed slavishly, with left-hand threads on the left side and right-hand threads on the right, but only for a good reason. The pedals and the pedal axis bearings precess or loosen under bearing forces, requiring this thread arrangement.

In the same assembly, the bolts holding the cranks to their centre shaft are both right-hand threaded. A left-handed thread would serve no purpose; and it allows more parallelism and saves money and time to make and stock just one version of the bolt (1.18).

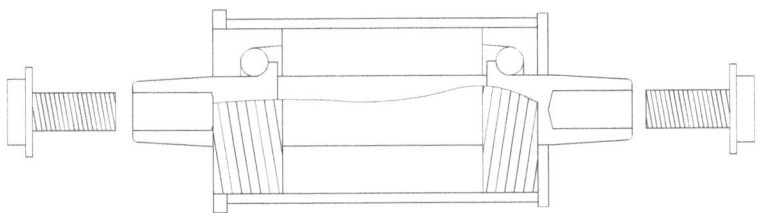

1.18   Symmetry in bottom bracket bearing includes symmetrical threading.

Brake actuators are often very similar on each side, in fact so similar that, within a set, a left-hand lever works just as well on the right-hand side, and vice versa. So manufacturers could make just one version of a brake lever, and supply two of them as a set, but that does not happen for reasons of symmetry and appearance. Brake actuators are fitted so their mechanism is hidden from the outside of the bike, which is more aesthetically pleasing. It may cost slightly more in tooling for the parts, but parts manufacturers are in business; they just get on with it.

While the way brake actuators look on handlebars is symmetrical, with few exceptions, the way they act on the bike is not. One lever acts to stop the front wheel, and the other acts to stop the back wheel; and bicycle dynamics causes tipping under heavy front braking. This hidden asymmetry is like left and right handedness in people.

Some braking systems don't have this asymmetry: bikes I have developed have both brakes on the front wheel with a different weight distribution preventing tipping, and tadpole recumbent trikes have the right brake retarding the right wheel, and the left brake retarding the left.

Bicycle frames are symmetrical with the exception of some threads and bosses. However, the chain is mounted asymmetrically on the right side, causing asymmetric forces. Pinarello have calculated chain forces within racing-cycle frames and design them asymmetrically. This reduces weight by removing material in areas of reduced stress (https://road.cc/content/feature/227118-design-classic-pinarello-dogma-and-how-it-came-dominate-tour-de-france).

Cantilever wheels

For a small machine, a cycle has a multitude of bearings. They are on wheels, pedals, bottom bracket, steering and suspension.

Pedals are an example of a bearing set supported on one side only or on a cantilever. Conventionally, bike wheels are supported on both sides, but there's no good reason why they can't be cantilever-supported. Heavy duty (14mm diameter) BMX wheel axles permit this without making a custom axle.

On bikes, having wheels held on one side only is asymmetrical, something requiring acceptance because we are not used to it. Perhaps the best known cantilever bike wheel is the Cannondale 'Lefty' fork, and Mike Burrows uses them extensively on his designs including the 8-freight longtail load carrier.

Wheelchair wheels, most trike wheels and all car wheels are supported on a cantilever. On cycles, cantilever support for a wheel:
- allows tube replacement without first removing the wheel from a frame
- can have aerodynamic and weight benefits
- permits a compact fold for folding bikes.

Function

Some people are healthy with good balance, and for them bicycles are functioning machines for transport and exercise. But for those with balance issues bicycles can be non-functioning, and only recumbent trikes have the stability they need for cycling. This is selection based on need, but we often have choices too, and choices are still part of function.

In 1970, Victor Papanek described a 'function complex', dealing with assessing objects. Papanek's descriptions are a start on making sense of design. He breaks design function into digestible chunks of Need, Use, Method, Association, Telesis, and an overriding simple aesthetically pleasing element called Elegance.

Need: When inventions first become popular, they do so in unembellished forms fulfilling needs. The rear-wheel-drive safety bicycle — or just 'bicycle' as we know it today — fulfilled immediate needs for economic transport for a wide range of people and situations. Unlike a horse, it did not need to be fed, watered and cleaned up after, and unlike its high penny farthing predecessors it was not precarious. To many people including women and the elderly, it was the first working (rideable/affordable/useable/safe) personal transport device. Later, cars and motorcycles became working transport options and cycling inventions filled lesser needs.

Necessary products don't require proper engineering to be useful; it is just that we can be conditioned that way. For example a local cafe started selling take-away coffee when Coronavirus restrictions started. People waiting for coffee were provided with outside seating in the form of milk crates, which the cafe dealt with anyway for (no surprises) handling milk bottles. They used the crates expediently (1.14) because of need.

Use: Answers 'Does it work?' When a product has reached its intended user, and they are applying it for its intended purpose, does it do its job well? This may seem like a designer's core and only task, but reaching a point where the product is in the user's hands is a huge and significant struggle as well.

Method: Described by Papanek as the interaction between tools, processes and materials, this promotes an honest use of materials, never making them seem what they are not. This is promoting harmony and ease in the way things are made; not struggling to achieve results.

Association: We have grown up in a world made by human beings, and are conditioned by what we see and consider normal. What we like we consider desirable. What if something new comes along? It will require thought and consideration of appearance and use before acceptance. However, some elements of design can be associated with familiar objects, softening the impact of complete novelty. In bicycles, high riser bars echoing the styling of a dragster bike, or layout evoking the shape of a motorcycle petrol tank can create positive associations. Using timber as trim creates environmental associations, and some Cruzbikes and other highracer recumbents maintain association with more familiar racing bikes by using racing bike wheels and parts collections or groupsets.

Telesis: Defined by Papanek as deliberate, purposeful use of nature's and society's processes to obtain particular goals, this is a fitting-in with society and economic order. Telesis helps explain why some ideas and products work well in one culture but not others.

Elegance: Aesthetics involves creating forms that move and please us, and are exciting and beautiful. Achieving aesthetics in the simplest form to satisfy Need, Use, Method, Association and Telesis is a statement of Elegance.

Upcycling, simplicity and do-it-yourself

Upcycling or 'do it with already made stuff' (DIWAMS) is a philosophy promoted by Paulo Hartmann in *Open Design Now*. Conventionally designers consider that thousands of their item will be made, so they make samples and prototypes in the best possible way, even if it costs more. Money is lost on the first item because of the trouble taken. But, DIWAMS is not designing with a blank sheet of paper; you are adapting what's already available, potentially using what could otherwise become waste.

When Cruzbike first marketed a recumbent bike, it came as a kit to attach to a suspended mountain bike. The cheap, common customer-supplied bike helped make an exotic machine, and saved on the labour, freight, sourcing and buying involved in delivering a complete bike. Choosing a donor bike and assembling the new bike involved the customer in do-it-yourself or DIY design and creation, making them a proud fan of their Cruzbike.

An approach that can be used in design is to 'do it with already made energy'. For several years I have been a fan of separating bikes that use gravity assist in the action of the frame join. Tinkering with the design led to familiarity, copying and eventually to my own version in a separating trike. This trike is shown in 1.14 and also features brake levers reversed to sit in the palms of the hands. Instead of relying entirely on hand grip, actuation is helped by the natural forward body motion of deceleration.

Upcycling parts to make cycles can be called a tool of simplicity. Other tools of simplicity include avoiding and disentanglement. 1.19 shows the example of old cantilever brakes and newer V-brakes. The V-brakes avoid the need for cable supports required in cantilever brakes. They also eliminate the cable running vertically above the brakes, disentangling the reflector bracket from the brake.

1.19   Cantilever brakes (left) are more complex than V-brakes (right).

Series/parallel

These terms are used in electronic circuitry, where two light globes connected in series (in a row, one after the other) along a wire produce different electrical currents compared to the same globes connected in parallel (on separate connected circuits). In bikes, spokes act in parallel to support rims, and brake components (brake lever, cable, V-brake arm) act in series to put pressure on a rim to decelerate.

Series and parallel activities are part of many things we do. As we start an oven-cooked meal, we preheat the oven, prepare what needs to be put in the oven, put it in the oven, and then go about our business. Later, when it's only half an hour or so before serving we do other things needed to complete the meal, like peeling, boiling and mashing potatoes, setting the table and pouring drinks. The meal can be seen as a project with serial (potato peeling, boiling, mashing) and parallel (oven cooking) activities blending together.

Making buildings, bridges and bicycles are all projects that are only completed on time through planning. This means timely starting of all parallel, potentially simultaneous activities needed for completion. 1.20 shows activities needed to get prototype electric motors out of a factory. Planning got effective results, and having the tasks visible was good for creating a team effort and communicating problems. Having tasks completed early is good and beneficial, but tasks running late compromise entire schedules.

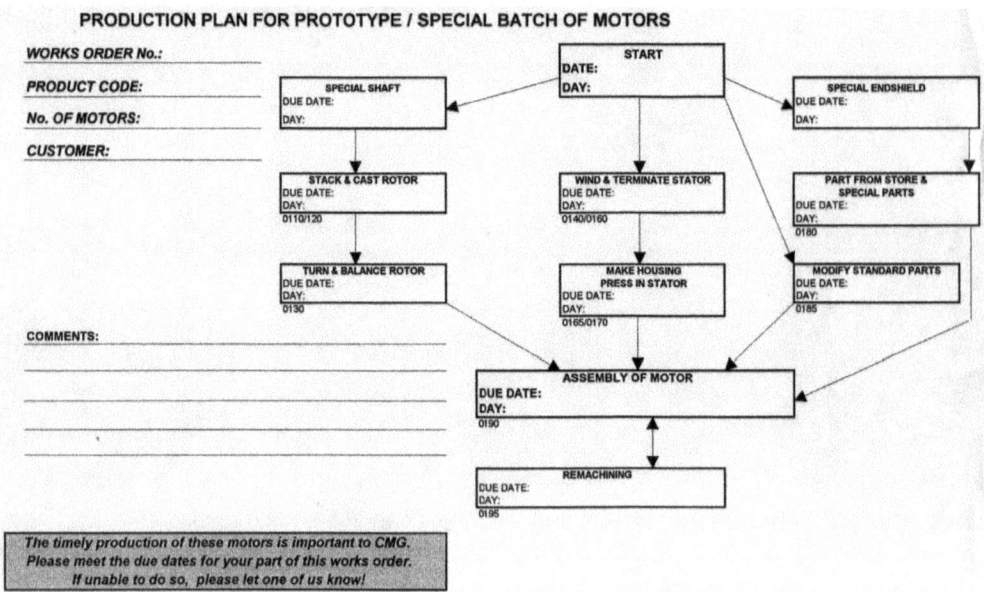

1.20 Electric motor production schedule showing serial and parallel activities.

For bridges, bicycles and buildings, this sort of planning is computerised, and ensuring timely delivery of events and goods is called expediting. This can be a full-time job in industry, but there's no reason the same logic can't be applied to your small-scale bike project.

The design of stems (fork and handlebar clamps) for bicycles has changed in recent years, with a clamp surrounding the fork tube replacing a post wedged into it, and a two-part handlebar clamp replacing a single-part clamp (1.21). What do these changes do?

1.21 Clamp and wedge type handlebar stems. Fork threading is eliminated in the clamp stem.

The fork tube clamp eliminates large (approx. 25mm) diameter fork threads, simplifying parts and assembly. The two-part handlebar clamp means handlebar assemblies including brakes, handgrips, bar tape, gear shifters, bell and reflectors can be put together before fitting to the clamp. This allows more parallelism and simpler assembly. It allows the critical steering alignment to be set before the handlebar is assembled onto the bike, and allows it to stay set even with the handlebars removed to compact the cycle for transport. The changes are hidden engineering changes and have no immediate benefits for the rider.

The bike helmet add-ons I have designed and use give another parallelism example. By doing several things, the helmet becomes so useful I like to use it. It is the highest thing on my bike when I ride, so a good place to put lights, reflectors and bright colours to make me more visible. It has a rear-vision mirror supported by Corflute. The Corflute forms a visor protecting my eyes from glare, and face from sun. The helmet's primary role is active head protection, but it only does that job during an accident. The other roles contribute in parallel to function, making me want to wear it except for the very shortest of rides (1.22).

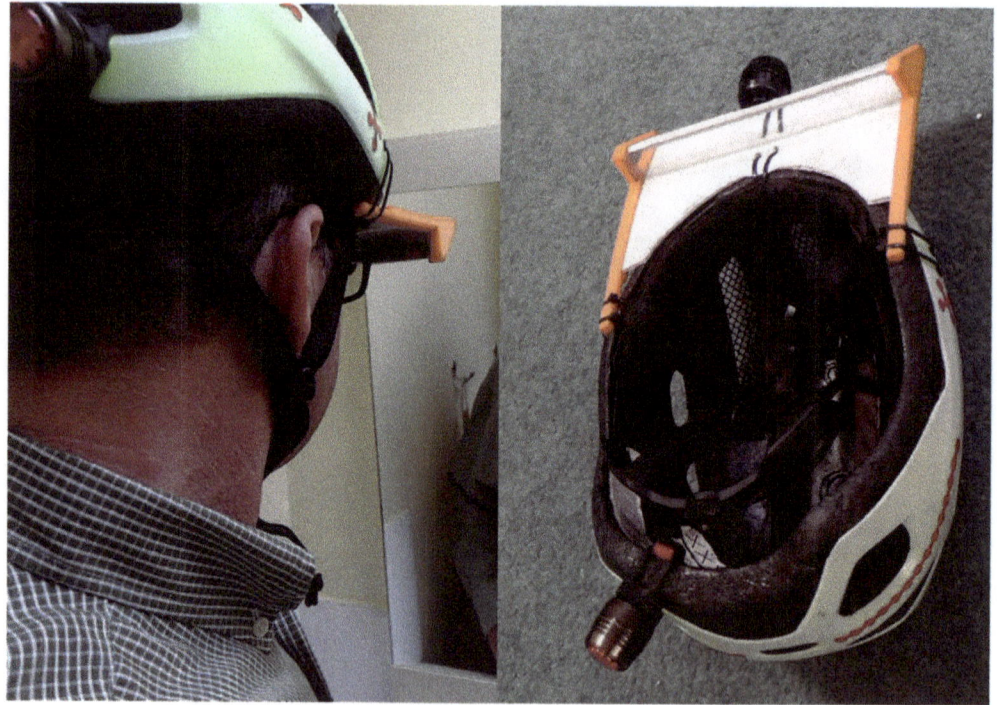

1.22   DIY bright visible helmet with reflective tape, lights, visor and mirror.

Cycling's primary use can be transport, but its secondary aspects add up, operate in parallel, and can tip the balance to make cycling an everyday activity. Cycling is environmentally friendly, can be highly social, and gets you into the neighbourhood so you can see what's going on. Making and fixing bikes can be an interesting hobby, and even short commutes and shopping by bike help maintain fitness.

So when is doing things in parallel not good? Trying to do several things at once can be a problem. When repairing bikes we can be confronted by a new issue and need to work with both hands to complete it in reasonable time. Working in an uncomfortable way or holding on to unneeded tools or parts are obstructing parallel activities. As we repair an item, our brain becomes more wired to do that activity, and we become better at it. So it makes sense in terms of learning tasks to do repairs (say fixing wheels by tightening spokes) in series, one after the other. This makes sense in terms of setting up the task as well: tools for the job must be found, set up and later put away. If they are used many times in a row, this set-up and shutdown happens only once.

Conclusion

Hopefully this mash-up of different principles and concepts is helpful. Cycling is the result of all of them at work, a rolling together of science, history, art, society, engineering; but most of all human tenacity.

References

Bijker, W.E. 1997 Of bicycles, bakelites, and bulbs: toward a theory of sociotechnical change, MIT Press, Cambridge, MA.

Burrows, M., Hadland, T. & Ballantine, R. 2008, Bicycle design: the search for the perfect machine, Snowbooks Limited, Thame, UK.

Jencks, C. & Silver, N. 2013, Adhocism: the case for improvisation, MIT Press, Cambridge, MA.

Goreng B.E. & Tinyou R. Steel designers handbook, New South Wales University Press, 1970.

Maeda, J 2006, The laws of simplicity, MIT Press, Cambridge, MA. Retrieved July 2020 from https://designopendata.files.wordpress.com/2014/05/lawsofsimplicity_johnmaeda.pdf

Papanek, V. & Fuller, R.B. 1972, Design for the real world, Thames and Hudson, London. Retrieved July 2020 through https://designopendata.wordpress.com/portfolio/design-for-the-real-world-human-ecology-and-social-change-1976-victor-papanek

Sharp, A. 2003, Bicycles & tricycles: a classic treatise on their design and construction, Dover Publications, New York. Retrieved July 2020 from http://www.survivorlibrary.com/library/bicycles_and_tricycles-an_elementary_treatise_on_their_design_and_construction_1896.pdf

Thingiverse files for visor by Stephen Nurse: https://www.thingiverse.com/thing:3548763

Van Abel, B., Evers, L., Troxler, P. Hartmann, P. and Klaassen, R., 2014. Open design now: why design cannot remain exclusive. Bis Publishers. Retrieved July 2020 through https://scholar.google.com/scholar?hl=en&as_sdt=0%2C5&q=diwams+hartmann&oq=diwams

Walker, D & Cross, N 1976, Design: the man-made object, Open University Press, Milton Keynes.

2 Bicycles and Components

Bicycles are highly evolved, with many designers and factories creating them. Because of this mass manufacture, building a bicycle from scratch may not be worth the hours spent. After all, inexpensive bicycles are available second-hand and in bike shops. However, repairing, restoring and researching bicycles is enjoyable, and selling or repairing bicycles can earn money or benefit local schools or charities. As well, working on bicycles teaches skills for building human powered vehicles — their more bespoke cousins.

This chapter goes from the front of the bicycle to the back, describing common designs. My riding is shopping, commuting or recreational riding in central Melbourne with no snow, temperatures 0–40°C, not much rain, few unavoidable hills, and paved roads. Less frequent are night riding and long day trips, and naturally I favour bikes that suit my rides.

1970s bicycles

Bicycles with the outward appearance of those we see today became standard by about 1890. Despite this, inventions and trends improving their design have never stopped, and still continue. Here are some observations from the 1970s concerning the best bikes of the day:

Lighting: 'There isn't any good or even barely adequate lighting system.'

Brakes: 'When it's raining ... I ride the one speed coaster brake because rim brakes are not as reliable in wet weather.'

Gears: Although two- and three-speed hub gearboxes were common, there were no wide-range hub gearing systems. Wide-range gearing was derailleur gearing with a rear sprocket maximum range of 13–30 tooth and two or more front chainrings. This gearing does not have simple sequential control, as it requires changing the front chainring when traversing the full gear range. This gearing is still common today.

Shoes: 'Feet should be shod with hard soled, light cycling shoes, with bowling or light leather walking shoes preferable to rubber tennis shoes.'

Today's bicycles

Lighting: LED lighting can be bright and use little power. LED lights can be powered by built-in USB rechargeable batteries, bottle dynamos or sophisticated hub dynamos, which cause little drag.

Brakes: Compared to older steel rims, now-standard aluminium rims are lighter and work better with less drag coefficient reduction in the wet. Disc brakes are readily available. They don't lose performance in the wet and don't depend on precise rim alignment. Thru axles do a good job of securing disc brake wheels in frames.

Gears: Rear sprockets with a range of 11–42 tooth are inexpensive, and high-end mountain bike group sets such as SRAM Eagle have a range of 10–52 tooth. These allow a single chainring to be used on a bike with a wide gear range. Bicycle gearboxes include the Rohloff hub gear with a 526% range and the Pinion frame-mounted gearbox with a 636% range. These are derailleur, hub gear and frame-gearbox options for simple-to-operate, sequentially controlled wide-range gearing.

Shoes: Made-for-cycling shoes are available with or without cleats for clipping into pedals. They are available for commuting, road racing and mountain biking, and many can double as shoes for off-cycle use.

Weight

Weight plays a role in cycle performance. However, cycles do not have to be extremely light to serve most people well. Instead of spending $1,000 more on a bike that is lighter and possibly less durable, it is possible to ride for an hour extra each week, perhaps lose some weight, get fitter and 'go faster' that way. An example is a basic racing (drop-bar) bike weighing 14kg and costing $500. The deluxe version of this bike may weigh 10kg and cost $1,500. Initially, the weight difference may seem huge (40%), but when riding, it's the weight of rider plus bike that counts. If you weigh 80kg then the laden cycles will weigh 94kg (basic) and 90kg (deluxe). The weight difference comes down to 4.4%.

Frame style

The two classic bicycle frame styles are 'diamond frame' with a horizontal top tube (2.1), and 'step-through' (2.2), with a lower top tube meeting the seat tube halfway down. With a higher top tube, diamond frames are harder to mount and dismount, but can be more structurally sound. Mounting step-throughs needs less effort. Although step-throughs are more prone to frame damage such as seat tube bending, it's really only abuse or decades of riding that will cause it.

The 'mixte' (2.3) is a step-through with a clever, stronger frame design. Which style of bike you choose should depend on your mobility, how far you are travelling and how much luggage you carry, with step-throughs better for short laden city cycling. Unfortunately, Australian men can be vain and disinclined to ride step-throughs.

More modern frame styles are often seen in mountain bikes and include diamond frame bikes with a downward sloping top tube, sometimes called a compact geometry frame. These are easier to mount, but often have a large unsupported seat stem (2.4).

Some recent bikes for city riding and easy access emphasise not only frame stepover height but also the foot position when sitting on the saddle and stopped. Juliane Neuss has written about the ergonomics of this style of bike and calls them (City-Rad or) City Bikes. Allowing a flat foot position when stopped gives a sturdy, relaxed position for waiting at traffic lights and starting. This is usually achieved by positioning the seat further behind the pedal cranks, so optimal distances from seat to pedals can be maintained while shortening the distance from the seat to the ground. A low bottom bracket also keeps the seat close to the ground, but this can require shorter pedals with less overall width to avoid pedal-ground strike on bumps and in cornering (2.5, 15.3).

2.1   Diamond frame cycle with horizontal top tube.

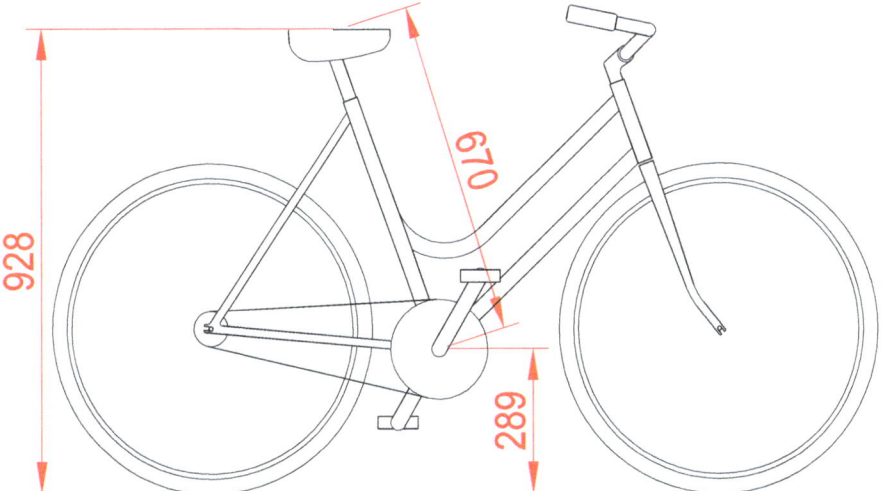

2.2   Step-through bicycle.

2.3   Mixte step-through bicycle.

2.4   Compact geometry bicycle.

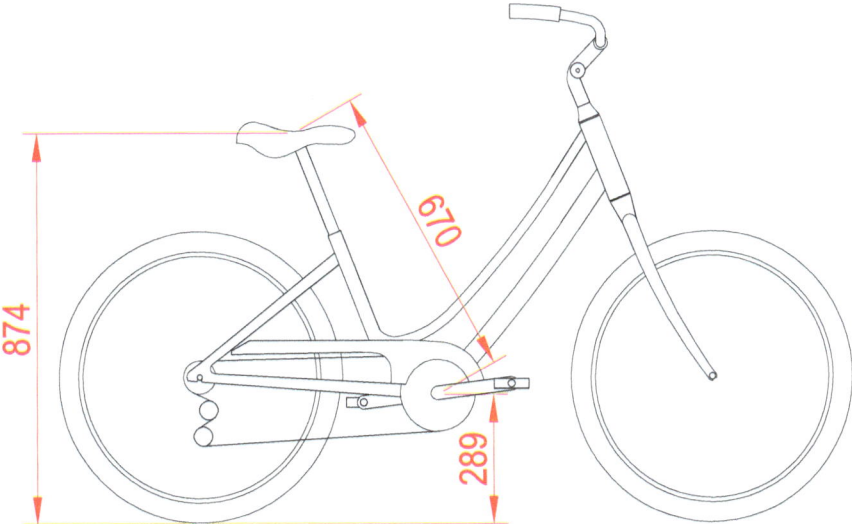

2.5 City Bike step-through.

Folding and small wheeled bikes

Modern folding and small wheel bikes have evolved from a range of early compact and military folding bikes. The compact bikes include Moultons, invented by Dr Alex Moulton in the early 1960s. They were made light and comfortable by combining small wheels with suspension. Although small, their ride is comparable to or better than standard cycles.

By the early 1970s, Moulton designs had been simplified and made worse by English cycling firm Raleigh and others. The resulting bikes were small-wheeled cycles for adults, generally with a low stepover height and no suspension. The Raleigh Shopper is an example, including a hinge for folding in the tube joining seat post and head tube. This increases weight but simplifies carrying in car boots and on trains, buses and trams (Figure 2.6). Folding bikes should be lightweight, not to increase road speed but as part of their portability. They are useless if they cause back pain when lifted onto a train or into the back of a car.

2.6   Folding bicycle with top views on hinge.

Folding bikes have progressed greatly in recent times, and modern folding bikes are designed to perform various jobs very well, for example:

- Bromptons fold small quickly, and are perfect for commutes including cycling and public transport, and for storage in offices or flats. Similar bikes include the Dahon Curl, Tern BYB and Bike Friday Pakit.
- Bike Friday make tandem folders, and some come in a suitcase to which wheels are added to form a bike-towable trailer. The trailer/suitcase and bike form a self-contained touring combination. A quick fold time is not one of the main aims in these designs.
- Tern is a world cycle brand offering folding cycles in 20", 24" and 26" wheel sizes. The larger wheeled Terns are capable touring bikes, and Tern also sell electric bikes.
- Folding recumbents trikes include the Terratrike traveller and Greenspeed GT20. The Trident Twig, Performer Front Wheel Drive and HP Velotechnik Grasshopper are folding recumbent bikes.

Bikes can be made into compactable travel bikes by adding S&S couplings. These are installed in at least two frame tubes and allow the frame to come apart at the coupling using special tools.

Shopping and folding bikes are popular on the second-hand market because they fulfil a need, are relatively rare, and can be quite stylish. Their new counterparts are not always available at low cost.

New folding bikes are available through eBay (selling internationally, i.e. https://www.ebay.com.au) and Ali-express (mainly selling from China, https://

www.aliexpress.com). Sellers get products in front of an interested public without a storefront, save on costs and so can sell competitively.

New bikes sold through the internet may not be well-known brands with complete warranties, so let the buyer beware. Be alert for expensive freight costs and new bikes for less than $100. Bikes with wheel sizes less than 16" are also a problem. They may be very portable, light and promise much, but their lack of rigidity, suspension and sufficiently high gearing can make them unsafe and not much quicker than walking.

Wheels

Tyres: Should have minimal tread and be capable of withstanding high pressures. High-pressure, slick tyres lead to low rolling resistances, and tread is rarely needed on made roads.

Schwalbe, Primo, Continental and Maxxis all make durable tyres that have little tread and withstand high pressure. At relatively low pressures (30psi), Schwalbe 'Big Apple' tyres offer both a small amount of suspension and low rolling resistance.

The rubber on a tyre is not at its most durable when tyres are new, and I have spoken with a road cyclist who deliberately ages tyres for 2 years before putting them on a bike, then moves the tyres through use for competition and commuting before abandoning them after a planned 6-year cycle!

Tubes: Standard tubes with car-type valves are good for most applications. On wheels that are complex to remove or when punctures are particularly undesirable, self-healing (slime) tubes can be used. Tubeless tyre systems using slime are also available. Tubeless systems reduce weight, particularly when large fat tyres are used and a large fat tube is eliminated.

Rim tape: The protective material between a bike rim and the tyre tube. Usually a bike rim has spoke heads protruding through it, and tubes will puncture if exposed to them. For these rims, a cut-up bike tube or strong sticky tape is just about as good as commercial rubber rim tape.

When the wheel rim is double-walled/hollow, the spoke heads can only be seen through the holes in the rim, and strong, cloth rim tape is needed to cover these holes and stop the tube from being forced into the rim by tyre pressure.

Rims and spokes: Aluminium rims are much better than steel rims because they are lighter and stop better in the wet under V- or side-pull (rim) brake pressure. In general, I only like steel rims on the back of 'clunker' or cheap folding bikes where a back-pedal brake is fitted and rim braking is not used. Aluminium rims designed for use with caliper brakes are machined (2.7).

2.7   700C Shimano wheelset with custom aero spokes, 16 front, 20 rear, radial spokes except for rear left-hand side. Spoke nipples are central where they have less drag. Machined rim suits caliper brake.

Disk, drum and hub brakes act at the centre of cycle wheels. These brakes remove requirements for rims designed as a brake surface, and for precise rim alignment. However, like driven rear wheels, disk, drum and hub brakes transmit torque from hubs to rims, creating rim-distorting forces. These forces require stronger tangential spoking, not weaker radial spoking (2.8).

2.8   700C Rear wheel for disc brake, 32 generic spokes. Unmachined rim does not suit caliper brake.

Hollow-rim wheels with deep sections are structural, and can be incredibly strong and slightly more aerodynamic than plain section rims. However, the rims can leave a very small part of the valve stem exposed or require tubes with long valve stems. This can lead to difficulties pumping tyres or obtaining tubes.

Looking at a bike from the front, we see some triangles made up of spokes on each side and the hub at the bottom. The top of these triangles are at the rim. On small spoked wheels (20" and 16"), these triangles are strong and have a large angle at the rim when compared to the triangles on large (say 28") wheels. This strength helps counter wheel distortion caused by potholes and stones on the road.

2.9   Hollow-rim 16" 349mm rim front wheel with strong triangulation.

Spokes can be zinc-plated steel, but stainless steel spokes are the most durable and proof against rust. I had a set of 20" Velocity 'Deep V' hollow-rim wheels with stainless steel spokes made up by Greenspeed about 15 years ago. They have done trojan service on load-carrying bikes, tandems and recumbents. They are exceptionally strong.

Spokes should be checked for tightness regularly, and tuned to make sure the wheel is round and not buckled or running out. Although lowering spoke count is a way of improving aerodynamics, it's also a way of weakening the wheel, and is not recommended. Instead, flattened, aerodynamic spokes can be used.

Very low spoke counts should be avoided. On 28" wheels, 32 front spokes and 40 back spokes were used up till the 1980s. Strong wheels can have *slightly* fewer spokes than this today, as hollow aluminium rims can make up part of a wheel's strength, but this shouldn't go too far. Although aerodynamic, wheels shown in 2.7 have bespoke spokes, which could be hard to replace. Spoke adjustment is at the hub, so in the rear wheel both disc and cluster must be removed to tighten spokes. On the 16-spoke wheel, the loss of any one spoke could compromise the whole wheel.

Brakes

I often use V-brakes on bikes I build, and these provide reliable stopping. However, brakes that work on wheel hubs (back-pedal, disc, drum) are best because they are less prone to fouling with muck, act independent of rim conditions and don't wear the rim. Drum and coaster brakes are sealed from dirt, and back-pedal brakes have the additional benefit of allowing the cyclist to brake well while indicating for a turn with one hand off the handlebars.

Rim brakes such as cantilever and side-pull brakes can work well. However, side-pull brakes become less effective when the brake arm is large, and work best on racing bikes where they fit tight around a skinny tyre. Brake pads should never be allowed to wear right down because metal brake shoes (left after the rubber pad has gone) wear rims very quickly.

Disc brakes operate in the centre of the wheel and are modular in allowing different wheel styles to be swapped over in the same frame. They allow wheels to be made without a rim braking surface. They have the added benefit of requiring greater wheel strengths, as the hub and wheel transmit high braking torque (higher than pedalling torque in emergencies) through the wheel to the road. Disc brakes are usually not much affected by road dirt, but to be fully secure should be held in by thru axles.

Gearing

To use leg power efficiently and make good progress, most cycles have variable gear ratios. Any given ratio provides more or less 'distance travelled per metre of foot movement'. The best gear ratio depends on slope, road condition, weight and profile of bike and rider, wind, and tyre type and pressure. The ratio of the distance travelled by the rider's foot to the distance travelled by the cycle itself is affected by the crank length, the number of teeth on the driving and driven wheels, intermediate gearing and hub gears, and driven wheel diameter. Good gearing keeps cadence (pedalling frequency) close to natural running tread frequencies.

All cycles have at least two gears, the lowest of which involves pushing the cycle while walking. If you are running out of low gears at 5 or 6km/h, this is always an option.

Sequential gearing is the simplest to operate, with the rider having one control for all gears. Most modern hub gears are sequential, as are derailleur gears with single chainrings. Hubs with internal gears can have an efficiency of 98% per stage of gearing, and keep the gear mechanism free from road muck. They tend to be a rare and more expensive option on Australian bikes but are widely accepted on 'town bikes' in continental Europe. Derailleur gearing works well when clean and properly tuned, but is prone to inefficiency when dirty or if there is a big misalignment between the chainring and the cluster cog in use.

The number of gears available on the rear cluster of derailleur systems has risen in recent years. Reasons for this include:

- Racing cyclists wish to pedal at optimum cadence to preserve energy and win races. This requires close gear ratios and therefore a high number of gears.
- Derailleur gear mountain bikes, which previously had non-sequential front and rear derailleur systems, now have sequential rear derailleur-only systems, but their gears must still cover considerable range with only one cluster. Mountain bikers need to concentrate on not banging into trees, so sequential gearing is important.
- Novelty — and more gears on the rear cluster — is a driver of sales for new bikes and parts. If people didn't buy new bikes and expensive replacement parts, the bike companies would not be in business. However, as more gears are placed on the back wheel (9, 10, 11, 12, 13 speeds), the space between the cogs narrows, and matching proprietary, non-generic chains must be used. For this reason I stick to eight-speed drivetrains for my city and on-road touring cycles. These can be separated and reattached with standard tools and without special rejoinable links. I don't need the large range of mountain bike groupsets, or the close spacing of road bike groupsets, or the lighter weight of narrow chains. Instead I prefer durability, repairability and compatibility.

The following is a guide to gearing ranges and equipment for different cycling styles. The two components of gearing are range and lowest gear. A '2:1 range' means the highest gear makes the bike go twice as far per pedal revolution as the lowest gear.

A single gear on a bicycle is usually enough for flat country or short distances. Common Australian bikes with a single gear include:
- fixed-gear bikes, which have no clutch, and pedals always moving when the back wheel moves
- simple bikes with coaster (back-pedal) brakes, including kids' bikes.

2:1 range: is okay for short distances around town and most riding on the flat. This gear range is supplied by three-speed hub gears and five-speed derailleur bikes using a 13–26-tooth rear cluster. When fixing a derailleur bike with multiple front cogs, it is possible to remove the front derailleur, and its control and cable. This makes sequential gearing with only the rear derailleur and its control. Usually it's best to leave the chain on the front ring with the least number of teeth so only the highest gears are disabled. Sometimes retaining the front derailleur helps keep the chain in place.

4:1 range: is sufficient for most town riding and light touring. It is offered by mid-range (8 speed) hub gears and Enviolo/Fallbrook continuously variable transmissions. It is the maximum ratio available with a single front chainring and inexpensive large range rear eight-speed clusters (such as Sunrace CSM680 8AY 11–42 tooth or CSM680 8AX 11–40 tooth).

5:1 range: should be sufficient for all but the most arduous cycling on heavily laden machines. It is offered by many simple three-chainring derailleur systems and the expensive, complex and respected 14 speed Rohloff speedhub. The SRAM Eagle derailleur system has 12 speeds, a single front chainring and a 10–50 tooth sprocket.

Ranges higher than 5:1: are offered by hybrid systems incorporating both hub and derailleur gears. Their main application is on trikes, which are statically stable and tolerate low speed and large loads. Some of these systems include Schlumpf geared bottom brackets, which have an epicyclic gear installed in the chainring. The epicyclic gear can be switched on and off by moving a pin running through the pedal axis (Just on their own, Schlumpf bottom brackets can contribute a 2.5 times range to the overall gearing). Pinion sell gearboxes with up to 18 gears and a 636% range. These gearboxes are part of the frame, and bikes using them have only one cog on the back wheel. In rear suspension mountain bikes, this allows the back wheel to be light with a wide hub. This gives a small unsprung wheel mass and strong spoke triangulation.

Cycles should have their lowest gear set to climb most expected uphills. Single-speed bikes can't really have their gear set to climb hills, but bikes with wider ranges can have a lowest gear such as:

- A 1:1 sprocket ratio on a 28" wheel bike will allow a well-laden bike to travel up steep hills. On derailleur gears this ratio can be achieved using a 32-tooth chainring driving a 32-tooth sprocket, and is a good lowest gear for a bike with twin or triple front sprockets. The sprocket ratio changes to about 1.3:1 for a 20" wheel bike.
- A 1.5:1 sprocket ratio on a 28" wheel bike will allow a bike to tackle most steep hills, especially when ridden with gusto. On derailleur gears this ratio can be achieved using a 48-tooth sprocket driving a 32-tooth sprocket, and is a good lowest gear for a bike with a single front sprocket. The sprocket ratio changes to about 2:1 for a 20" wheel bike.

A benchmark to judge gearing is useful, and I compare set-ups with what is fitted on my recumbent trike. It hasn't changed for several years since 11–40 tooth eight-speed cassettes became available. This set-up (2.10) is:

- Single 52-tooth front chainring with 170mm cranks: These are available as part of 52/40 tooth chainrings, which were practical on 28" wheeled cycles with a smallest cog size of 13 tooth. This was before clusters with 11-teeth cogs became common making the high gear on most 52/11-tooth 28" bikes too high.
- 20" front wheel with a diameter of 520mm. This fits in well with the overall trike design.
- 11–40 tooth eight-speed rear cluster. On some bikes an extender may be needed to help a standard derailleur cope with the large 40 tooth cog.

Overall these parts give a minimum gear of 26.6" equivalent diameter, or 2.1m per pedal revolution. The maximum gear is 96.8" equivalent diameter, or 7.7m per pedal revolution.

2.10   Benchmark recumbent cycle drivetrain.

Warnings, see and be seen

Bells: It's always worth having a bell to warn pedestrians and other cyclists of your approach, especially on bike paths. They are fairly ineffectual in the middle of car traffic but better than nothing. I prefer the ones that just hit a clapper onto a bell and are fairly indestructible. Bells should be instantly accessible from your normal hand position, otherwise you could lose control at a critical time or spend too long getting your warning out.

Visibility and lighting: Day or night, cyclists should be clearly visible. When riding at night away from streetlights, cyclists should illuminate the road ahead to see road edges and upcoming obstacles or patches of glass.

Bright jackets or vests help daytime visibility. Yellow or orange workwear is common, inexpensive and works well. Recumbent riders should have a bright flag on their vehicle if their eye height is below about 110cm (approximately eye height of motorists in sedans).

There is no longer any excuse for not being visible on a bike at night. Light emitting diode lights (LEDs) have come down rapidly in price. Battery-driven flashing lights for visibility start at about $5 for back lights and $10 for front lights. Camping stores stock front lights designed to be attached to helmets. Jackets for night riding should include silver reflective strips. If two front lights, front and rear reflectors and two rear lights are used, some lights will be redundant, and there will still be adequate lighting even if a light fails. Reflectors on pedals, spokes and tyre rims are effective, and signal 'bike' to motorists and pedestrians.

Lights with removable batteries usually use AAA size batteries. These last a reasonable amount of time, and rechargeable AAAs are common and inexpensive. Lights with an even number of batteries are best, as many battery chargers will only handle an even number of batteries. Rechargeable AAA batteries have a lower voltage (1.2V) than single-use batteries (1.5V). Single-use batteries are best reserved for rear flashing lights because they are brighter, last a long time and self-discharge more slowly.

Lights with inbuilt batteries are usually recharged with a phone charger-style USB cord. The best of these usually provide a warning flash pattern before running out of charge completely. I have found some plain inexpensive USB rechargeable lights to be better than brand name equivalents. They may still fall off, but at least they don't get stolen!

For extended riding at night, illuminating bike paths and unlit roads, you may need lights driven by a dynamo or larger rechargeable batteries. Dynamos are usually of the bottle or hub type. There are excellent, efficient (Busch and Mueller) bottle and (SRAM, SON, Shimano, Shutter Precision) hub dynamos available. SON (Schmidt's Original Nabendynamo) manufacture very efficient hub dynamos as well as models that fit on special wheels such as 16" wheels on folding bikes and cantilever-axle trike wheels.

Handlebars

Handlebars come in five basic shapes:
- moustache — for step-through bikes/roadsters.
- racing/bull — bull handlebars are racing bars swivelled through 180° and

sometimes seen on older gentlemen's cycles. Yes, the cycle and the gentleman may both be old.
- flat — wider handlebars used on mountain bikes.
- hi-rise — found on some small wheel cycles for adults and almost all chopper bikes.
- BMX — a wide, reinforced, hi-rise bar.

Tri-bars are an add-on to flat or racing bars that allow a rider to assume a fast, tucked position with the forearms resting on the tri-bars.

Generally, the lower and narrower the hand position, the more aerodynamic the cycle. Wide handlebars give good handling and enable a high front-wheel steering torque. Materials for handlebars include steel, aluminium and carbon fibre. Traditionally, town bike handlebars were 22.2mm (7/8") diameter at the ends and 25.4mm (1") at the centre, but the new clamp stems have led to new centre diameters for handlebars, such as:
- 31.8mm: by increasing diameter and decreasing wall thickness, bars can be made lighter and stronger. This diameter is becoming a new standard for racing and mountain bikes.
- 22.2mm: the two-part handlebar clamp means it's not necessary to wriggle handlebars through a hole till the centre is under a clamp, so handlebars with only one diameter are now possible. For kids' bikes, whose riders are light and don't exert much force, Byk introduced handlebars with a 22.2mm diameter all the way through, avoiding the process required to increase the centre diameter.
- Road bike handlebars are slightly different, with 26mm or 31.8mm centres and 23.8mm ends.

Pedals

The three types of pedals are those with a cleat binding the foot to the pedal, those without a cleat, and folding pedals.

Cleats clip specially designed shoes to the pedals and allow riders to pull as well as push. Pulling needs a conscious muscle motion, and isn't always done. However, wearing cleats always positions feet well, and this helps experienced riders. Pressing the shoes into the pedal in the right spot clips in, twisting the shoe clips out, and these actions become automatic. Cleats carry the feet on recumbents, and without them it's tiring riding long distances. It's worth practising clipping and unclipping cleated pedals when using them for the first time, as awkward falls can result if feet are stuck in cleats.

Without cleats, the rider's foot always absorbs energy when travelling upwards, but for short rides this is fine. Rubber pedals with reflectors make the best plain, uncleated pedals. Older pedals of this style are fully serviceable and allow bearings to be cleaned and regreased. If possible, avoid pedals with plastic bodies. They are inexpensive but often break. Aluminium body pedals are much more durable.

Folding pedals suit folding bikes. They are quick to remove from the bike or fold, meaning pedals do not add to the bike's folded package size. Wellgo make a range of good quick-release pedals. Cheap plastic folding pedals can wear out quickly and are not recommended.

Cranks and bottom brackets

Modern cotterless cranksets secure the crank reliably to the axle and are an improvement on the cotter-pin cranksets they replaced. Cotter-pin cranksets should only be left on historical bikes or those used for short distances. Ashtabula-style cranksets have a single piece of bent steel, which is cranks and crank axle combined. They are sold on the cheapest of bikes, are heavy and should be avoided.

Sealed bottom brackets are cartridge-type elements, and a reliable, dustproof and waterproof housing for crank bearings. They are inexpensive and more reliable than open/greased ball bearing systems.

Some modern bikes are equipped with eccentrically mounted bottom brackets that allow a chain to be tensioned without using slotted rear wheel dropouts, a system recommended for single-speed and hub-gear cycles. This is a feature borrowed from traditional tandem cycles.

Seats

I favour wide, sprung saddles for my bikes. These carry body weight on the 'sit bones' and not so much on the genital area. *The Penguin Book of the Bicycle* has a good section on bicycle saddles.

Actuation

Brakes and gears are usually actuated by tension cables (inner) running inside a compressed cable outer. Pairs of lugs allow cables to run in free air, eliminating the cable outer, reducing weight and saving cable friction.

A spring action on V-, cantilever and caliper brakes keeps the pads just off the rims unless the brake levers are squeezed. Tension on the brake cable inner actuates the brakes, and this can be done:

- conventionally, with a brake lever
- by separating two parts of the brake cable outer using a lever, or
- by moving the inner (like an archer's bowstring) when it's running in free air.

A spring action on derailleurs is balanced by gear change lever friction, and the cable stays put unless the gear change lever is moved.

Gear indexing is the separation of switching between gears into discrete steps. It is essential on hub gears and now standard on derailleur gears. Indexing is not needed on derailleur gears, and most of my bikes use older friction shift parts.

Brake and gear levers can be combined, but I don't like this. If one part of the mechanism fails, the whole thing needs to be replaced.

Hydraulic actuation is used on some disk and rim brakes. Hydraulics make brake action almost friction free but can be difficult to repair.

Caution should be taken when mixing V-brake levers and side-pull brakes and vice versa, as V-brake actuation distances are longer than those for side-pulls.

References

Eland, P 2009, *Bike Buyer's Guide*

S and S couplings http://www.sandsmachine.com

Bike World Magazine Editors, 1974, *Traveling by Bike*, World Publications

Harland, J., 1992, *The Australian Bicycle Book*

Watson, R and Gray, M. 1978, *The Penguin Book of the Bicycle*

3 Cycle Commuting

Cycle commuting eases pollution, reduces road traffic, keeps you fit, breaks up your week at work and relieves stress. It is a great thing to do. A daily 20km round trip cycle commute is doable for many people. If trips are longer, you can commute 2 or 3 days a week, or use public transport some of the way, and still benefit.

The modern Western world has come so far that the norm is to be isolated from wind, weather and seasons. When cycle commuting, wind and weather matter, and you can observe the level of streams and the blossoming of flowers, and reconnect to the environment.

Depending on distances and traffic, cycling to work can take longer than driving, but it is simultaneous travel and exercise. It will almost certainly take less time and cost less than a drive to work and a trip to the gym. Cycle commuting is my normal exercise, and keeps me fit enough to enjoy active sports like surfing. To prepare for big rides such as Melbourne's 210km Round the Bay in a Day, I ride extra kilometres.

My commutes have been a 50 or 70km round trip 2 days a week, and a 30km round trip 5 days per week.

My 50 or 70km commute was 'wet', meaning showering on arrival, and this goes with longer distances where cycling clothes give more benefit. Planning started the night before, by laying out cycling clothes to ride in, and putting work clothes in the bike. Forgetting belt, shirt or trousers led to comical attempts to find halfway decent alternatives the next day at work. Fortunately my employer was sympathetic. Using cycling shoes was not a problem, as my work required steel-capped protective boots, which I left at work and changed into as I finished showering.

The morning commute started as a 5km bike leg to Richmond Station, then a trip on a near-empty train to outer suburban Glen Waverley and a 10km ride after that to work. I showered, changed and shaved at work, and was at my desk just before official start time. I always rode all the way home and tried to leave work soon after knock-off time, especially on short winter days. It was dark when I got home from the 35km ride but at least some of that ride was in daylight. Friday was a good day to ride because I got off work earlier and could visit a favourite shop on the way home. Later, I quit using the train in the morning and just rode all the way, making the overall commute 70km.

My 30km trip was a dry commute, without showering, and ridden in work clothes. Even on the hottest days, it was cool enough to ride in the morning without too much sweat. Riding in the clothes I spent the day in required less planning than riding in cycling clothes. Often I'd see and chat to cycling work colleagues on the way. At the start, I wore cycle shoes riding, then changed into other shoes at work. This didn't work out. I was comfortable enough in the non-cycling shoes and would forget to change into cycling shoes at the end of the day. I'd realise my mistake 2km or so into my home trip, and then be stuck riding without cleats all the way home. The solution was just to wear mountain-bike-style cycling shoes all the time.

While commuting, I used big roads (4 lanes each way), quieter roads and bike paths. On roads, car traffic really isn't a problem as long as you are visible, behave predictably and keep to the left as much as possible. Some off-road bike tracks aren't worth riding on and are constantly interrupted by creek crossings, road crossings and meander without getting anywhere quickly. And on some roads, cycle lanes don't have penalties for cars parking on them and so aren't bike paths when I ride them. All this said, there are some good, worthwhile bike paths — you just need to seek them out — and the more circuitous bike paths are still very pleasant on weekends when there's no hurry.

Some roads are just not bike friendly, and it's fine not to be brave or foolish and use pedestrian lights or a hook turn (3.1) at intersections that are just too dark, scary or choked with traffic to do a normal right-hand turn.

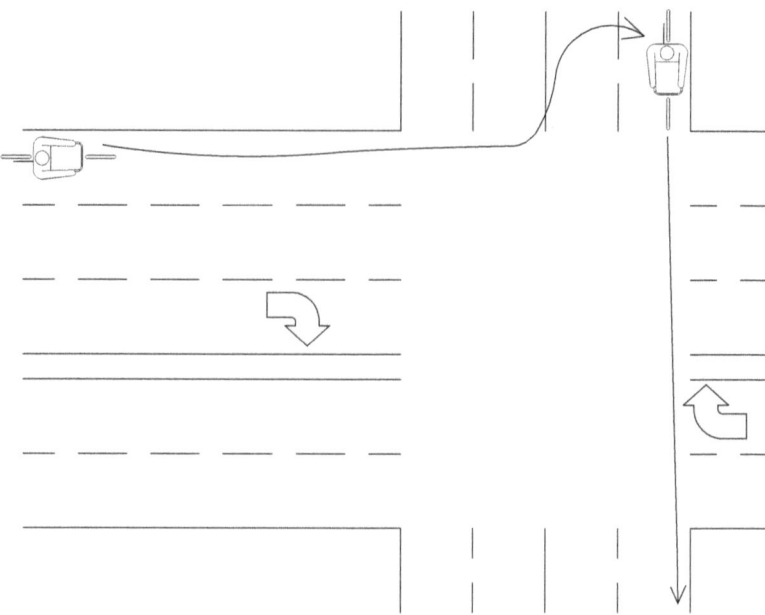

3.1   Hook turns. Keep left through intersection, turn and wait on far side, proceed with green light.

Riding contrasted with driving to work, when I would listen to the radio and concentrate on the surrounding cars. I was completely powerless to change traffic conditions. This is not boring, but not exciting either.

However, when riding there is usually something interesting. Almost always there is a smile or a wave and a chat with a fellow cyclist. Less often there is missing a train, destroying clothes when they rub on a bike wheel, draining my water bottle on the train floor, accidentally dropping my helmet on the train tracks, breaking the gear cable, bike breaking and having to proceed by taxi, a puncture, getting rained on, riding through a thunderstorm and flood, catching the wrong train, running over a dog turd, riding in 42°C, or spilling a casserole in the back of the panniers. These are the small everyday problems that cyclists resolve, helping keep them sane and resilient.

I'll always indicate on roads or cycle paths, holding my arm out for a long while before turning. I have a mirror installed on my helmet, which avoids needing a mirror on every bike I ride. Using the mirror, I know when there are no cars behind, and can do speedy left-hand turns by veering right to increase turn radius (3.2, 3.3).

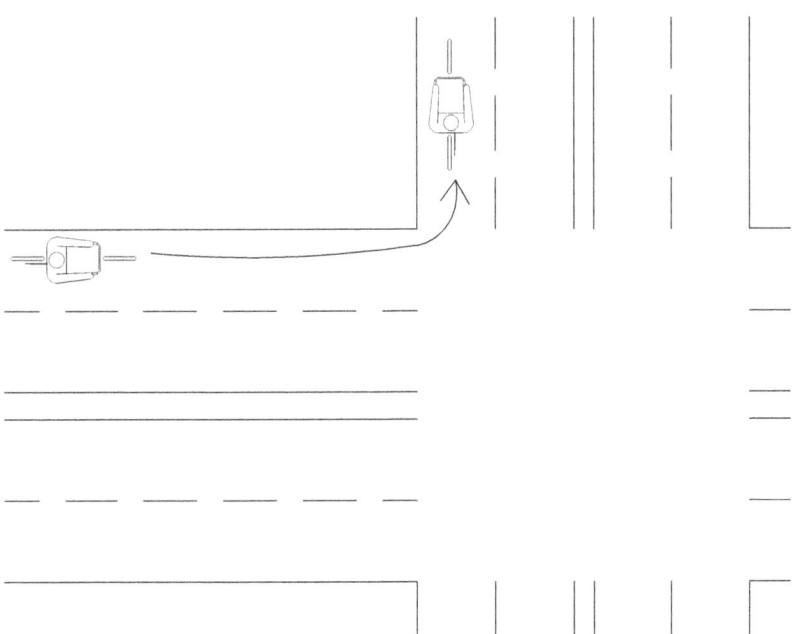

3.2   Slow turn without mirror.

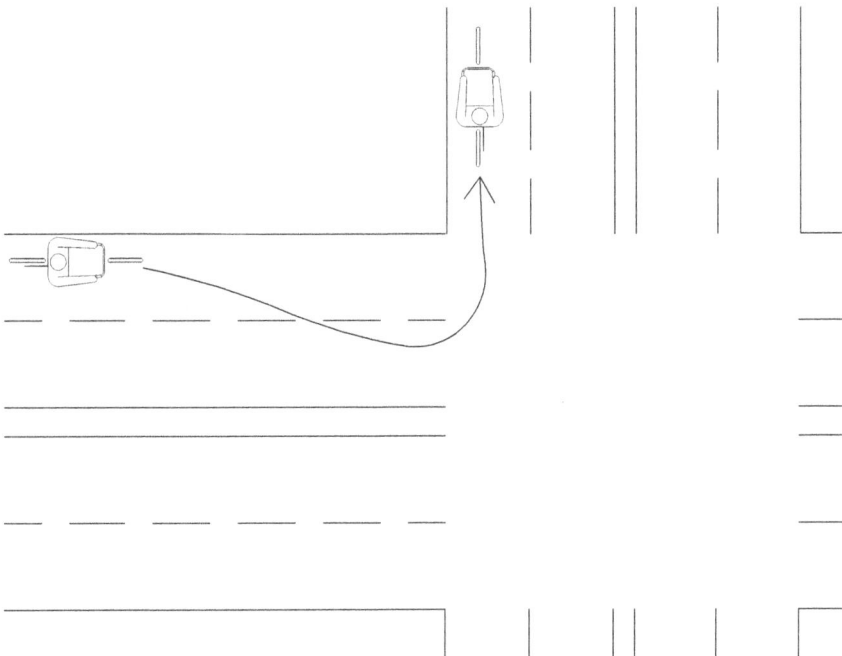

3.3   Faster turn uses mirror to ensure safety.

'Dry cycling' is more sustainable than 'wet cycling', as the distances aren't as long or debilitating and can be ridden daily. A good option to increase the distance range of cycles is to use an ebike. They can improve performance without adding much weight. Light electric assist on a good bike can increase the range for daily commuting from 20km per day, 10km per trip to 40km per day, 20km per trip. Unfortunately some electric-assist bikes are not designed for easy pedalling or low air resistance. These bikes are better classified as small motorbikes and don't offer the fitness advantages of hybrid human-electric cycles.

4 Electric Cycles and Vehicles

Electric cycles have recently become popular, with several 1990s inventions making batteries, motors and controls smaller, lighter and outwardly simpler. These inventions include improved torque sensors, power controls, and motor and battery technologies.

Like load-carrying and recumbent trike technologies, adding electric motors opens cycling to more users for more purposes. Delivery jobs, distances and commutes not sustainable on unassisted bikes can be ridden comfortably on rechargeable ebikes. Electrification overcomes hills and allows significant load or family carrying. It assists the elderly or those with physical or balance issues with cycling socially, exercise and transport.

Alternatives

Although cycle electrification has been readily accepted, other technologies can sometimes replace it. For example, an unassisted, designed for purpose freight cycle improves load and family carrying even before electrification is added.

Similarly, a light aerodynamic cycle reduces forces holding a bike back, and can perform comparably to an electrified bike, which has more forces pushing forward. This applies especially on flat ground. Cycles with both good aerodynamics and electric assist can be fast and use less battery power. The technologies don't need to fight each other and can be used together effectively.

It is worth considering wheel size, stability, load carrying and aerodynamics before electrification. Purely human powered cycles are less expensive and easier to maintain and improve than ebikes. If electric assist is required later, it can often be retrofitted.

Power and configurations

Although some ebikes have more power, most Australian ebikes are legally limited to motor outputs of 250W (0.25kW). This is a small fraction of the outputs of small petrol (2019 Kia Rio 74kW) and electric cars (2018 Nissan Leaf 110kW). This means ebikes still use much less energy than automobiles.

The diagrams show some electric-assist cycle arrangements. Ebike batteries, which were once heavy petrol-car-style lead acid, now use higher energy density NiMH, NiCd or Li-ion chemistry. These battery technologies are in electric cars and buses, which are forecast to replace petrol vehicles on our roads within decades. This means there is ongoing battery development. Ebike batteries are commonly mounted in or on the frame, or in a rear luggage rack. When batteries are mounted in the frame, the bike is likely to have been designed from the ground up as an ebike. Examples include electric mountain bikes and some electric town bikes.

4.1   Ebike battery positions.

Electric motors for ebikes have benefitted from improvements in electronics and wire insulation, allowing electronic commutation, compact size and light weight. These motors can be mounted to add electrical power at the pedal axis, back wheel or front wheel. As well as the siting of the battery and motor, ebikes are formally classified as ebikes (throttle control) or pedelecs (automatic electric assist provided when pedalling), although "ebike" is a term that covers both.

4.2   Ebike motor positions.

4.3   Ebike controls: pedelec controlled by assist level and pedalling, and ebike controlled by throttle.

New technologies and mass manufacture have let ebikes become more popular, affordable and reliable. Ebike technology has been applied to human powered vehicle styles including racing bikes, recumbent bikes, recumbent trikes, skateboards, scooters, unicycles and velomobiles.

4.4   Bachetta and Cruzbike recumbent ebikes.

E-assist can make vehicles more viable, including fat trikes, fat bikes, and scooters for last-mile transport. For example, some riders who would not contemplate powering the weight and high rolling resistance of a fat trike (all terrain trike with wide tyres) can now use electric versions.

Costs and retrofitting

Ebikes vary in cost, with DIY conversions of standard bikes less expensive than bikes designed with electric assist from the ground up. Complete ebike kits of battery, motor and controls costing from A$600 can be installed on a second-hand $100 bike for an all up ebike cost of about $700. There are even cheaper options. For example, my friend Ben Moore makes ebike power supplies from discarded battery-driven vacuum cleaners and power tools, and uses them on bikes for himself and others.

Readymade ebikes are no longer expensive, with Peter Wells recently reviewing a $1,000 ebike favourably. Expensive electric mountain bikes, town bikes and family/freight bikes cost many times more, with an Urban Arrow family bike advertised for $9,000 in Australia. This may seem expensive, but this bike often replaces a small family car and costs less in registration, parking space, fuel resources and pollution. In the same way that car owners have called on moving companies or hire a van when shifting house, ebike owners can call on car or van hire or taxi services to meet their transport needs.

Using and needing an ebike

My ebike is a conversion of an existing recumbent cycle. I wasn't getting full use of all my recumbents and decided to have one converted to electric. This was done by having a kit installed, with a rechargeable battery, controls, display, wiring, electronics and front-wheel motor. My bike is front wheel drive, and the front-wheel motor would be a rear wheel motor on almost any other bike. It is a pedelec, so to ride with extra power I set an assist level between 1 and 5, pedal away, and automatic electric assist helps out. There's more power at higher levels, but I must pedal for any assist to occur. As well I have a throttle used to start without pedalling or to maintain power through awkward corners. I use higher assist levels when needed on hills.

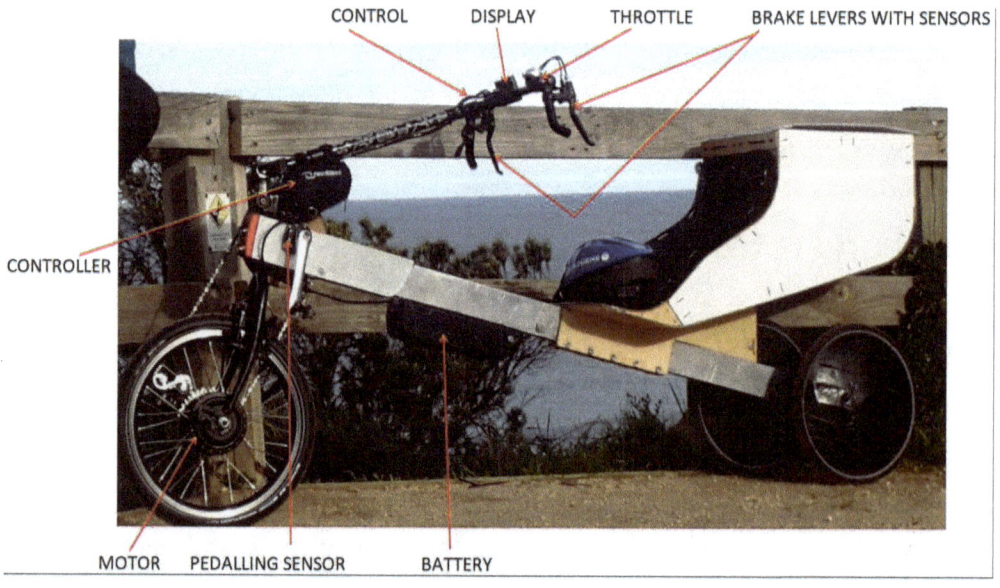

4.5 Motor retrofitted to my recumbent.

I'm 60 years old and usually ride unassisted, but occasionally the powered recumbent is useful. If it's very hot and I need to ride or have appointments several kilometres away, I can still cycle without excess exertion. Although I may not now need it, in 10 years when I do, I will already be used to electric bikes and won't be forced to suddenly buy one.

Discussion

Electrification of pedelecs hardly changes the riding; it just means more than human power drives the bikes. Electrics changes some vehicles more dramatically. For example, electric unicycles reduce the balancing required and remove pedalling. Compared to unpowered boards, electric skateboards are harder to perform tricks on, are becoming a transport option, and are often controlled by smartphone.

Electronics may soon change cars fundamentally as well, with self-driving cars predicted to be common in 20 years. This furthers the trend where electronically controlled petrol car engines have become more efficient but also too complex for home repair. In recent years cycling has become a haven of simple, user-repairable transport, and this will continue.

If there are doubts technologies can change things quickly, we should consider mobile phones. Twenty years ago, phones only sent texts and made phone calls. Now they still call and text, but also play movies and music, guide us, communicate sound, video and images to the world, and keep us in touch with each other.

In the next 20 years cycles won't change as much as that. Some cycles won't change at all, and still work as well as they do now. However, future ebikes may include the emerging technologies of solar recharging, series hybrid drives and multifunctional materials. Combined with 3d printing, these technologies could make low-pollution, low-powered cycles rival automobiles in most circumstances, especially when overall travel times and congestion are considered.

There are plans for wide-scale, carbon-pollution-free road travel with electric cars. However, pollution-free air travel with today's aircraft speeds, flight distances and passenger numbers isn't possible. Technologies to enable electric flight are still being developed. These include multifunction materials combining structural strength with electrical power storage — they are currently in use to extend the flight times of unmanned drones. These materials are predicted to increase the flight distance of electric aircraft by 66 per cent and could also be used to make velomobile shells. This is not as silly as it sounds. Like aircraft, cycles need strong, light, bodies, and good aerodynamics is preferred. The earliest aircraft by the Wright brothers were developed with bicycle technology, and carbon fibre is used extensively in both aircraft and cycles. Until recently, the Rans corporation made both recumbent cycles and aircraft, and the Australian manufacturer of Glyde velomobiles also makes aircraft.

Velomobiles could make an ideal test platform for multifunction composites. They cannot fall out of the sky, and could be used for safe testing of combined structural and battery materials. Today's lightest velomobiles like the Alpha 7 weigh about 21kg. With aircraft industry backing and a shell acting as a battery, an e-velomobile could weigh only a few kilos more.

There is a promising future for cycles whose sole motive force comes from an electric motor with no direct human power to the wheels. This form of serial hybrid cycle was developed by Andreas Fuchs and Jurg Blatter, who had built a side-by-side faired tandem with electric assist for hilly terrain in Switzerland. They reasoned that the whole cycle could be simplified if each rider pedalled a generator that powered the cycle's battery and motor along with regenerative braking. Solar cells were nominated as another potential power source. In the future, perovskite thin film solar technologies could make solar cells cheaper, able to be fitted to curved surfaces, more efficient and therefor more applicable for cycles and velomobiles.

Solar is already used as power input for ebike motors and batteries, and cyclists in the July 2020 Suntrip used hybrid human–solar–electric cycles to cycle 3,000km round France. One of the Suntrip competitors is the TiltDragonFly, a tilting solar powered delta trike with series hybrid drive and full suspension. The following report is from tests of the TiltDragonFly, where pedalling charges a battery instead of driving the wheels:

> 'We have to face facts, after decades pedalling mechanical transmission machines, our reactions are so entrenched that using serial hybrid transmission is confusing. Despite at least 1,000km travelled with this device both on a tandem trike and the new "TiltDragonFly", it is still difficult to get rid of habits.

Natural instincts take over as soon as the guard is dropped.

Rather than maintaining a regular effort, it is the vision of the countryside that takes over the brain. I find myself correlating the force exerted on the pedals to the slope of the road. I still note some improvements, pedalling downhill, certainly at reduced power, begins to be done much more naturally.'

4.6   TiltDragonFly Photo www.sunrider.fr.

Summary

The outlook for cycles looks good as our vehicle fleet becomes more electrified. Non-assisted cycles will remain a refuge of simplicity, self-expression and autonomy as other transport modes become more complex. Electric assist will continue as a technology making cycles more useful for more people. Cycles should be involved at the cutting edge of technology because they are, and will remain a vital part of sustainable transport. Researchers into solar cells and multifunction composites have a duty to put their technologies into bicycles and velomobiles as exciting, challenging applications for their technologies.

References

Alpha 7 Velomobile website https://www.velomobileworld.com/product/alpha-7

Ecosunriders Websites https://www.ecosunriders.com/ and http://www.sunrider.fr

Kia Rio petrol car specification https://www.kia.com

Nissan Leaf electric car specification https://en.wikipedia.org/wiki/Nissan_Leaf

Nurse, S Context and methods for improved velomobiles https://www.australasiantransportresearchforum.org.au/sites/default/files/papers/ATRF2019_resubmission_31.pdf

Urban Arrow Electric Cargo bike https://dutchcargobike.com.au/brand/urban-arrow/

Wells, P. *Ebike Review* https://www.smh.com.au/technology/can-you-get-a-reliable-electric-bike-for-less-than-1000-20190520-p51pc5.html

5 Cycling for a Cause with Gayle Potts

Gayle Potts is a founder and volunteer for the Wecycle social enterprise, which rehomes bicycles. In Australia bikes are inexpensive compared to cars, so are sometimes given to friends or charities after they are replaced or children outgrow them. Wecycle is a charity in Darebin giving volunteer-refurbished cycles directly to refugees. Every attempt is made to give bikes that are fit for purpose, and Wecycle has successfully rehomed everything from mountain bikes to kids' pedalless balance bikes to tilting trikes to upright trikes to tandem recumbent trikes. In 2017 and 2018 Wecycle rehomed 80 bikes and that number jumped to 100 in 2019.

    I met Gayle to discuss Wecycle and her cycling life over breakfast at Ballarat Station. Jamie Friday was with me as a touring companion. Jamie and I had arrived by train and he took some photos on a wet, windy day.

* * *

5.1   Stephen Nurse with Gayle Potts, Ballarat Railway Station.

SN: Hi Gayle, you have had a lot of experience with bikes and I just wanted to talk about it. So to start, you were a cycle commuter in Melbourne, is that right?

GP: Yes, so I moved back to Melbourne in 2006 and got a job in the city and was living 12km out at Reservoir, and was wondering how to bike to the city and was a bit scared of that.

SN: And have you been a bike rider all your life?

GP: Yes, but not in a big city like Melbourne, more in New Zealand and up around Brisbane, so the idea of riding and commuting in Melbourne was a challenge. But I did that and found it was fine, I found some alternate routes to the city, found I could go mountain biking before work and started using that beautiful morning time for riding and my job had showers and I used to keep my wardrobe at work, and so for 12 years I cycle commuted to work.

SN: And obviously your confidence increased with all sorts of cycling. And I found out that there's people you have met on your commute and you know to talk to, and I found that amazing, I have commuted a bit but never got to that.

GP: Yes, I've met quite a few people who've become friends, and Mike Williamson on the Wecycle team was one of them, because he used to commute into the city; and another Italian fellow, he's a good long-time friend now. Yeah. I think as commuters you see the same people at the same time each day and you get a connection.

SN: I commute on a recumbent and I think people would just notice me for the bike, and I recognised people I saw often, but it never got to that level.

GP: It's always at the lights, like that intersection of St Georges Road where it meets Merri Parade. There's a long wait there.

SN: And some of that is on a bike path too, so you are isolated from cars and that would help a bit I imagine.

GP: Yes.

SN: And recently you've started taking on bikes as a profession but also you've set up a whole voluntary enterprise, haven't you?

5.2   Peter Kelly, Simon Batterbury, Gayle Potts, Wecycle Northcote.

GP: Yes, my job in the inner city was working for consulting engineers and deadly boring, and also the workload was often quite light so I just felt I needed to do something more fulfilling. So in 2016 I did the Community Leaders in Sustainability course with the city of Darebin. That was the catalyst enabling me to get from wanting to give back to the community to actually forming an idea and following through. Another fellow on the course, Craig told me his father was involved with a church group in Geelong rehoming bikes for refugees and asylum seekers.

SN: Okay, I see.

GP: So Craig kind of had this model that his father was involved with, and he wanted to set up the same thing in Darebin. I thought it was a terrific idea, and so we teamed up and it progressed naturally.

So in early 2016 we started. Craig's a better bike mechanic than me, and my job was mainly to make contact with refugee and asylum group support agencies. We were working out of our backyards. Craig's garage turned into this crazy, jam packed shed full of bikes hanging from the roof and everywhere. We were picking up and dropping off bikes every weekend, and my backyard turned into a bikeyard as well, and so we got it going, and then a notice went into the Darebin Sustainability Newsletter saying we needed bikes, and they started rolling in. There was no trouble getting bikes, and it seems like everyone has a bike sitting in their backyard that hasn't been used, hasn't been loved, hasn't been ridden in some time.

So the donations just started coming in. I spent that first year looking for a venue, and I was working with the council saying you must have a place somewhere around Darebin to use for this project, so we were scouting, and eventually one of the team from the Transport Department suggested there was a little building in Batman Park. So we looked at it and thought what a perfect place. It had been used as a Greek women's group meeting place previously. After that it was empty and kids broke in and graffitied it. Council was happy to have somebody take occupancy. Once we got the place, we put a sign up on the bike path on adjacent St Georges Road saying volunteers wanted to work on bikes for rehoming.

SN: Yes.

GP: And there was really good response to that. In fact I think we could probably do that again now, put a little sign out, because there are about 5,000 trips a week just down that St Georges Road bike path. The shed location is perfect because we have a tram stop next to us, and a train station 500 metres away, so the locality has been terrific for us for accessibility.

SN: And it's very good in particular for clients. They have transport needs, they might not be able to just jump in a car.

GP: And a lot of them who live in Craigieburn come here and then go to Southern Cross railway station and then get back with their bikes. And the transport can be such a difficult thing for new arrivals in Melbourne, just trying to move around the city like that can be really difficult and that's been our problem. Often our clients have trouble getting to Darebin.

SN: And so do you get reports back about newly arrived people and their experience with the bikes?

GP: Yes, and that's been a wonderful thing. It enabled our clients to ride to English classes, to go to the shops, to get to work, for their kids to ride to school. It's really sustainable and affordable transport. Sometimes just having enough money for transit cards can be difficult, so having a bike means not getting fined for travelling without transit cards.

SN: Yes, if you don't have enough money it's one thing you would do, not pay your fares rather than not put food on the table.

GP: And with help. A number of mostly young men from City Mission have been referred to us by one of their social workers, and having that bike has meant they can travel without fares, and they can keep a job or get to work, so having that bike can make the world of difference.

SN: And I'm amazed sometimes by the standard of donated bikes, like last Saturday some 3-year-old top of the range bikes came in and they were all going, all there, and just having the Wecycle shed there is an enabler. It motivates moving bikes on, because they are going somewhere useful. They might just stay in garages if they weren't going to a good cause.

GP: Yes. Bikes could be put on a website like Gumtree to raise money, but some people actually feel like if it's going to a good home it's greater value.

SN: Yes, for me sometimes it's more effort than it's worth to try to sell bikes. It's easier to drop it somewhere for people who need it more. So for a while you've lived in the country, and it's been a weekend commute to Wecycle, hasn't it?

GP: Yes, and even when I was cycle touring for 2 months last year up the coast of Western Australia, I was still able to do the administration, I could manage the emails, keep in touch with the team, do the ordering of spare parts for bikes, and so it's possible to work remotely with the bike shed and still be actively involved, and that's been really good. So I've been doing that weekend commute for a year now. I get to the bike shed most Saturdays, but now I've moved to Ballarat it's harder, but I do spend probably 5-10 hours per week on Wecycle emails, ordering and keeping up with things.

SN: Yes it's easy for me to put in my 3 hours a week volunteering as a mechanic, but the other end takes real contact with people, putting out the word that cycles are available and organising for clients to visit to try refurbished bikes.

GP: Yes.

SN: And besides Wecycle, I think you've had a couple of other bike related enterprises including going on a small business course, is that right?

GP: Yes, so giving up my house, my job, my partner last year has meant some big changes, and I lived and worked on a farm for a year. That was one of the best things I've done and I enjoyed that and realised I'd rather not live in a big city any more. I was looking at career change and how my life's going to be, so I had the opportunity to do the New Enterprise Incentive Scheme (an Australian Government small business incubator), so I have support for my business ideas for the next nine months, giving me the equivalent of a Job Seeker allowance.

SN: So that's really your income while you're up here?

GP: Yes.

SN: And one of your ideas is the sort of bike tour you organised last weekend?

GP: Yes, that was a great adventure.

SN: Did it go well? Did you get enough people along?

GP: We wanted 20–30 minimum, and we had 22 sign up and another two at the last minute. And on Saturday morning it was absolutely pouring with rain at Woodend Station, and we were looking at the rain radar on our phones, and there was this crazy amount of rain coming through. And so we had four people say it was too wet and they wouldn't do it, and the rest were standing there, so we delayed it a little, but thought it's not going to get any better, so we thought we had better do it.

SN: Well if you choose to bike tour, that's actually what it's like, you do have to suck it up sometimes.

GP: Well obviously this is not the best weather today for you guys. But I think you're going to have a tail wind.

SN: Yeah, I think we're going to be alright.

GP: So the event was terrific. I organised it with Russell from the Woodend Cycles bike shop, Jeremy who runs minivan tours for overseas visitors down the Great Ocean Road and mountain bike tours, and Jimmy who's a Woodend local bike mechanic. So the four of us organised it — Russell had had this idea of a Great Divide cycle ride for years, he used to run 24-hour races and he does shuttles driving downhill mountain bike riders back up the hills around Maldon.

SN: Right, so he's across all sorts of bike tourism.

GP: Yes, and he's done bike touring including the 1,000km Munda Biddi trail in Western Australia last year, which I did part of. So we love the adventure, and that's what people are really interested in, adventure cycling, getting out on gravel roads, quiet roads, and really tripping around. So this was an introduction for people. They ride consecutive days but their gear was carried. We had this amazing farm out at Mt Franklin with a huge barn, it was such a good venue for it.

Everybody arrived at the barn about 4 in the afternoon after stopping for lunch at Trentham, soaking wet, and inside the barn we had a feast cooked up. It was 56km for the long route and 46 for the short route for the first day from Woodend to Mount Franklin via Trentham. There was a huge woodburner in the barn, so it was warm and we'd brought in portable showers and toilets so everyone could have a hot shower. And in the morning on the platform, the enticement to do the trip was that the barn was big enough for sleeping in, you could set up your sleeping mat and bag on the floor, so that was good. Then by the evening it had actually cleared up, so some people set up their tents outside.

The next day was from Mount Franklin to Castlemaine via the dry diggings track, which is technical, rough, tricky single track mostly, and then along the water races. So it's beautiful riding but a mountain bike was the best bike for the day, but we did have a smoother option as well. So we had one girl come off, and she had concussion, and we took her to Castlemaine Hospital. But she's fine, they were worried about her head but she had some friends there and between all of us we got her to hospital and safely home, and she got back to Packenham on the other side of the city by about 9:30 on Sunday night. They had kept her under observation for 4 hours. So once we got to Castlemaine, everybody had their vehicles at Woodend, so we had a bike trailer hooked up to the Sag wagon with 12 bikes and we got nine bikes on the train between Castlemaine and Woodend. That was pretty good for that rail line. We spoke to some platform staff and they let the train conductor know and they let them all get their bikes on.

SN: They are probably nicer with a little bit of warning. And this morning we had our rather strange bikes on the train and everybody was really nice, Jamie's bike took over half the aisleway.

GP: But if you had a group of 10 it would be harder!

SN: Will you run that ride again?

GP: Well the feedback so far was it was so much fun and they'd do it again, so we want to run it next year ... It was a great lesson, and we might use Mount Franklin as a base. People drive there with bikes and then ride out, so you don't have that transporting bikes back from the station. It was such good feedback and a lot of them said they would bring friends. Yes, I think we've found something we could develop and take further. And we've learnt lessons from it, we will make it better.

5.3   Volunteering at a Ballarat mountain bike ride. Photo Gayle Potts.

SN: Now we're in Ballarat, and you're organising some bike tourism here, is that right?

GP: Yes. I looked at a few different areas for it, but Ballarat seemed best. I would love to have done it at the Macedon ranges but the roads there are not safe enough for novice riders or families. So I looked at rail trails. Bendigo-Heathcote was one, but there's not a lot happening, there's not a lot of towns on the way. People kind of pass through Heathcote and as far as I can see it's not really a destination.

SN: So you've picked Ballarat as a medium-sized town with good cycling facilities, or roads that are okay.

GP: Yeah, and a rail trail, Ballarat-Skipton Rail trail, have you ridden that?

SN: No.

GP: I think I should organise a Wecycle team ride up here to do the Ballarat to Skipton Rail Trail.

SN: Yes. Why not?

GP: It's 57km just one way, and that's where we come in. So 114km might be too much for some to do in a day, so the idea is for support so riders can do a one-way trip and be collected and returned to their Ballarat accommodation. The next day they can do a lovely heritage tour around Ballarat, Lake Wendouree. Have you ridden around beautiful Lake Wendouree?

SN: Yeah, lots of times. I've been up here about seven times in late February for an organised cycle relay around Lake Wendouree for the Fiona Elsey Cancer Research Institute.

GP: Great, I'd like to be involved with that.

SN: And you're trying to develop a phone app to help people get around Ballarat?

GP: Yes, I want a scavenger hunt around Ballarat. You know Ballarat is an old gold mining town, so I think a treasure hunting theme would go well in an app. People can have the app and it will suggest historic and scenic places to be marked off, with a photo, or a quiz question, and then they will get a reward for completing the treasure hunt.

SN: It reminds me of Pokemon Go, which was a super sophisticated smartphone game, and it was location sensitive. It was a craze for a while.

GP: Yeah.

SN: You don't want a craze; you want an enduring tourist venture.

GP: And geocaching is similar, you go out in the bush or something and you'll find there'll be a point and you have to collect virtual tokens.

SN: And sometimes they're real tokens. People collect and leave things.

GP: Right, yeah. Maybe I could turn it into a little geocaching treasure hunt around Ballarat as well. So I think it would be a buzz and it will be really engaging and it could be for families or a team building exercise. Eventually it could be a whole weekend package or 2- or 3-day trip. In that time customers could come up to Ballarat and do the phone app activity, ride around Lake Wendouree or do a bit of the rail trail. So I'm going to package it up and sell it!

SN: Well we might wrap it up there. Thank you very much.

*   *   *

After breakfast, Gayle guided Jamie and me to the edge of Ballarat on our trip south.

6 City Cycling with Nell Sudano

Nell Sudano turned up at the Wecycle bike shed on a rainy Saturday in search of a replacement seat post. It was raining, so a few of her appointments had been cancelled and we had time to sit down to talk bikes. Since the interview, Xtracycle have stopped selling cargo bike conversions to concentrate on selling complete cargo bikes.

* * *

6.1   Nell Sudano with Simon Batterbury, Wecycle shed.

SN: Hi, I'm with Nell Sudano and we're at Wecycle. Nell's had a lot of experience with bikes and I wanted to capture some of that. So what brought you here Nell?

NS: I guess Wecycle is the latest chapter for me being involved in all things bike. I've been riding since I was a little kid and had to share bikes with brothers and sisters. Especially the brothers would return bikes with mechanical faults and flat tyres. I learnt quickly if I wanted to ride I'd have to learn to repair bikes and I quite enjoyed it. And then as a teenager I drifted away from that to other distractions. Then in middle age I just got involved with bikes again as a volunteer, initially with not for profit bike education groups, teaching children and adults to ride if they'd never ridden before, particularly people from different cultures, refugees, new Australians.

SN: And could I just stop you there, that was a huge gap, so you said you were fixing bikes as a kid and within the family. Did you stay a cyclist?

NS: I lived in Sydney, and if you wanted to ride a bike in Sydney you really needed a death wish. I tried hard to keep riding as a teenager but couldn't keep it up. And I rode to work there but it just felt too unsafe.

SN: Hopefully things have changed these days so you don't really need a death wish to ride in Sydney …

NS: Well I think it's definitely improved, but it's not like Melbourne, so the renaissance of riding for me was coming to Melbourne in 2005. I had no money, and a friend lent me a bike, and that just opened up a whole new city for me. I could get around safely and easily. There is great bike infrastructure on terrain that lends itself to riding, and a grid pattern of streets, so I wasn't concerned about losing my way, and very quickly that became my transport of choice.

SN: So it was after that you became a pushbiker again?

NS: Yes, exactly.

SN: So then you were able to branch out when you needed to, and there were organisations around helping people learning to ride.

NS: Yes, because I also revived my fixing skills a bit and used to fix bikes for friends, and then a friend who was aware of a bike education charity referred me for some volunteer work and that was it, that was my niche. I really enjoyed the work and could contribute. Coming close to retirement, I was a bit burnt out and hadn't really expected to be able to contribute in a meaningful way at that stage in my life. So it was really like a second wind and one role dovetailed into another and the charities that I worked for sent me along to Austcycle to get accredited to lead rides, and I did a couple of training courses. One set of rides I led was called 'Breeze', which aimed to get women back on bikes. My cohort came from those rides, women my age with various riding histories who lacked confidence and had been encouraged by menfolk in their family to ride but weren't set up with correct bikes. And there was not a lot of understanding given to their concerns and fears around riding.

SN: So to some extent, you were a sort of born-again biker, put off by things in Sydney and had that bad experience and had come back.

NS: Very much.

SN: So some of your cohort's experiences were relatable?

NS: Yeah, the thing about rediscovering biking as an adult — I mean when I first picked up cycling again I lost 8kg and kept that weight off until menopause but that's another story! Also I'd suffered depression on and off throughout life and because of easy exercise and getting out and about more for meaningful volunteer work, I found it a lot easier to manage those issues and just went from strength to strength. And when I was reflecting, I thought there were lots of other women in the same position, who just had reservations and just need a little bit of understanding to overcome issues, which I was seeing all the time.

SN: Yes. And did you get paid work out of all that volunteering?

NS: Yes eventually it did become paid, sort of few and far between and very seasonal, but there were opportunities to be paid, which was great. And then the next thing was that I had some physical issues. I have quite a bad lumbar spine and read about electric bikes but they were absurdly expensive. Then I found someone who imported and fitted electric bike kits, and they were offering training courses to let you fit a kit to your own bike, which I did, and I've not looked back.

SN: So was that Rev ebikes?

NS: Yes.

SN: And you work for them now, is that right?

NS: Yes, but at the moment I'm tapering down. So as a result of that training course the boss Rebecca asked me if I'd be interested in any work that came up, so I said absolutely, so I did a lot of kit fitting. I talked to some of my cohort of middle-aged women, who had bikes under the house gathering dust, about my electric bike conversion, and they got interested and had the same experience as me. With the electrics they didn't have to worry about getting tired or carrying loads. So I worked consistently for Rebecca two days a week for a year, and I've just dropped back to one day a week because I've got work locally in community transport.

SN: Well it's very good to have that skill and to know about ebikes. Somebody suggested to me that ebikes are going to go away because the batteries will die and then people would not stump up for a new battery at $600 or so. Maybe they thought that after the batteries die ebike users will go out and get a 'proper' bike. What do you think?

NS: With ebikes the technology is like we had with computers from 2000 to about 2005, where technology is going ahead exponentially. Batteries are becoming smaller and lighter, with greater energy density. There are also technologies like Revbikes LoVo where instead of shoving all the energy possible into the battery in charging and then draining it completely they have a battery management system that switches off charge by about 0.1 volt which means maybe 5% less range. But because the batteries aren't stressed, they last longer. A quality ebike battery should last 700–900 charge cycles, so that keeps the battery out of the waste stream longer, and the performance stays better for longer.

SN: So something like LoVo preserves the battery?

NS: Yes, and if you use a bike recreationally, you might recharge it once a week. So that's a lot of recharging. Also battery management is getting a bit less fussy. It used to be when you weren't riding ebikes you should leave them plugged in. You don't have to these days, and batteries come with battery management electronics, so they've got a circuit board in there that checks the battery health, that balances the cells

SN: Okay, so it's like a built-in caretaker for the battery?

NS: Exactly.

SN: So it talks to the cells and says, 'Hey guys, what's happenin'.'

NS: Yes, it's like a feedback system or car computer that monitors things and might eventually show a warning light. Sort of a simplified version of that. And batteries are really improving. Ebikes have outsold regular bikes in Europe and South-East Asia and now in North America (for example see this article https://www.theguardian.com/world/2019/mar/01/bike-country-n0-1-dutch-electric-record-numbers-e-bikes-netherlands), so they are definitely the future and we will see some really amazing changes in the next 5 years. There are some prototypes out there that have the motor, the controller and the battery all together in the wheel hub.

SN: Yes, I've seen one of them. The electric bike show had one, and it had a smartphone as the control (https://www.zehus.it/bike/).

NS: Yes, that becomes your display, and the range on them is quite limited, but they are great for a commute or between the train and your place of work, and a great, lightweight solution. So it's all coming and it will be huge.

SN: Yes.

NS: And in the time I've been in Melbourne the increase in traffic congestion is hard to believe.

SN: So that's car congestion.

NS: Yes, not only are houses disappearing so on a single house block they are now 5, 6, 7, 8, 10 units, each unit can have more than a single car, so just moving around the streets here, 5km out of the inner city, it's become a lot more congested.

SN: For bikes that's not a problem?

NS: Much less of a problem.

SN: It's a sort of a tipping point to push people away from cars and onto bikes.

NS: Bikes can seem inconvenient or exposed, but as traffic slows down and you are just crawling along, a bike becomes the most efficient way to do things.

SN: And you find that yourself personally?

NS: Absolutely, without question. I can get a load of shopping home and done in probably two-thirds of the time it takes to do it in the car. I'm not trawling for a car space, and can get in and out quickly, and cross streets at pedestrian crossings. And there's a lot of great infrastructure in Darebin. They're one of the few councils that actually put their money where their mouth is with bike infrastructure.

6.2   Happy Xtracycle rider. Photo Martin John Brown.

SN: Yes I was at Simon Batterbury's cycling seminar yesterday, and Heidi from Darebin council was there … and she was very encouraging, and she was the person who actually had lived experience with bikes as compared to others who were quite academic about it.

NS: … and her partner who's also Simon, I've worked with him at Squeaky Wheel and Cycling Network for a long time and he is a very strong cycling advocate. And that's what I find is that some people in those transport roles walk the walk, they are passionate about it, live locally and are well versed in the benefits of bike riding. And you know it's just the perception of safety now that is the main impediment, and it is becoming safer because traffic is slowing down, and there's better and well-considered bike infrastructure.

SN: Yes, it would be good to get all the councils on board. I've thought when riding on bike paths why don't they have a bike path council who control them overall in the city of Melbourne. You cross a creek or something into another council area and things are done in a different way.

NS: And another thing is signage. They expect people to use a smartphone to find the way. That's not my forte, and I can't manage a phone when I'm riding.

SN: Well it's enough to manage the bike.

NS: Yes and it's a shared space. You've got dogs, kids, people with headphones on, you've got all kind of things out there. You've gotta be a good cycling citizen for that whole concept to work. You can't get out there and say, 'Right, bike path, too bad for pedestrians,' and just tear around. It's just not going to work.

SN: You sort of want bike paths to accept riders who are beginners so they are not put off. To get onto another topic, you've built up an electric load-carrying bike, can you tell us about that?

NS: Well the beautiful thing about bikes is their recyclability. A quality bike can be reused and rebirthed uncountable times. I started in Melbourne with a bike given to me, and it was only when I upgraded that I realised what a dog it was, and then I went for one that had a particular technology known as flat-foot technology, which is a claimed proprietary feature.

6.3   City Bike.

6.4   City Bike with Xtracycle.

SN: A slightly more backward sloping seat tube?

NS: Exactly, but that coupled with an open, step-through frame. It turns out that's a sweet spot particularly for mature women. For those who've had knee, hip, back problems it just makes riding easier. Women in particular have a terror of falling and breaking something, and the fact they can just put down a substantial part of their foot and then ride without having to get out of the seat and still have reasonably correct leg length makes for a perfect solution. So, riding round on that bike, really enjoying it, quite upright torso with a big squashy comfortable seat, which is the other thing women find really vexing.

SN: So just to say what your current bike is, you have a longtail extension on the back of your electric flat-foot cycle, right?

NS: Yes, and the extension is called an Xtracycle free radical.

SN: Okay, and are they still available?

NS: They are, and they are now on Generation 2 of that concept. An MIT engineering student who travelled in South America worked out that a load-carrying bike could really revolutionise life and the economy down there. So he came back and promptly designed this bolt-on addition, which could adapt any bike to become a load-carrying bicycle. By removing the back wheel, fitting this framework into the rear-wheel dropouts and moving the existing back wheel into the back of the framework, you've created a longtail cargo bike (See http://www.worldbike.org/about-us).

SN: So you've used one of the Xtracycles, but have the electric motor fitted as well. And the thing is to start with the right bike to make it a good overall proposition, with the sloping seat tube letting you put feet flat on the ground when you're stopped.

NS: Yes, that suits me and my electric load carrier and my cohort too. When I put middle-aged women on flat-foot bikes, their whole demeanour changes and they start smiling. You know you can get seriously out of condition when you have had kids and put on weight post menopause. On standard bikes they need to use their upper body to pull themselves up and step down, and they don't do it, and they sit there propped on the seat with their very tippy toes trying to support themselves, it's going to be a disaster. Sooner or later they will overbalance and be unable to stop and down they come and fall heavily and feel stupid. If they don't actually hurt themselves they feel embarrassed and convince themselves, they can't balance.

I'd love a dollar for every woman who's come to me and says, 'Oh, I can't ride a bike, I don't have the balance.' So my way of teaching proves to them that of course they have the balance, what they don't have is confidence. Once you prove to them their balance is absolutely fine, then it's just so satisfying. It takes maybe an hour, an hour and a half to get those women pedalling on their own, and you get to relive the first time you did it, so it's really a lot of fun, and they're just astonished at what they can do.

SN: What's the supply of those sort of bikes like, I mean we're here in a bike shed and there's not any of that type here.

6.5   City Bike with ebike kit.

6.6   City Bike with Xtracycle and ebike kit.

NS: There's only a few manufacturers I'm aware of, and one of them's Electra.

SN: Yeah they have a Townie?

NS: That's exactly the one I'm thinking of, they also have one called the Loft and another one called the Amsterdam. Electras come out of Taiwan. They are a quality build bike, with a nice blend of aluminium and good components, and mine's bomb-proof. I'd bought it second-hand, it had lived near the beach, but once I had the bearings sorted it was a great bike.

SN: Okay, so are they all for sale in Melbourne?

NS: Yes, they are not as common as Giant, Trek or the others, but you can look up and find a dealer. And Giant used to have a copy of the Townie called a Suede, and that had a raked seat post too.

SN: Woohoo, nice name. Gotta get one of them! I think we can wrap it up there, but thank you very much.

NS: A pleasure.

7 Recumbent Bikes

Recumbent bikes are two-wheeled cycles where riders are laidback or horizontal. Most recumbents have the rider head up, feet forward — that is positioned as for car driving or couch lying. A combination of low frontal area and slippery shape can improve aerodynamics and make them faster than bicycles. This was documented beyond reasonable argument in Scientific American by Albert Gross and Chet Kyle in 1983. The article drew on contemporary and historical human powered vehicle records.

In the 1930s, Francis Faure broke world cycling records on Mochet recumbent bikes. Recumbents were subsequently banned from cycling competitions, temporarily stalling their development (7.1, 7.2, 7.3).

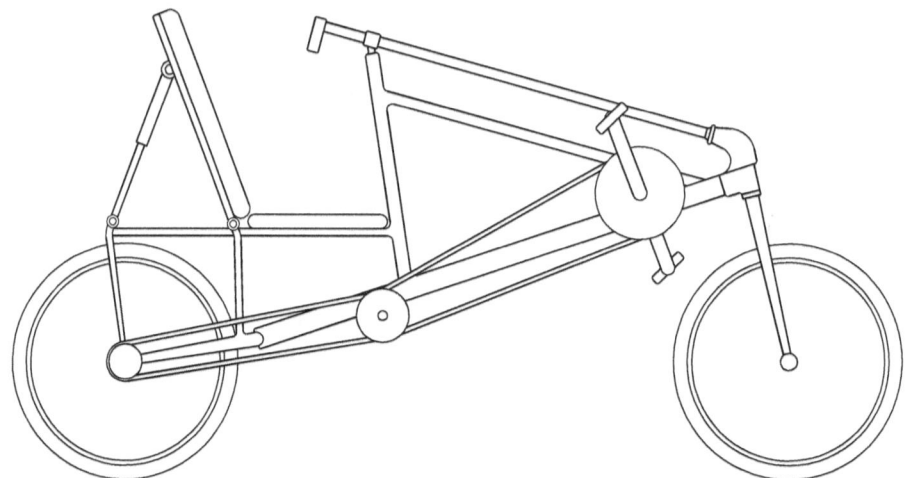

7.1   Mochet recumbent bike with seat in upright tour position.

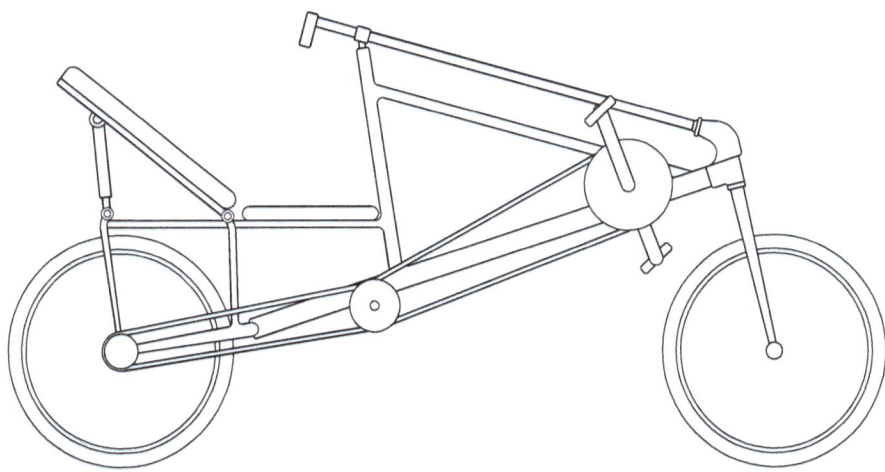

7.2   Aerodynamic laidback race position.

7.3   Megan Hamilton on Mochet recumbent. Note load-carrying tailbox. From Player's cigarette cards 1939.

Widespread development of recumbent bikes only resumed in the 1970s with formation of the International Human Powered Vehicle Association. The association sanctioned recumbent races and speed records, resulting in a wide range of new bikes. By the early 1990s, commercial recumbents were available, and they depended on cycling inventions and trends of the 70s and 80s. Clipless pedals and matching shoes, V-brakes, precision Japanese parts manufacture, aluminium rims and frames, and wide-range gearing all helped the newer, faster and heavier-than-bicycle recumbents to start, stop and remain in control.

In the early 2000s, recumbents were made in Europe, America and Australia and were expensive. Now they are made in bicycle manufacturing hubs in Taiwan and China for a world market, are available online, and so are less expensive. This has only gone so far. Mainly because they lack sales volume, recumbent bikes are still more expensive than bicycles. They are definitely harder to test and obtain. For example, I know of only one bike shop in Melbourne (population 5 million) stocking recumbents.

Recumbent bike designs pay attention to aerodynamics and ergonomics, and I find them fine for everyday cycling. However, because they are rarely seen, they are less understood than bicycles. Some riders take up recumbent bikes because they relieve non-traumatic cycle injuries such as wrist or back pain, and for this reason they can be seen as cycles for older people. But what is good for strained bodies is good for all bodies, and there is no practical reason why there are not more recumbents on the roads.

Recumbent bikes make great home building projects. They are simpler than most recumbent trikes, can be made from scrap bicycle parts, and almost every recumbent bike builder gets some pride of achievement. Today, recumbent bikes hold outright speed records ranging from 200m (Todd Reichert, 144.17km/h in Battle Mountain, Nevada USA) to 15,000km (round Australia unsupported, Peter Heal, 48 days, 23 hours and 37 minutes). Recumbent trikes hold a few records in the middle ground, for example the world 24-hour cycle speed record is 1,219km held by Christian von Ascheberg in a modified velomobile trike.

This chapter explains different types of recumbent bikes. Unlike bicycles with one basic drivetrain/wheel/steering geometry, recumbents have many variations. However, many recumbent bikes share steering geometry with bicycles. That means a head tube angle close to 70°, a front wheel trailing the steering axis, and a front wheel flopped to a low potential energy position (7.4, 7.5). Recumbent bikes can be classified by wheelbase, steering, seat height, drivetrain and aerodynamics.

7.4   Bicycle showing trail: front wheel trails steering axis.

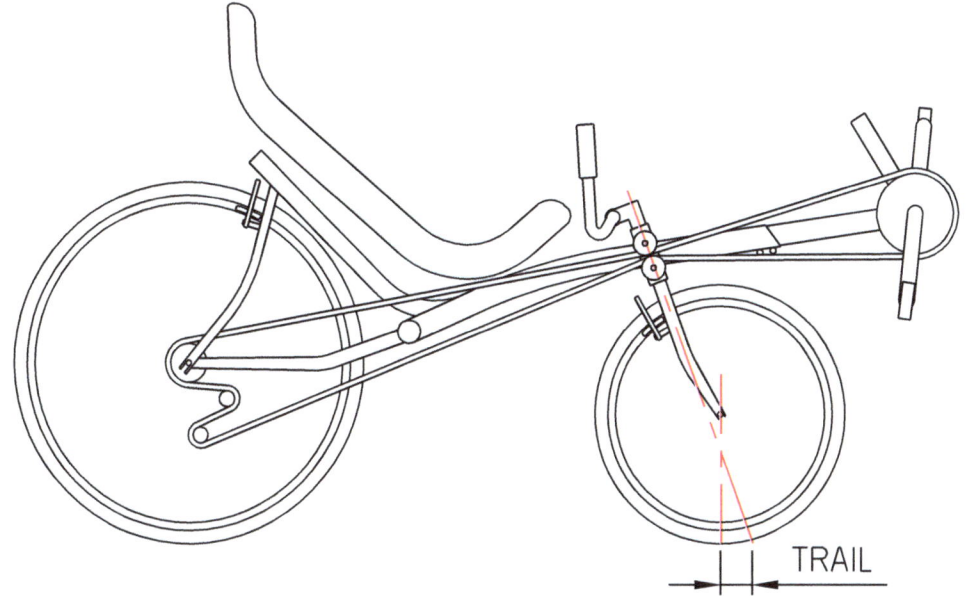

7.5   Actionbent recumbent bike showing trail.

Rear-wheel-drive recumbent bikes have the same drivetrain configuration as bicycles, and there are two categories of front-wheel-drive recumbents. These are the front-wheel-drive recumbents with pedals fixed on the rear frame (called fixed bottom bracket/FBB), and those with pedals on the moving front wheel frame (called moving bottom bracket/MBB). MBB recumbents have leg steer, that is legs influence steering to some extent.

Wheelbase

Cycles 7.5, 7.6 and 7.7 are recumbents with short, medium and long wheelbase. Long-wheelbase bikes have the front wheel in front of the pedals, short wheelbase bikes have the front wheel behind the pedals, and medium (or compact long) wheelbase bikes have the front wheel near or over the pedals. Long-wheelbase bikes are associated with relaxed, slower riding, and generally have a larger turning circle than the shorter bikes.

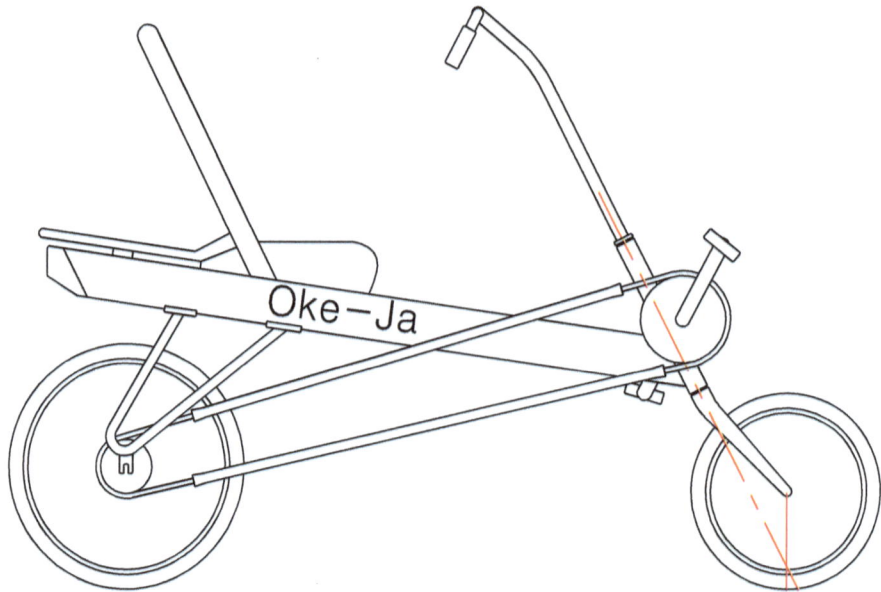

7.6   Oke Ja medium-wheelbase recumbent bike.

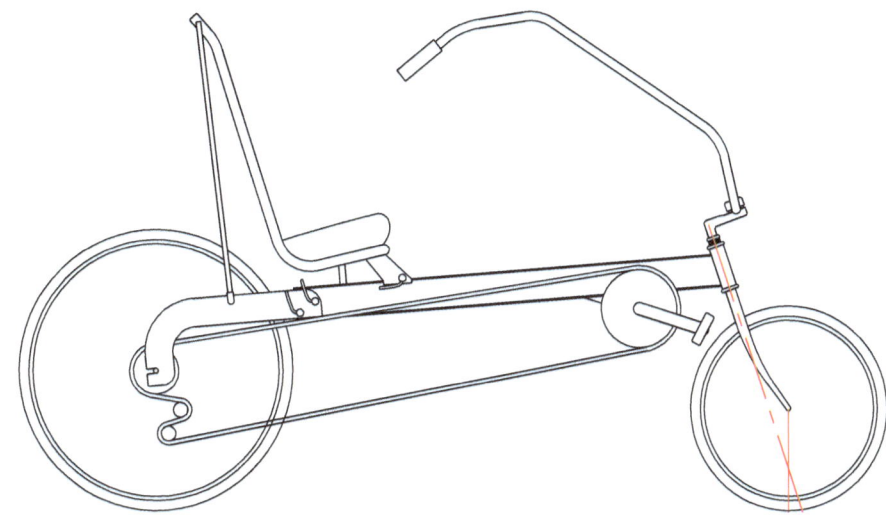

7.7   Linear long wheelbase with overseat steering.

Steering

7.5 and 7.8 show bikes with underseat/under-the-legs steering, while 7.6, 7.7 and 7.9 show overseat/over-the-legs steering bikes. 7.5 has direct underseat steering, while 7.8 has indirect steering with a rod connecting front forks to handlebars. 7.7 has tiller steering handlebars, which require sweeping sideways to steer. These long handlebars can be favourably associated with dragsters or chopper bikes. In 7.9, the fork is on a greater angle giving more handlebar rotation and less sweep.

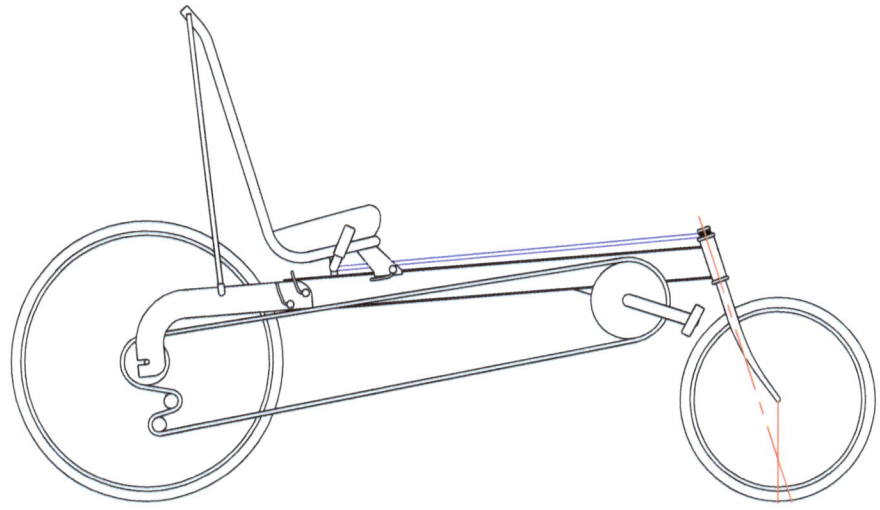

7.8   Linear long wheelbase, with underseat steering and linkage shown in blue.

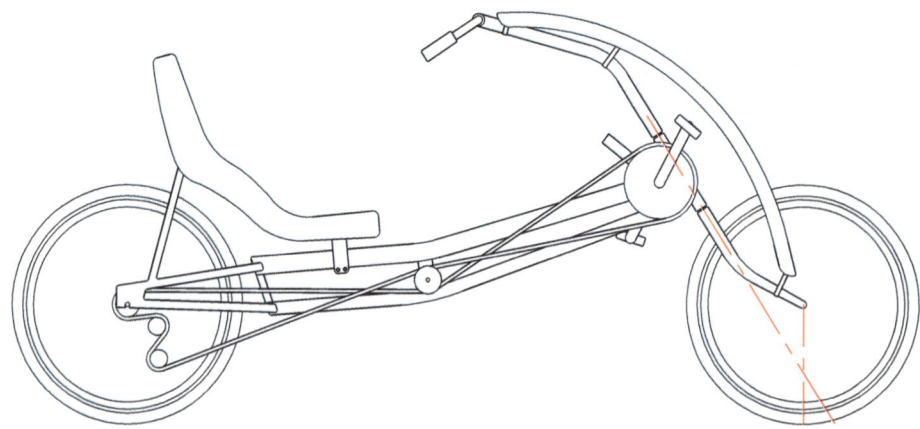

7.9   Rans with raked back steering and fairing.

Overseat steering bikes are simpler for novices to ride because the rider's feet can easily reach the ground without handlebar interference. Overseat steering bikes can be more aerodynamic because the rider's arms are not at the side of the body, adding frontal area and contributing to wind resistance. Underseat steering bikes offer a relaxed and comfortable riding position.

Seat height

The lower a recumbent's seat, the faster it will go. This is because a low seat leads to a low body position and improved aerodynamics through reduced frontal area. Lowracers (7.10) are low enough to allow the rider to support themselves with their hands when stopped, and often include a 20″ front wheel. Very low bikes can be hard to see on the road, so lowracers are rarely used as city transport. Highracers (7.11) are higher and generally have 700C wheels and racing bike parts. Common components and component knowledge makes for simple transition between road race bicycles and highracer recumbents.

I ride cycles with a seat height of 48cm giving an eye height of 110cm, and feel safe riding in city traffic. As all cyclists should, I proceed slowly in city traffic where cars and SUVs can stop riders being seen by pedestrians and cars. 110cm is about driver's eye height in a car, and city riders of lower recumbents should consider using a flag to aid conspicuity.

7.10   M5 Lowracer with 20" front wheel.

7.11   Pelso Brevet highracer with racing bicycle 700C wheels and groupset.

Drives and transmission

Recumbents shown in 7.1 to 7.9 are rear-wheel drive. This gives a simply understood transmission layout, but the chain needs to be long to reach from front pedals to rear drive cogs. The long chain can run over pulleys or in plastic tubes to prevent flopping, accidental derailment and oil stains on trousers. Power is transmitted on the top side of the chain so the top side is the only one that will strain pulleys.

To shorten the chain and stop it running exposed to road grit under the seat, recumbent builders made fixed bottom bracket front-wheel drives. In the commonest commercial FBBs, the chain reaches the drive cluster via two pulleys near the fork crowns. The chain twists when the bike is steered, but this does not cause problems because chains are already designed to flex in derailleurs (7.12, 7.13). The Bevo bike had a variation on this arrangement, with the crankset near the fork crown, a direct chain drive, and a pulley in the non-drive side of the chain (7.14).

7.12   Toxy lowracer fixed bottom bracket front-wheel drive. Small chain angle at top pulley causes high forces.

7.13   Toxy lowracer, Spezi, Germersheim, Germany. Photo Kim Aagaard.

7.14   Bevo bike has chainring above fork crown avoiding need for drive side pulley.

With the exception of the back brake, front-wheel-drive recumbents have the drive and controls at the front. This minimises entanglement and makes them good candidates for folding and modularity, where parts are swapped out to make new configurations. The Performer Conquer is an example of a folding front-wheel-drive bike.

Moving bottom bracket (MBB) front-wheel-drive bikes have both cranks and front wheel mounted on the moving frame at the front, meaning legs influence steering, and the legs can *be* the bike's steering. Commercial models include Cruzbikes, which come in touring and highracer formats, and have bicycle steering geometry. The Atomic Zombie frontrunner is a similar foldable bike, available as a set of DIY plans in PDF format for $17.

7.15   Cruzbike front-wheel-drive bike.

Another DIY MBB bike style is the Albatros, a French highracer design. Drawings of the bike are available free on the internet, and the bike has been built in steel, plywood and bamboo. My friend Simon Watt built his own Albatros with the help of Peter Heal. Simon researched recumbent bikes designs before building his bike, and made his version foldable to fit on trains and inside his small car.

7.16   Albatros DIY front-wheel-drive bike.

7.17   Ian, Peter, Simon in Katunga Australia with Simon's Albatros.

Flevobike designed and made centre-steer moving bottom bracket front-wheel-drive bikes. They made two different frames that both fold: a racer, and a beginners' bike that can convert to a load-carrying trike. Engineered rubber blocks are used to aid suspension and steering. I helped Aki Kubota make his Flevoracer rideable and tried it myself (7.18, 7.19). Initially it is awkward to ride, as it involves some unlearning of bicycle riding.

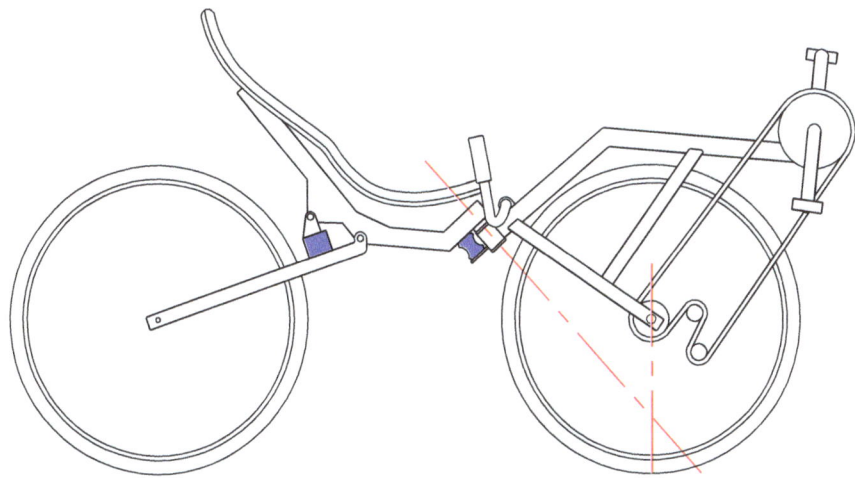

7.18   Flevobike centre-steer race bike with steering and suspension elastomers shown blue.

7.19   Success! Aki on the altered Flevo.

The Python is another challenging centre-steer moving bottom bracket bike. These are almost exclusively home built. They are lowracers by default and an old-school email list and open source website keeps riders and builders informed of progress on Python projects worldwide, including bikes, trikes and leaning trikes. Pythons are stabilised by the riding position being a low, minimal gravitational potential energy position. Trail is negative, with the steering axis behind the front wheel centre.

7.20   Centre-steer Python bike.

7.21   Kervelo front-wheel-drive hubcycle with front hub gearbox.

A hub bike has the same configuration as Pierre Michaux velocipedes of 1865, that is with pedals on the front wheel axis. But Kervelos, MC2s and other modern hub bikes are updated two generations in materials and technology, and can have a wide ranging, variable speed, front hub gearbox. This makes them safer, stronger, lower and more ergonomic than their Michaux grandparents, and more versatile than their 1893 Crypto Bantam Gearbox parents.

Kervelo bikes were first made by adapting Pinion gearboxes, and later they used their own made-for-purpose Kernel gearbox. Kervelo have demonstrated versions of their bike with interchangeable ebike, trike and tilting trike rear sections. MC2s also feature modular designs and have been made in mini penny farthing, recumbent and direct rear-wheel-drive types. Modern hub bikes are still under development. They are an emerging type with few or no readily available commercial models.

7.22 1893 geared Bantam cycle. From Sharp 1896.

7.23 Kervelo hub bike, Spezi, Photo Kim Aagaard.

7 Recumbent Bikes

7.24 MC2 hub bike, Spezi, Germersheim, Germany. Photo Kim Aagaard.

Aerodynamics

Figures 7.25 to 7.29 show lowracers in order of increasing speed. The speed improvements shown can be made using DIY, which has long been part of recumbent bike culture. Bicycle racers are less likely to make DIY bike improvements, partly because more commercial products are available to modify bicycles.

Circular spokes on bike wheels are not good aerodynamically and cause speed-decreasing drag. So on fast bikes, spoke counts are minimised, spokes are made in aerodynamic sections, or entire spoke sets are covered with cloth, plastic or foam to form disc wheels (7.26). Covered wheels can cause instability in side winds. In particular, covered front wheels can be steered by strong winds, and are avoided and for this reason.

Fairings are used to optimise airflow over bike and rider to achieve minimum aerodynamic drag. 7.27 has a tailfairing behind the rider primarily to increase speed. This tailfairing is cut by the back wheel decreasing its usefulness as storage as compared with 7.3. 7.28 adds a front fairing to be fully faired, and a cloth fairing (7.29) can further decrease wind drag. Commercial faired bikes exist and these include the Lightning F40 and F90.

Practical fully faired bikes aren't self-stable and must be ridden to balance. This means they must allow foot- or hand- access to the ground, otherwise they could not be started or safely stopped. As well, they have a large side-area and can be difficult to control in cross winds.

For these basic control reasons, fully faired practical human powered vehicles are usually three-wheelers called velomobiles.

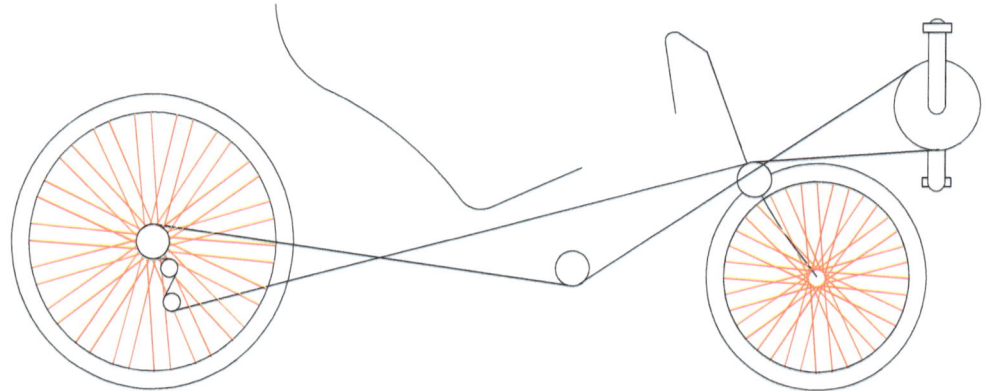

7.25   Stock lowracer bike with exposed spokes.

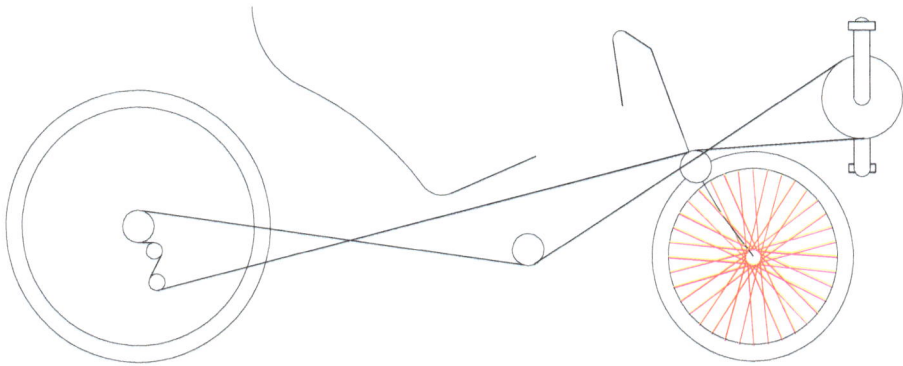

7.26   Disc rear wheel removes spokes from airstream.

7.27   Tailfairing decreases air turbulence behind rider.

7.28   Fairing improves aerodynamics of front of bike.

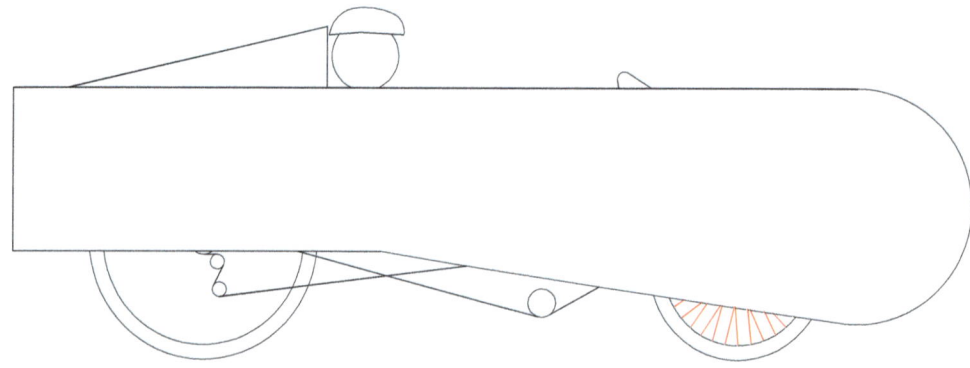

7.29   Cloth cover completes aerodynamic profile.

Speedbikes

At extremes of cycle aerodynamics are two-wheeled streamliners, cycles whose entire purpose is to challenge and break outright speed records. Holders of 200m and hour speed records are good examples.

Aerovelo's ETA Prime streamliner (200m record by Todd Reichert, 144.17km/h in Battle Mountain Nevada USA, 2016) is a lowracer surrounded by a full aerodynamic computer-designed fairing. A video camera and monitor are used for forward vision, as a clear windshield at the front would compromise aerodynamics. This configuration has become standard for single-person streamliners, and some examples are shown in Chapter 8.

Francesco Russo's Metastretto (hour record, 92.43km, Dekra Lausitzring, Germany) also has the rider laidback but facing head first and looking forward via a mirror and windshield. This position has the body's wide-point/shoulders at the front, fitting in with the smallest possible aerodynamic shape, also widest at the front. The Metastretto is a triumph of mechanical engineering, with a layout pioneered by Damjan Zabovnik. The outright hour record has been held by these style bikes for all but 2 years since 2008.

7.30 shows Metastretto's immediate predecessor, Eiviestretto. The pedal axis runs through the rear wheel, and transmission is through two chains, one of which reverses wheel rotation. The bike's outside shell is optimised for low aerodynamic drag.

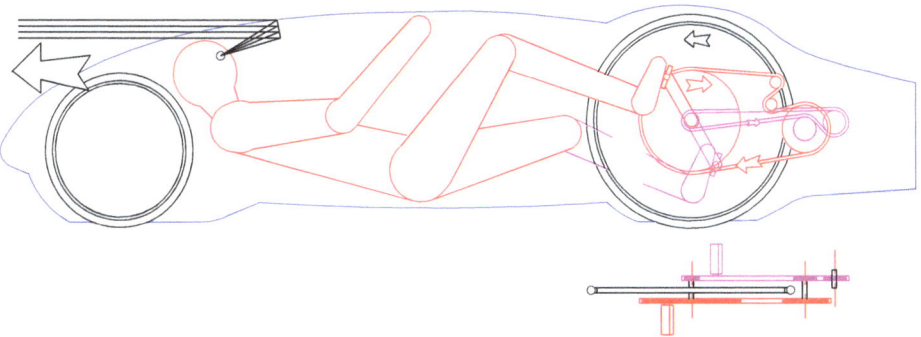

7.30 Eiviestretto schematic.

Summary

Recumbent bikes have developed alongside — and with — bicycles, and they offer great options for DIY and comfortable touring, Audax riding and load carrying. They do not have to be designed to be the fastest to be faster than bicycles.

References

Davidson, A. 1994, *Encycleopedia 1994/1995*, Open Road, Rotherham, UK. Retrieved July 2020 from https://issuu.com/encycleopedia/docs/enc01_opt

Davidson, A. 1996, *Encycleopedia 96*, Open Road, Rotherham, UK. Retrieved July 2020 from https://issuu.com/encycleopedia/docs/enc02_opt

Davidson, A. & McGurn, J. 1997, *Encycleopedia 4*, Open Road, Rotherham, UK.

Davidson, A. & McGurn, J. 1999, *Encycleopedia 99: the guide to alternatives in cycling*, Overlook Press, New York.

Davidson, A. & McGurn, J. 2001, *Encycleopedia 2001*, Open Road, Rotherham, UK.

Davidson, A. 2002, *Encycleopedia 2002*, Open Road, Rotherham, UK.

Eland, P. 2009, *Practical bike buyer's guide*, Snowbooks, London.

Eliasohn, M. 1991, 'Front-wheel-drive recumbent cycles', *Human Power*, vol.9, no.2, pp.11–14. Retrieved July 2020 from http://www.ihpva.org/HParchive/PDF/30-v9n2-1991.pdf

Fehlau, G. 2006, *The recumbent bicycle*, Out Your Backdoor Press, Williamston, MI.

Garnet, Jeremy: *Direct Drive Recumbent website Velotegra*: https://www.velotegra.com/directdrive

Gross, A.C., Kyle, C.R. and Malewicki, D.J., 1983. The aerodynamics of human powered land vehicles. *Scientific American*, 249(6), pp.142-153. Retrieved July 2020 from http://www.zzipper.com/documents/HPV_Paper.pdf

Heal, Peter, 2010 Roll down tests on bikes Retrieved July , OzHPV magazine *Huff*, https://www.ozhpv.org.au/HUFF/docs/huff066.pdf

Nurse, Stephen, *In-Hub gearbox front wheel drive cycles* Retrieved July 2020 from: https://www.hupi.org/HPeJ/0026/0026.html

Python Website and mailing list links: http://en.openbike.org/wiki/Main_Page

Rear Wheel Steering: http://en.openbike.org/wiki/RearWheelSteeringConcepts

Schmitz, V.A. and Hadland, T., 2000. *Human power: the forgotten energy*. Available through BHPC, https://shop.bhpc.org.uk/human-power-the-forgotten-energy-arnfried-schmitz

8   Speedbikes with Adam Hari

This chapter was written in late 2019 before COVID-19 virus restrictions. These restrictions included a worldwide aviation shutdown, cancellation of the 2020 Australian Ford — OzHPV Speed Challenge and of the 2020 World Human Powered Speed Challenge. Adam is continuing to build his speedbike and fitness for events in 2021.

Background

Adam Hari is in it for the long term and is playing a clever and slow strategy to be among the world's fastest 20 bike riders. Ever. In anything. In 2020.

He lives in Gosford on Australia's East Coast and took up cycling after a broken ankle left him unable to play soccer. He found standard cycling too slow, but a few internet searches led him to pictures and stories about the Battle Mountain speedbike Championships in Nevada, USA. There, on an almost flat, very straight, elevated, very smooth stretch of State Route 305, an annual competition takes place with fully faired streamliner cycles regularly reaching speeds of 100km/h. Adam was very motivated and visited the Battle Mountain event (officially the World Human Powered Speed Challenge) in 2015, where he was proud to sign off as an official witness to one of Todd Reichert's world record runs of more than 137km/h. He learnt more in a week than in all of his previous internet searches combined.

Since then, Adam has been building and racing recumbents and speedbikes, trying to make machines with the lowest frontal area and slickest shape to dramatically reduce wind resistance and allow more speed. He's a council electrician and gets access to the council's workshop, lathe and mills, and that helps ('I clean the tools up better than the guys who regularly work on them and they are all keen on my projects anyway,' he says).

8.1   Adam with front-wheel-drive highracer in Geelong.

Adam posted a few pictures of the bike he built for the 2018 OzHPV Challenge on Facebook, and I met him at the event itself in Geelong a few days later. The bike was quite a machine, with front wheel drive and a frame made of carbon fibre coating a foam core. The front wheel was mounted inside a pair of standard carbon bike forks and overall the frame was very stiff. Even then, Adam was focused on the sprint events and had a meter on his pedals letting him record his power output. He didn't care if he didn't do well in the longer races.

At this stage, Adam had already prepared moulds for a very high-end bike. These had been developed by measuring his body in his mountain bike riding posture, then rotating the measurements through 90° to size and build a speedbike mockup. Adam's body was scanned to 3d CAD in that position to define the minimum size for his Speedbike. Later, an aerodynamic shape was built up in CAD around that size. Results were put into a Computational Fluid Dynamics program and, after much tweaking and trialling, a final shape was decided on. Following that, a female mould of the fairing was made by Innovation Composites, a company making foiling yachts and aerospace components in Nowra New South Wales. Accurate carbon fibre aerodynamic fairings will be made directly from the female moulds.

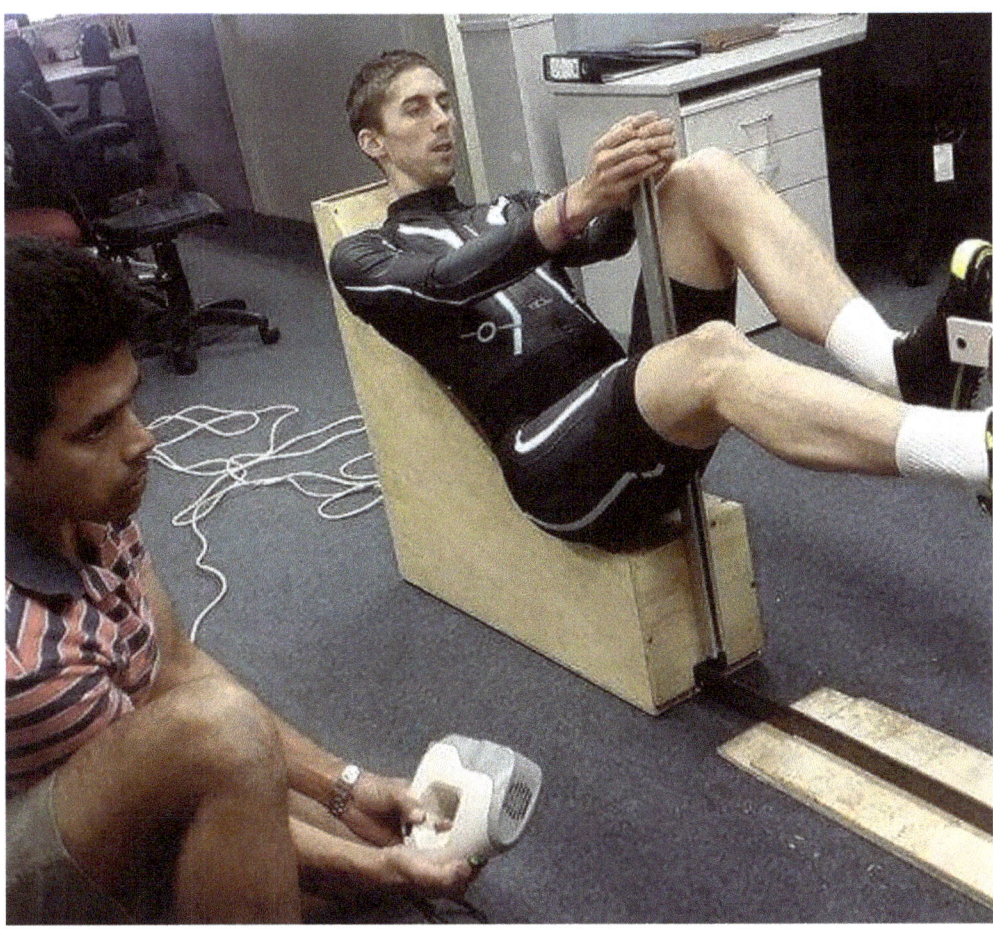

8.2   Body scanning Adam's for speedbike . Photo Adam Hari.

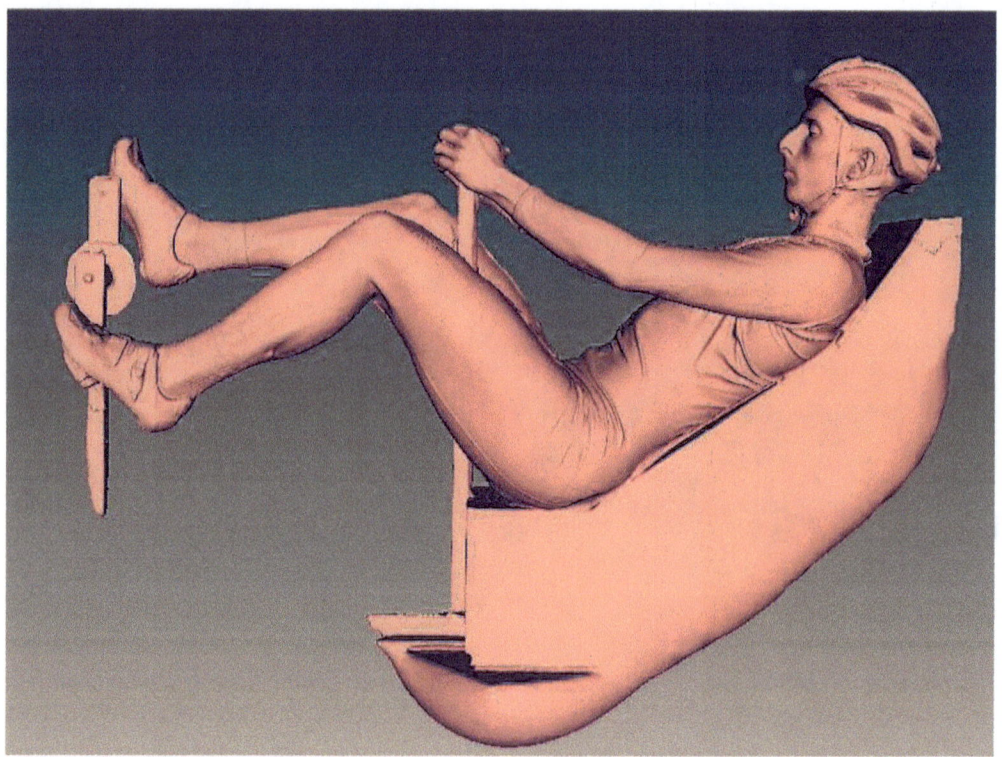

8.3   Body scan results. Photo Adam Hari.

WHPSC 2019

Before building a bike using the new fairing moulds, Adam decided to enter the 2019 WHPSC with a good but not fully developed bike. A fairing shell from a Kyle Edge streamliner had become available through Trisled in Melbourne, and that was converted to a structural shell (monocoque) by adding carbon fibre sections inside. The bike included a video camera outside and display unit inside. The camera and display avoid poor strength and aerodynamics that can come with clear windshields in speedbikes. This streamliner was completed a week before the event began. It was not tested until it reached Battle Mountain because starting requires balance assistance. It really is all about speed, and having simpler starting and stopping would compromise aerodynamics.

8.4 Hans van Vugt and Adam with repaired front wheel. Photo Jun Nogami

8.5   Ellen van Vugt. Photo humanpowerteam.com, basdemeijer.photo.

Adam had a few problems at WHPSC, but as a designer/builder/pilot was on the same level and had no barriers talking to, learning from and receiving help from much more experienced teams. His weak, 20-spoked front wheel broke, and it was rejigged by Hans Van Vugt to have 28 spokes. He had several training runs without his full fairing, meaning simpler launching and balance, but more wind resistance and lower speeds. Right at the end, Adam got through a full run with the fairing on, and reached 89.25km/h. This was a great achievement given that other teams considered it a victory just to get through the course's timing traps.

8.6   Battle Mountain speed run with partial fairing. Photo Jun Nogami.

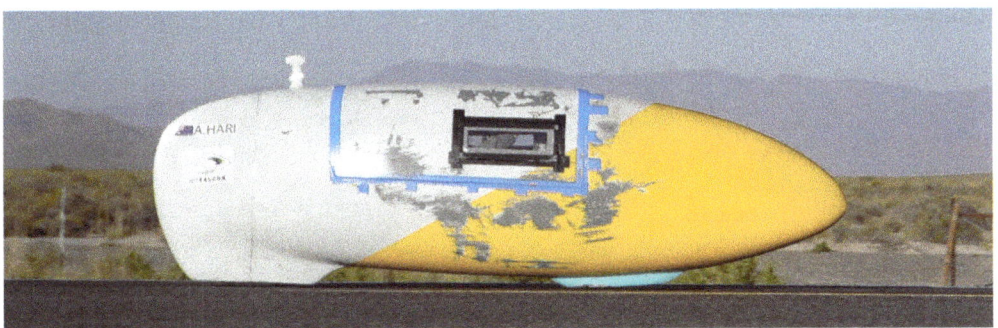

8.7 Run with full fairing and bike-top video camera. Photo Jun Nogami.

WHSPC 2019 was notable for great achievements and designs, and only a few are listed here. The women's speed record of 121.81km/h was broken by three riders from three different university teams, with Ilona Peltier finishing the meet with the highest speed of 126.52 km/h. Ilona and the other girls are learning fast from experienced riders such as Ellen Van Vugt.

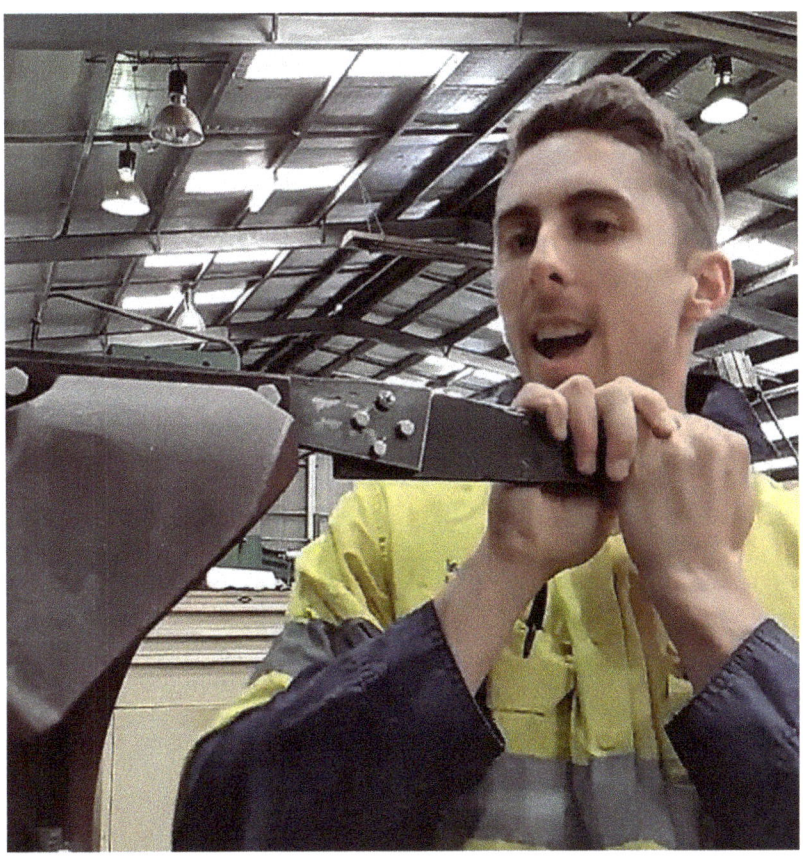

8.8 Adam tests a bike part in his employer's workshop in Gosford. Photo Adam Hari.

8.9   Adam's team in Battle Mountain Nevada 2019: Adam, brother David and father Michael. Photo Jun Nogami.

Despite some early crashes and technical difficulties, the tandem bike TITAN from Toronto set a multi-rider world record with 120.26km/h. Adam thinks the Titan could go faster and vie for the fastest machine outright. And the rather large, rocket-proportioned, five-rider Sprocket Rocket bike was a thrilling, rumbling sight on the track.

8.10   Ilona Peltier, Vittoria Spada, Ros Bas. Photo Jun Nogami.

8.11   All BM2019 teams seen from the front. Photo Jun Nogami.

8.12   BM2019 teams from behind, Sprocket Rocket dominates. Photo Jun Nogami

8.13 University of Toronto's TITAN is a back-to-back tandem streamliner. Photo Jun Nogami.

8.14 TITAN's high gearing allows speeds of around 130km/h. Photo Jack Wu, HPVDT, University of Toronto.

Plans for 2019

Back in Australia, Adam is building his WHPSC 2020 streamliner. He is currently working on a custom-made Arduino circuit-board-controlled gear changer. His gears will slide along an axle to keep chain lines straight and therefore more efficient. This year, several competitors wiped out their top mounted cameras in rollovers, and Adam plans to move the camera inboard in the new bike so it's less vulnerable.

When the streamliner internals are completely worked out, Adam will be assembling the bike using a shell made from moulds he has waiting. The internals will be structural carbon fibre laid over CNC machined foam. All parts are being developed by Adam using 3d computer-aided design. He plans to start assembling in December 2019, possibly having it ready for April 2020 when there is a chance of running it at an OzHpv event at the Ford proving ground at Lara, Victoria.

After that it is (of course) Battle Mountain in September 2020. Good luck Adam.

3d CAD bike building by Adam Hari

- Import scanned body shapes as basis for streamliner shell design.
- Optimise and specify streamlined shell, export specifications for contractor to build.
- Mock up pictures of streamliner for sponsors.
- Export CAD data for home-made 3d printed and CNC routed parts.
- 3d printer bike building.
- Make models of bike.
- Make camera mounts.
- CNC router bike building.
- Manufacture foam blocks as male moulds for internal struts and seats.
- Manufacture plywood bike mockups for training and gauging power output.
- Manufacture aluminium cranks and sprockets.

Programming jobs by David Hari

- Customise forward-vision camera displays to show speed, rider power output, target rider power output, distance covered.
- Program Arduino controlled gear changing unit.

References

Nogomi, Jun, *Biking in a Big City Blog*, Entries https://jnyyz.wordpress.com/2020/04/29/bm2020-cancelled/ and entries dated 1 to 18 September 2019, https://jnyyz.wordpress.com/page/2/?s=bm2019

Hari, Adam, *Website and Instagram*, http://hptfalcon.com/contact/ and https://www.instagram.com/hpt_falcon/

9 Recumbent Trikes, Velomobiles and Quads

This chapter covers non-tilting recumbent trikes and velomobiles, four-wheel light vehicles (quads) and delta (one wheel forward) and tadpole (two wheels forward) trike configurations. Stability, tilting trikes and passenger and freight trikes are covered separately.

Trike basics

9.01   Kids on trikes at a Canberra OzHPV event.

Riding recumbent trikes is easy for most people, with little learning required. Recumbent trikes support the body and are statically stable, allowing people of all ages and weights to exercise safely. Those with cerebral palsy or recovering from stroke can often exert full leg power on recumbent trikes despite having difficulties walking. They are also fun, and kids will lie almost flat on trike seats to reach the pedals and ride away with a huge grin once they achieve forward motion.

Trikes differ from bikes in stability and wheel forces. It is like they speak different languages! Bicycle stability is dynamic, depending on forward motion and leaning for balance. Bicycles only achieve trike-like static stability when stopped, propped and unoccupied.

Trikes don't need motion for stability: in fact trike motion leads to instability. When trikes' dynamic centre of gravity falls outside the triangle formed by the wheels, trikes go up on two wheels and can eventually crash. In trikes, this bicycle-style leaning/balancing is called tipping. It mostly occurs at high speed and is either undesirable or a party trick. But trikes' low-speed stability means they can travel uphill at speeds lower than the 3–5km/h required for bike balancing. Some trikes are geared low to enable this slow laden hill climbing. Trikes are rolling machines, and stability when stopped means a park brake is essential.

Extreme examples of gearing on recumbent trikes include:
- a three-speed hub gear combined with a 24-speed (3 × 8) derailleur drivetrain to give 72 possible gears and a 900% gear range.
- a Rohloff speed hub combined with a Schlumpf 2.5 times increasing gear system in the bottom bracket giving 28 possible gears and a 1,200% gear range.
- the inexpensive Terratrike Maverick i3 with a 3-speed internal hub gearing and a modest 188% gear range starting with a 32″ low gear.

Bikes lean when cornering, confining forces on their wheels to a straight line between tyre contact point and wheel axle centre. This usually means no side forces. In contrast, most trike wheels stay perpendicular to ground when cornering, causing side forces. For this reason, trike wheels must be built strong. The Schwalbe Tryker is a specialist tyre designed to deal with trike forces.

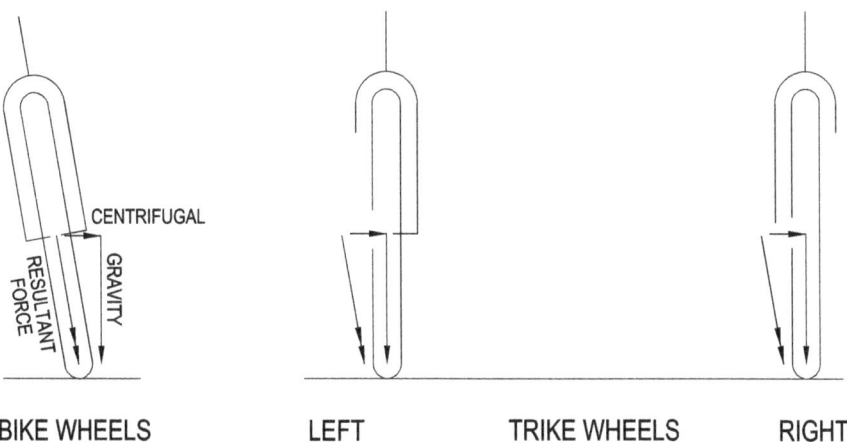

9.2　Forces on bike and trike wheels.

The highly dished spoke structure of small wheels can make them stronger than large wheels, and small (16 or 20″) wheels are common on recumbent trikes. Trikes can also use larger, disc brake, thru-axle 26″ rear wheels with widely dished spokes for adequate wheel strength. As well as advantages of wheel strength, thru axles (12, 15 or 20mm) become a structural part of the frame. These wheels are standard on mountain bikes and the Azub Tricon 26 trike. Thru-axle technology also works well for tadpole trike front wheels, allowing simple wheel removal despite the presence of disc brakes.

Early background

Trikes were developed alongside some of the earliest two-wheeled pedalled cycles. While high penny farthings were precarious, early trikes such as the 1881 Tricycle Carriage (9.3) offered stability and a low and large seat. Early tricycles introduced chains and rear wheel drive to cycling, inventions later used in bicycles.

Once rear-drive safety bicycles were established in the 1890s, they started dominating cycling. They were less precarious than high-wheel bikes, and lighter and less expensive than trikes. Bicycles became working, accessible machines for more people. As bicycles took over, available trike alternatives reduced in number until few remained. One that survived for personal transport (9.4) was the forerunner of today's Gomier trikes, essentially a bicycle with two back wheels using mass produced bicycle components (9.5). Compared to recumbent trikes, these upright trikes have a higher centre of gravity and are less dynamically stable. This is fine for low speeds, but cornering at speed causes stability problems.

9.3   Tricycle carriage. From Cassell's Magazine 1881.   9.4   Tricycle. From Sharp, 1896.   9.5   2016 Gomier trike.

Recumbent trikes background

In the early 1980s, Mike Burrows of England headed a Human Powered Vehicle race team, and entered the fully faired, recumbent 'Speed Machine' in an open design 200m International Human Powered Vehicle Association event in Brighton England. Andy Pegg rode the trike at 72km/h on the flat. Andy also trained on the designed-for-speed trike unfaired on public roads. At intersections he was forced to dismount and pick the trike up to turn. This was not great, and something new was needed.

9.6   Windcheetah trike.

9.7   Greenspeed trike, 1991. Courtesy Wayne Kotzur.

So Mike designed and built the Speedy or Windcheetah, an open version of faired Vector speed trikes he had seen at races. The design was fun, and soon more were made. Mike received feedback from a mate in Holland that the Speedy was practical transport, and more could be sold. Speedy trikes went into production and the recumbent trike was born.

By the mid-1980s Mike's Speedies had influenced Werner Stoyke from Germany, who with his students built a series of ever-improving recumbent trikes. These started off with Mike Burrows' centre steering design, but without some more exuberant flourishes such as the cantilever rear wheel. They included mesh seats, still present on trikes today. Some of Werner's students continued building trikes and exhibited commercial models.

In the early 1990s, Ian Sims from Melbourne Australia was also influenced by Burrows' machines and made his own recumbent trike. He rode it on the long-distance, multi-day Great Victorian Bike Ride. By the end of the ride he had a customer for a trike, and began making and selling them. Greenspeed trikes were soon manufactured for a world market.

Now numerous trike makers exist, with manufacturers based in Italy (Slyway) Taiwan (Performer) Australia (Trisled) Serbia (Steintrikes) Germany (Hase, Hp Velotechnic, Velomo) UK (Ice), USA (Terratrike, Catrike, Sun Bicycles, Trident), and the Czech Republic (Azub).

With surging popularity and manufacture in Taiwan and China, recumbent trikes have come down in price since the early 2000s. For example the Terratrike Maverick i3 is great value, costing $999 within the USA.

Velomobiles background

A velomobile is an enclosed trike or quad, and the vehicle's shell keeps the rider warm, dry and aerodynamic for travel at cruising speeds of 30km/h and above. Static stability and coverings make velomobiles ideal for snowy and icy roads where bikes slip and trikes are cold and exposed.

Chapter 7 describes recumbent bikes of the 1930s. Although open trikes were not part of the recumbent scene of the time, Mochet recumbent bikes did evolve from covered 3- and 4-wheeler 'cyclecars', velomobiles in current speak. Mochet velomobiles were manufactured from 1925 to 1944, with plywood bodywork and a steel frame. They suited the austerity of the time, costing the same as a motorbike but operating completely without fuel. One of the first velomobile riders was 10-year-old George Mochet, who found he could overtake every cyclist he encountered. Mochet velomobiles were part of France-wide cyclecar manufacture, where small manufacturers made human powered or modestly powered transport machines.

9.8   Mochet velomobiles, 1924 Photo Arnfried Schmitz, George Mochet archives.

Austerity in Europe lasted into the 1950s, and in Scandinavia the need for cheap cold-weather transport meant cyclecars continued to be built as DIY. One DIY builder was Carl-Georg Rasmussen from Denmark, who made an Ulf Cronberg designed cyclecar and went on to become a physicist, pilot and aeronautical engineer. As a senior engineer, Rasmussen responded to the 1979 oil crisis by saying, 'New and more sustainable ways of transportation, that use less energy, had to be found.' He then designed, built and manufactured the Leitra velomobile. From 1985, Leitras were made for the European market and are still sold today. Rasmussen himself was the first to complete the 1,250km Audax Paris-Brest-Paris bike ride in a velomobile.

9.9   Leitra velomobiles at Spezi. Photo Kim Aagaard.

In 1993, a velomobile called the Alleweder designed by Bart Verhees entered and won a Dutch 365-day Fiets competition for practical cycling. This led to the production of Alleweders by Flevobike of Holland. Alleweder provided a template for velomobiles that were to follow. Today, velomobiles are the fastest roadgoing human powered vehicles.

9.10   Alleweder velomobile.

Velomobiles can be 'head-out' or 'head-in' as per the Leitras in 9.9. Head-in velomobiles have the problems of moisture from the rider's breath condensing and fogging the windscreen, and can be claustrophobic. There is an aerodynamic penalty for having the rider's head outside the smooth shell, but it is a small compromise, and most commercial velomobiles are the simpler head-out type.

Velomobile wins in open rule cycle races are slowly convincing a wider cycling public of their abilities. An example is the win by Marcel Graber in an Alpha 7 velomobile in the unsupported, 6,800km 2018 Trans-Am cycle race. Velomobiles remain expensive, with the Alpha 7 weighing 21kg and costing 10,000 euros (A$16,500 before shipping) and the Trisled Rotovelo weighing 33kg and costing A$6,500.

9.11   Trisled rotovelo. Photo trisled.com.au.

Many young Australians get their first taste of human powered vehicles through their schools, where HPV (Pedal Prix) events involve building and racing pedalled vehicles. Races last up to 24 hours with multiple riders taking turns. Construction rules include restrictions on track width and inclusion of foot catchers, roll cages and seatbelts. All these can be necessary, as some teams consider HPV racing a contact sport!

Famous races on the Pedal Prix calendar include the Murray Bridge, Maryborough and Wonthaggi 24-hour events. These are huge festivals, and the biggest Human Powered Vehicle events in Australia, with thousands descending on country towns to supply, compete, support and officiate. Manufacturers such as Trisled, Trump Trikes, MR Components and Gtrikes supply trikes, plans and materials for HPV racing to schools.

Layout

This section deals mainly with trike steering and wheel configurations. Generally, what applies to open trikes also applies to velomobiles. While recumbent trikes all have frames, to which wheels, seat, brakes and pedals are attached, velomobiles can have either frame-plus-shell or monocoque construction. In the monocoque or structural skin version, the velomobile shell is the frame, an approach sometimes used in aircraft construction. A common DIY way to build a velomobile is to make a plywood or Corflute shell on top of an existing trike.

Simple billycart steering (front beam axle on a single pivot) is rarely used on recumbent trikes because it is prone to bump steer. The small wheels, high speeds and light steering mechanism of trikes conspire to make their handling difficult. However, some load-carrying trikes use billycart steering.

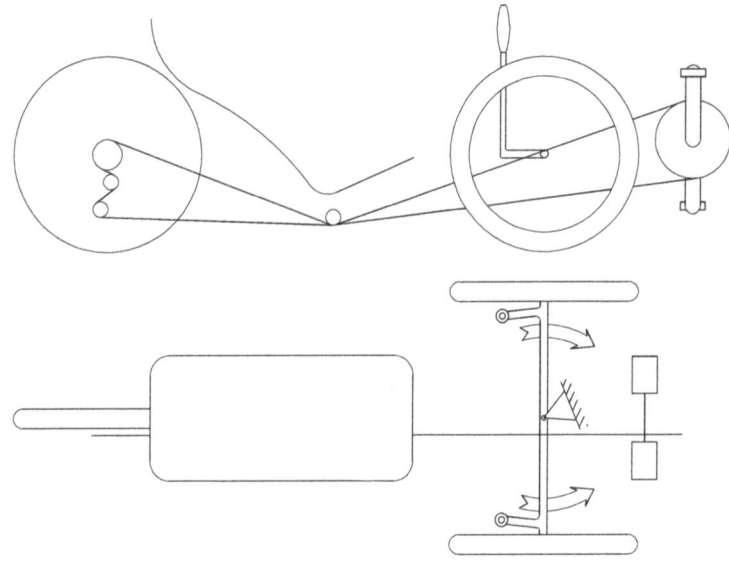

9.12   Trike with billycart steering.

Tadpole trikes have a simple drive mechanism with front cranks driving the back wheel and two steered front wheels. Stability can be enhanced when riders lean into corners, and tadpoles are generally stable in turns. They usually have a low seat and good aerodynamics. Both front wheels are linked, and turn together while cornering.

Ideally lines drawn through the axles of all three wheels always meet at a point, a principle known as Ackerman steering, which prevents wheel scrub. As well, the steering linkage must be tuned so wheels are not excessively 'toed in' or 'toed out', as misalignment scrubs out tyres and causes rolling resistance.

Tadpole trikes usually have brakes on the two front wheels, as weight is transferred to these wheels during stopping. They carry loads in a way common on bicycles, starting with a rack for pannier bags mounted over the back wheel.

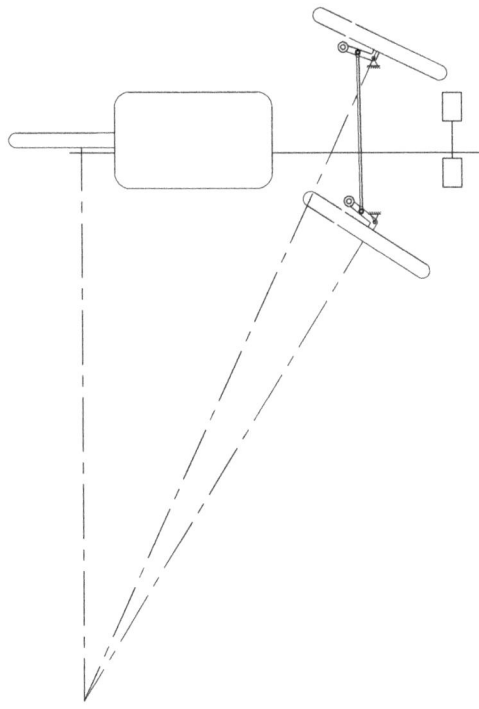

9.13   Tadpole trike, Ackerman steering.

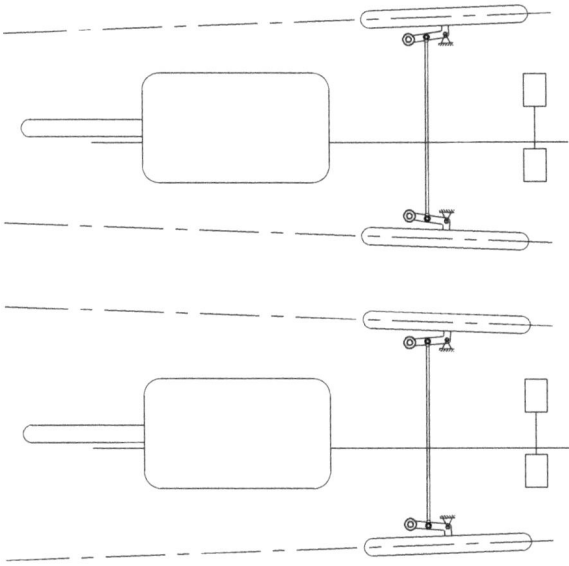

9.14   Tadpole trike wheel alignment, toe out top, toe in below.

Tadpole is the dominant configuration for velomobiles, partly for aerodynamics: the two wide wheels at the front fit in with the best teardrop aerodynamic shape. A delta velomobile would have two wide wheels at the back and either a large bluff end or two wheels sticking out.

Mesh seats are common on these trikes. Mesh seat frames can be structural, and the mesh is a simple type of suspension. Some clearance is required for a mesh seat so that a sagging bottom or back doesn't hit the frame. Mesh seats can be repaired, replaced and altered to include load carrying using DIY, and are generally robust.

Trikes intended for speed have moulded or composite seats with cushioning. These hard shell seats don't need much space, allow riders to be close to the ground and won't give under pedalling pressure. Fast tadpole trikes are generally light and low with front wheels close together, spoke covers on the wheels, and a very reclined hard shell seat. An option for hard shell seat covering is Ventisit/ACS10. This is an open-weave material, allowing the back to breathe.

Direct steering tadpoles are controlled by two linked steerers inboard of the front wheels, which include brake levers and disc brake mounting bosses. This steering is usually simple, compact and keeps brake cables short and tidy. Trisled have direct steering on their Gizmo model.

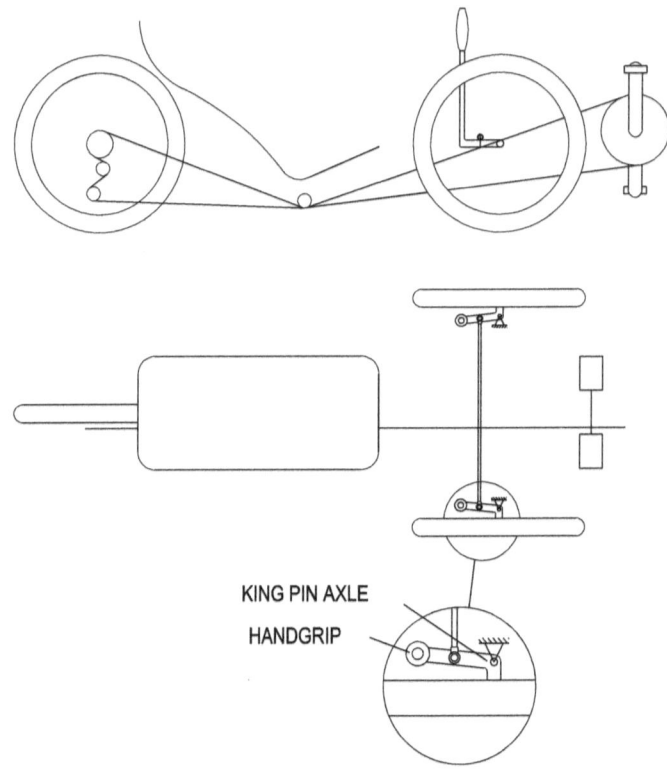

9.15   Tadpole trike, direct steering.

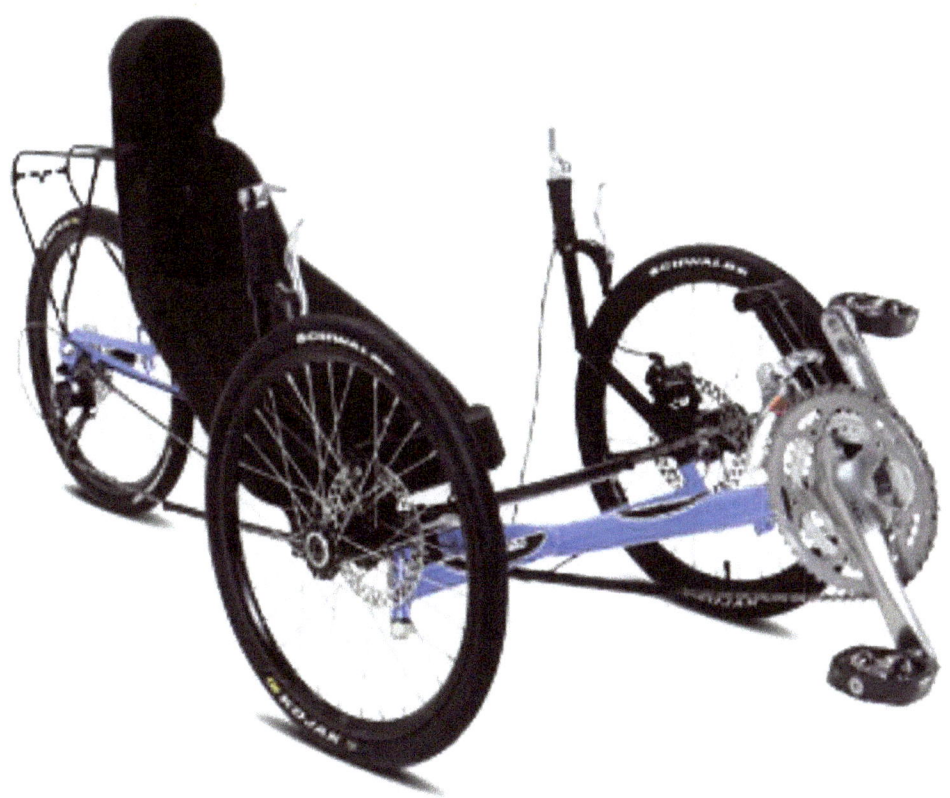

9.16   Trisled Gizmo trike, direct steering. Photo trisled.com.au.

Indirect steering on tadpole trikes is similar to underseat steering on recumbent bikes, and the wrists are isolated from road vibration. Ice trikes have indirect steering on their touring 'Adventure' models.

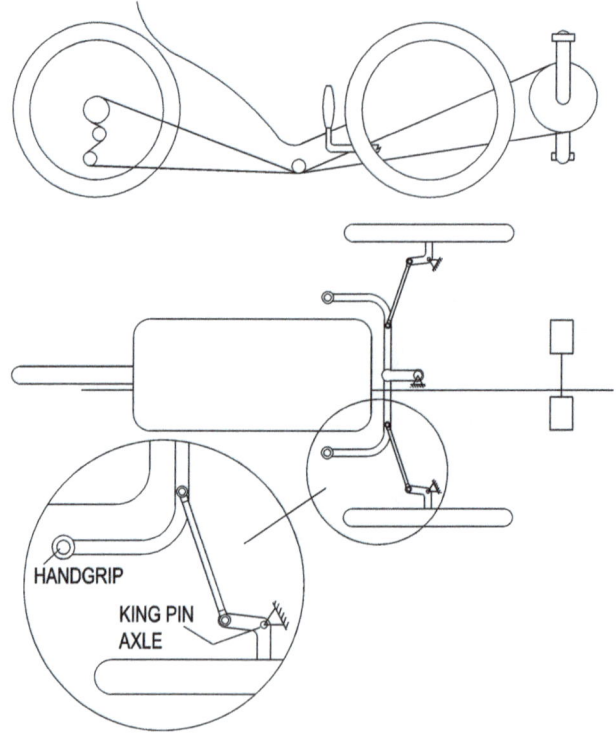

9.17 Tadpole trike, indirect steering.

9.18 Indirect steering Ice Adventure trike. Photo www.icetrikes.co.

Suspension has been available on tadpole trikes for several years on models including the sprung Ice Adventure and the Azub Ti-Fly 20 with a flexible titanium crossbar between the front wheels. Fat trikes are for off-road use and have large, low-pressure tyres providing significant suspension. Many velomobiles have suspension, as high speeds and high-pressure front tyres combine to make riding velomobiles feel rough otherwise. As well, suspension damps velomobile shell vibration.

Seat height is important in trike selection, and 9.19 shows examples. With a low seat, the Greenspeed Aero is more stable and aerodynamic, while the Terratrike Rambler is higher, wider and easier to access.

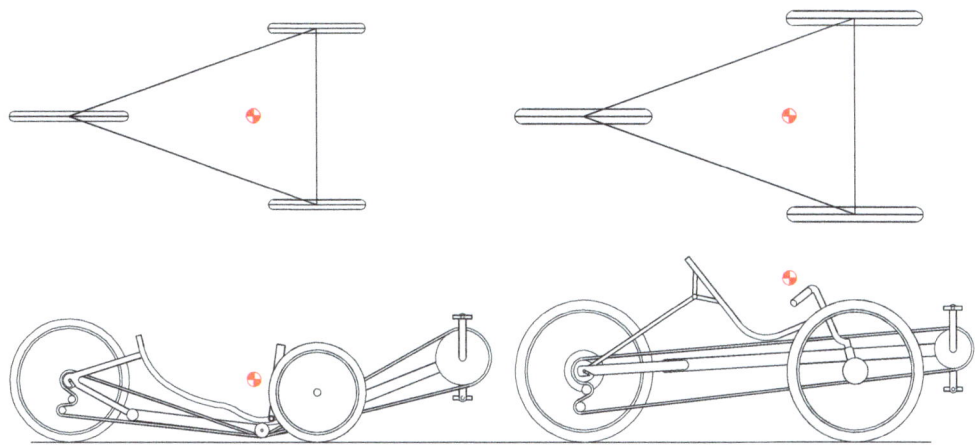

9.19 Contrasting trike layouts showing estimated centres of gravity in red: Greenspeed Aero and Terratrike Rambler.

Larry Varney mentions accessibility and handling and in his Rambler review, 'There are many of us in otherwise good condition, who find that the older we get, the heavier, and the less-able to squat down low and get back up without some assistance. This seat height is going to make you smile – it's like the chair at the dining room table,' and 'The higher that top [seat] is, the more careful you need to be when going fast through turns. Yes, with a seat height of over 17 inches, you're piloting a pretty tall pyramid! The track width is wider than most trikes on the market – it is matched by the Ice Adventure HD, at 31.5". This does help with the handling in general and turns, but I would advise to take it easy until you get more experience on the trike.'

There is more detail on trike handling in Chapter 15.

Delta recumbent trikes have been available in Germany since 1994, when Marec Hase produced 150 Easy Glider trikes. They became more readily available in Australia when Greenspeed started selling Anura trikes in 2007.

Delta trikes have simple steering but complex drive. With one wheel steered and a straight line axle at the back, Ackerman steering geometry is achieved automatically. Most deltas have rear wheel drive, with a chain driving one or both of simplify rear wheels. There are different methods of achieving this, and ideally it should be done with the least cost and compromise.

A solid axle between the two back wheels is inexpensive but compromised. With both wheels driven in corners, the outer wheel travels further, causing torque buildup in the axle and eventually wheel slip and potential loss of control.

When only one wheel is driven, traction is compromised, as two drive wheels and higher traction is possible. For some light duty trikes this is okay.

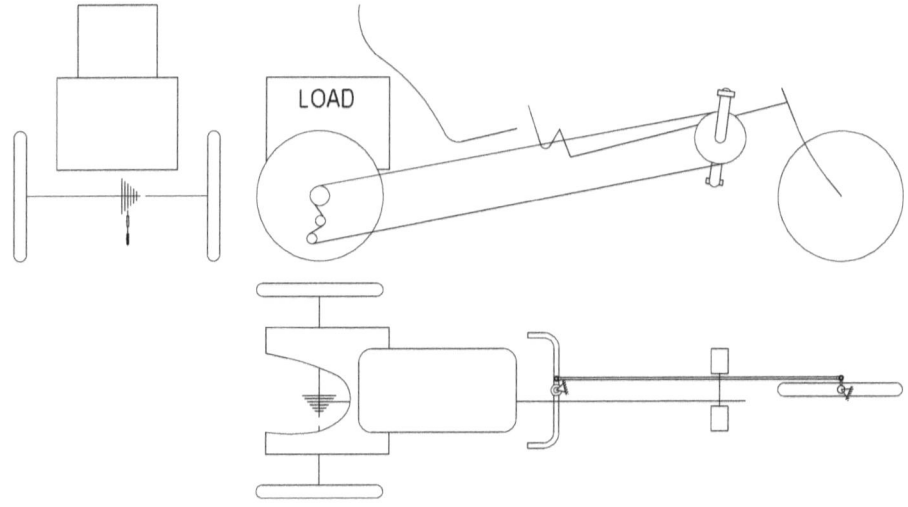

9.20 Single-wheel-drive delta trike showing steering linkage and load area.

Two wheels can be driven with a single driven rear axle, and a clutch on each wheel. This provides two-wheel drive in a straight line and still provides traction even if one wheel is slipping.

Lastly, a differential gear provides reliable traction on both wheels of a delta.

A new development is front-wheel drive on a delta recumbent trike. Trisled have used their experience with front-wheel drive recumbent and freight bikes to make the Sidestep delta with fixed bottom bracket drive. This is a trike for those with limited mobility. The rider doesn't need to step over the frame to mount the trike.

9.21   Trisled Sidestep front wheel drive delta. Asymmetric frame improves access.

9.22   Sidestep drive detail.

All deltas have a good, unbikelike spot for luggage behind the seat, and with an attachment point behind the back wheels, deltas can be hitched up to form a train. Some deltas can be parked vertically, using their two back wheels and the seat as props.

Deltas can have hub or derailleur gearing, or a combination of both. Deltas with derailleur gearing should be checked carefully. Low derailleur parts between the rear wheels mean they can be vulnerable to damage no matter how mild the conditions (9.20).

Handcycles are usually deltas driven and controlled solely through the arms and hands with a moving bottom bracket drive. They allow paraplegics to ride at cyclist speeds and to participate in longer tours and events. When hand cranks are in the standard bike arrangement (spaced 180° apart) steering isn't easy, so cranks and hand-pedals are usually next to each other. Gearing is low to match arm strength rather than leg strength. There are usually catchers on the front for leg support, but handcycles are always highly customised to match abilities and needs of riders.

9.23   Varna Handcycle.

Some four-wheel human powered vehicles or quads are available, and these cycles must have suspension if all wheels are to stay on the ground on rough surfaces. Quads are available based on deltas, tadpoles and velomobiles. Compared to trikes, quads have a larger area on the ground bounded by the wheels. This makes them more stable and less dependent on rider position for stability. With an area behind the rider free of wheels, potential for load carrying is good. Here are some examples of quads:

- The Anura delta-based quad from Greenspeed replaces the Anura trike's telescoping single front wheel and crank assembly with twin articulated front wheels and a crank. The front wheels are lightly loaded and without brakes. Larry Varney from Bentrideronline.com reports improved stability and a slightly higher turning circle compared to the delta trike version of the machine.

9.24 Side view Greenspeed Anura quad. Photo Larry Varney bentrideronline.com.

9.25 Back view Greenspeed Anura quad. Photo Larry Varney bentrideronline.com.

- Quads based on tadpole recumbent trikes include load-carrying and fat trikes. The rider position and weight is over the front wheels. 9.26 and

9.27 show a quad from Velomo including mesh seat, indirect steering and carbon fibre leaf spring suspension (http://www.velomo.eu/quads).

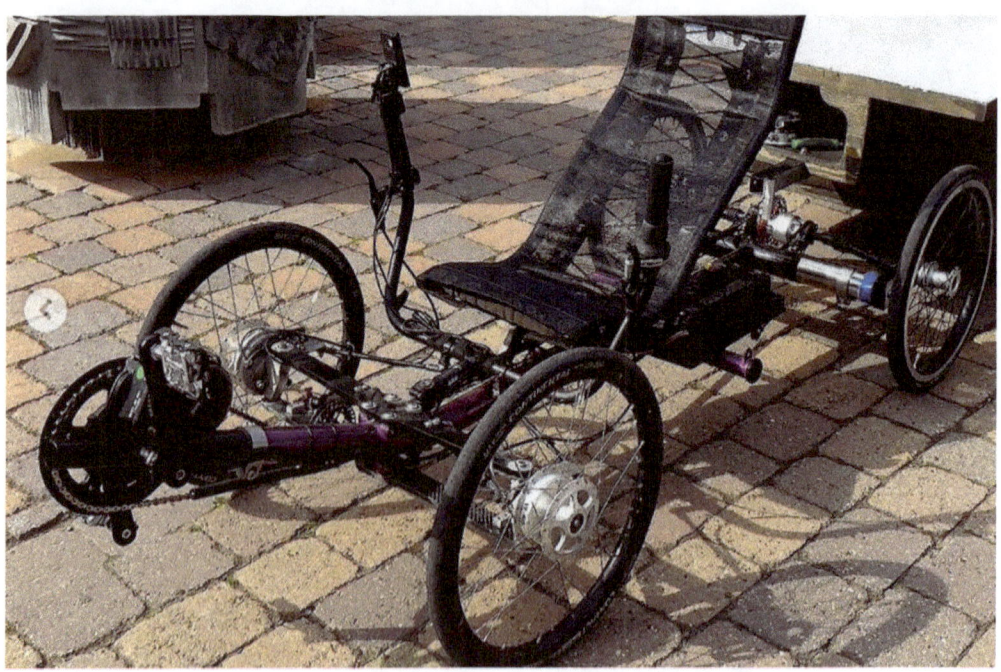

9.26   Velomo tadpole-based quad. Photo Kim Aagaard.

9.27   Velomo quad. Photo Kim Aagaard.

- The pioneering velomobile quad is the Quattrovelo with advertised features of excellent stability, huge luggage space, confident high-speed cornering, two driven rear wheels for traction, easy access to luggage space and the possibility to safely and comfortably bring a child along.

9.28   Quattrovelo. Photo Kim Aagaard.

- Velomo are building Velomobile Quads as well, and revert to the word 'cyclecar' to describe them. They state (http://www.velomo.eu/quads/cyclecars) 'Velomo CYCLECARS — The next evolutionary stage in cycling is aerodynamic weather protection. With a quad-based cyclecar you get even more than a velomobile. Especially at high speeds, you don't want to miss the tracking of a second rear wheel. Cyclecars are becoming hybrids: half bicycles, half e-cars. It combines the advantages of cycling (movement, lightweight construction, zero emissions) with those of the car (weather protection, luggage, shelter, motorisation — S-Pedelec up to 45km/h).'

DIY potential

With few exceptions, recumbent trikes are more complex than recumbent bikes, and only the most ambitious DIYers attempt designing and building trikes themselves. However, a large range of delta and tadpole trike plans are available from Atomic Zombie ($17 each).

Conversion of a recumbent trike to a velomobile makes a good DIY project, and support is available from online forums. Modern materials such as Corflute plastic sheeting and fibreglass struts simplify DIY velomobile construction, and making plywood velomobile shells is also possible. The original Alleweder kit is still offered for sale at http://alleweder.de.

And the rest, and the summary

There are more types of trikes, just a few of these are: front wheel drive, front wheel steer tadpole (http://www.aha.ru/~ykpro/index.htm), front wheel drive, rear wheel steer tadpole (https://trikeasylum.wordpress.com/2010/02/19/sidewinder), and rear wheel steer delta (http://www.ihpva.org/Projects/tstrike/rws.htm). In a survival of the fittest world, these variations haven't prospered. However, there is still a great and diverse set of quads and trikes available with some DIY options available.

References

8th European Velomobile Design Seminar Dornbirn — October 2015 Historical Introduction Presented by C.G. Rasmussen, accessed August 2020 from https://velomobileseminars.online/wp-content/uploads/8th-Velomobile-Seminar-Dornbirn-2015-partial.pdf

Alpha 7 velomobile cost retrieved August 2020 from https://www.velomobileworld.com/product-tag/velomobiles

Atkins, Richard, *The Leitra Velomobile Story*, retrieved August 2020 from https://spycycle.uk/the-leitra-velomobile-story

Azub Tricon 26 Website, accessed August 2020 from https://azub.eu/recumbent-bikes-and-trikes/trikes/26-wheels/tricon

Bentupcyclingjournal on *direct v. indirect steering* https://bentupcyclingjournal.blogspot.com/2017/11/direct-vs-indirect-steering.html

Bikebug *Thru Axles*, accessed August 2020 from https://www.bikebug.com/blog/the-buzz/everything-you-need-to-know-about-thru-axles

Catrike front wheel removal video with thru pin technology retrieved August 2020 from https://www.youtube.com/watch?v=nRn4zJMFYNU

Eland, Peter *Website including trike Steering geometry*, a home-made tandem trike and a front wheel drive tadpole trike, accessed August 2020 from http://www.eland.org.uk/index.html

Giuliani, Simone, Cyclingtips, *Breaking records at the 2018 Trans-Am Endurance Race*, retrieved August 2020 from https://cyclingtips.com/2018/06/photo-gallery-breaking-records-at-the-2018-trans-am-ultra-endurance-race

Hase Delta Trike information from *Encycleopedia 94/95*, retrieved August 2020 from https://issuu.com/encycleopedia/docs/enc02_opt/34 , p.17

Ice Adventure Trike retrieved August 2020 from https://www.icetrikes.co/products/adventure

Kanowitz, Stephanie: *Hot Wheels*, Washington Post, retrieved August 2020 from https://www.washingtonpost.com/lifestyle/wellness/hot-wheels-todays-adult-tricycles-are-low-sleek-and-speedy/2018/10/09/58570dd4-bdc6-11e8-8792-78719177250f_story.html

Kotzur, Wayne, *HPV Times #3*, retrieved August 2020 from https://www.ozhpv.org.au/HUFF/docs/HPV_Times_3_1991.pdf

Pohl, Michael *HPV Chronik 10 Jahre HPV, Ein Chronik und mehr*, Zypresse 1995

Plywood Velomobile building blog by Kai, retrieved August 2020 from http://plycar.blogspot.com

Schmitz, V.A. and Hadland, T., 2000. *Human power: the forgotten energy*. Available through BHPC, https://shop.bhpc.org.uk/human-power-the-forgotten-energy-arnfried-schmitz

Sharp, Archibald, 1896, *Bicycles and tricycles, An elementary treatise on their design and construction*, retrieved August 2018 from http://www.survivorlibrary.com/library/bicycles_and_tricycles-an_elementary_treatise_on_their_design_and_construction_1896.pdf

Terratrike Maverick i3 retrieved August 2020 from https://www.terratrike.com/leisure/maverick/

Trisled Gizmo, retrieved August 2020 from https://trisled.com.au/hpv/gizmo

Trisled Rotovelo, retrieved August 2020 from https://trisled.com.au/hpv/rotovelo-2

Van De Walle, F 2004, 'The velomobile as a vehicle for more sustainable transportation', Master of Science thesis, The Royal Institute of Technology, Stockholm, Sweden. Retrieved August 2020 from https://www.delo.si/assets/media/other/20130304/VELO_thesis.pdf

Varney, L, *Greenspeed Anura Quad review*, Bentrideronline, retrieved August 2020 from https://www.bentrideronline.com/?p=6335

Varney, L, *Terratrike Rambler review*, Bentrideronline, retrieved August 2020 from http://www.bentrideronline.com/?p=12761

Williamson, Peter, *Planet Pride in the South Pacific including DIY Anura quad velomobile* http://peter-williamson.blogspot.com

10 Tandems

This chapter deals with bicycles and human powered vehicles (HPVs) with two or more pedalling, whether in-line or side-by-side. This includes modular versions where an add-on transforms a solo into a tandem.

Background

Tandems have existed since the earliest days of the bicycle, and Archibald Sharp's 1896 book details side-by-side cycles, modular tandems, tandem bicycles and tandem tricycles, among others. For some, bicycles and their derivatives *were* personal transport, and design diversity helped.

By the 1920s, side-by-side cyclecars had been developed. Then, from the 1980s to the 2000s new tandem varieties emerged based on improved components and recumbents.

It's possible the need for traditional tandems has diminished with the arrival of electric bikes. Tandems let couples ride together, combining strong and weak riders to produce a compromise speed. But an ebike and a bicycle also allow couples to ride together. The ebike and bicycle pair are not a tandem, and can be used independently of each other, making them more versatile than most tandems.

Modular tandem technology of the 1990s has become mainstream and thrives today. As well, recumbent cycling has contributed to tandems such as counterpoints and Weehoo tag-along trailers.

The captain of a tandem is conventionally at the front, with the stoker behind. But now there are more tandem types and seating options — and the captain is more properly the cycle's steerer, and the stoker the non-steerer.

Technical issues in tandems include:
- stability and whether the stoker makes the bike less stable
- pedalling and whether the stoker must pedal with the captain
- gearing and whether riders can choose individual cadences
- modularity or how the tandem suits a range of riders, whether it can be used for freight hauling, and whether it can be disassembled for transport.

Tandems have riders arranged in a line, which is an aerodynamic configuration, and with twice the power available, tandems should be faster than individual cycles. Side-by-side cycles do not have the same advantage, as they have increased frontal area.

Tandem types

Standard tandems (10.1) are only one of a large array of HPV tandems and are now less popular than articulated tandems that have a child trailing along behind.

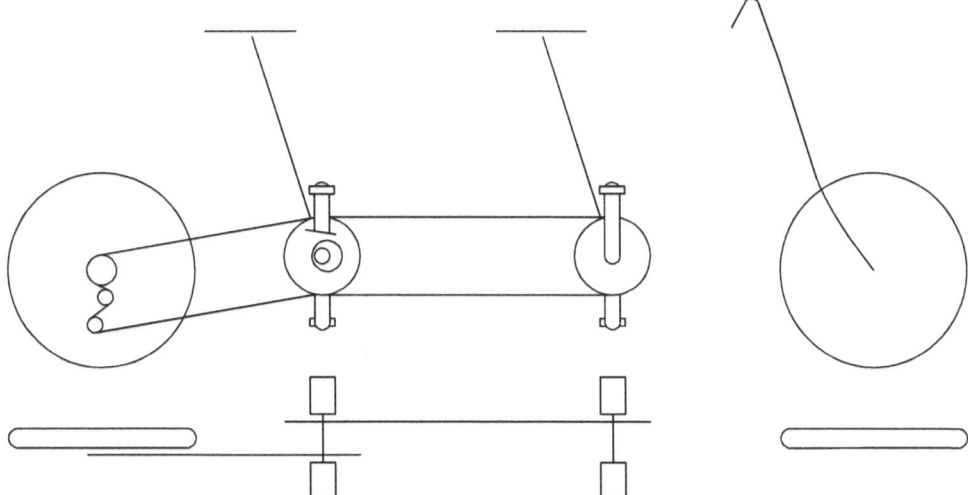

10.1   Traditional tandem schematic.

The tag-along tandem (10.2) and bicycle towbar (10.3) are machines often seen on our bike paths. Weehoo bike trailers (10.4, 10.5) are relatively new tag-alongs and have pedalling children supported in a recumbent-style seat. There are many types of tag-alongs with variations including the number of children carried, two wheels for added stability and bicycle towbar hitching. Wikimedia Commons shows a range of these.

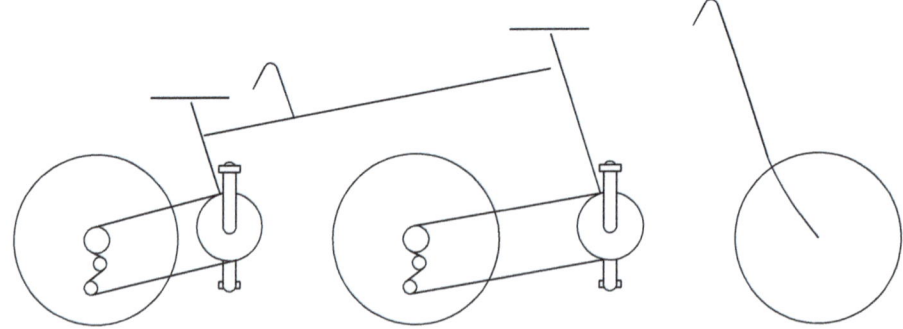

10.2   Trail-a-bike schematic.

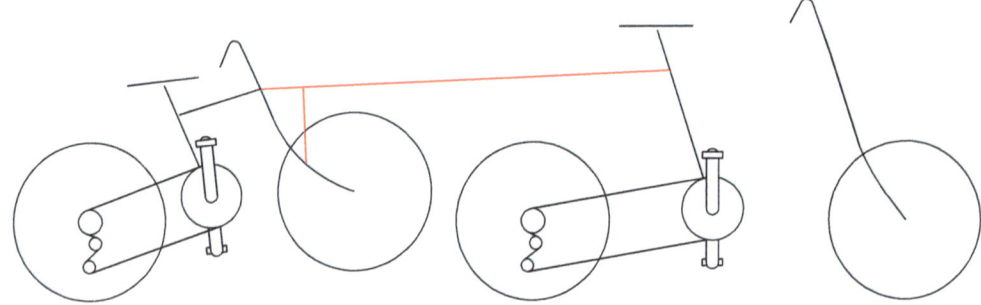

10.3   Bicycle towbar schematic (towbar in red).

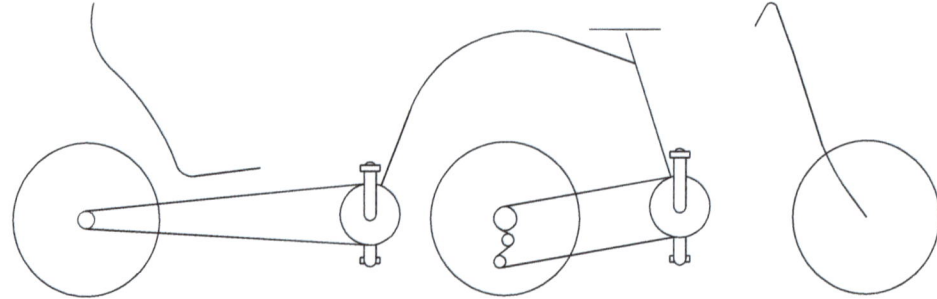

10.4   Weehoo trailer schematic.

10.5   Weehoo IGo trailerbike.

Traditional tandems have the chain on the left at the front and at the right behind (10.1). To tension the front chain, one of the bottom brackets is mounted eccentrically in an oversize housing. Left-hand cranks are non-standard, having a left-hand thread for pedals with chainwheels. Stresses on the rear bottom bracket can be high due to the two chains twisting in the same direction. However, the right-hand chainring at the back is not compromised and can carry 2 or 3 driving cogs. The alternative (10.6) has chains only on the right, uses a pulley as a tensioner, and decreases stress on the rear bottom bracket. The presence of two chains restricts the use of the rear chainring for multiple driving cogs.

Upright tandems can be steered from the back via a linkage (10.6) or large handlebars (10.7). 10.6 and 10.7 are bikes suiting a smaller rider at the front, allowing both riders to see the road ahead easily. Variations on the standard tandem include compact bikes by Cuddlebike. The rear handlebar is omitted and a motorcycle-style bench seat and long platform pedals mean the stoker's position is not fixed.

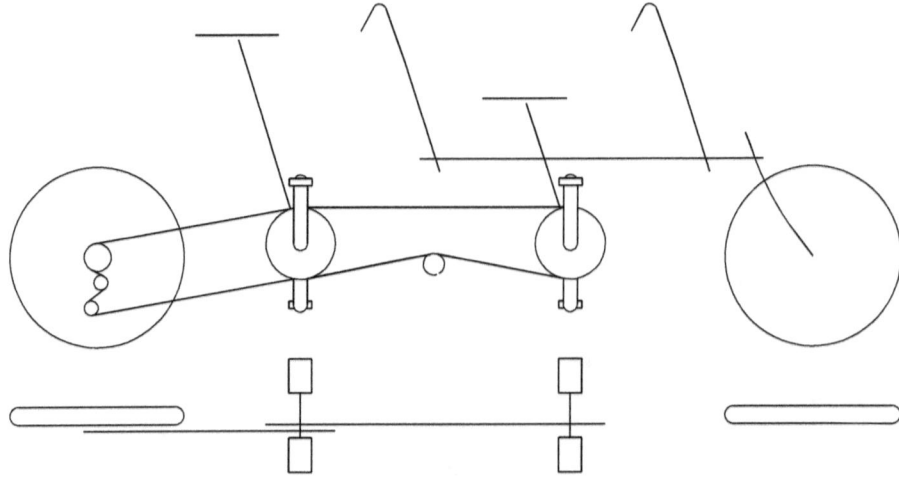

10.6   Steers from behind tandem with linkage and simplified right-hand side drivetrain.

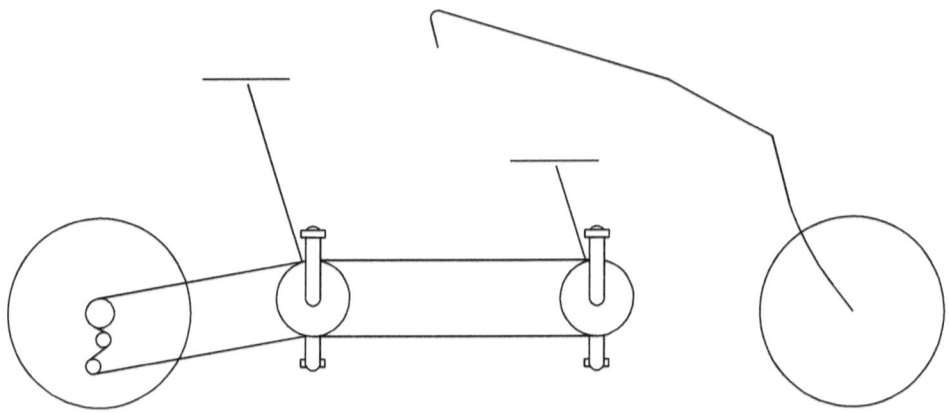

10.7   Steers from behind tandem with large handlebars.

10.8   Cuddlebikes. Photos Kim Aagaard.

The counterpoint tandem (10.9) has the captain upright at the back and the stoker recumbent at the front, allowing both riders to see well. The front rider has a lower centre of gravity enabling better control. The seat back encourages the front rider to sit still, and the front area can be used for load carrying when no rider is present. The Hase Pino is an example of this style. It has a clutch allowing the stoker to choose whether to pedal, options for electric-assist motors, and load carrying including a large freight basket sitting on the stoker's seat (10.10, 10.11).

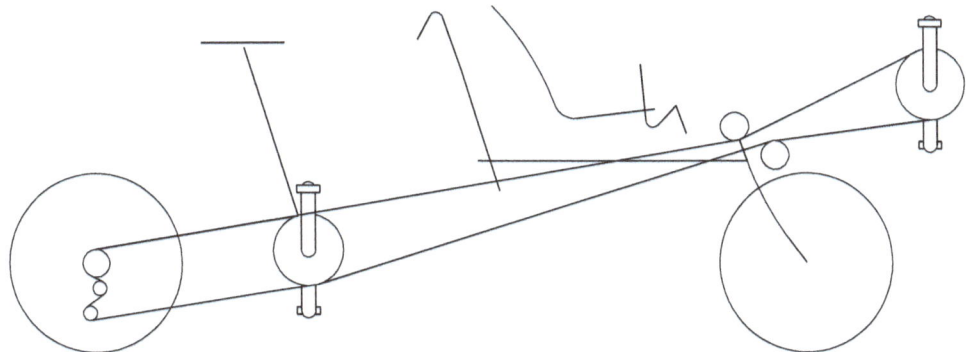

10.9   Counterpoint tandem schematic.

10.10 Hase Pino counterpoint as tandem. Photo Kim Aagaard.

10.11 Hase Pino counterpoint as cargo bike. Photo Kim Aagaard.

10.12, 10.13 and 10.14 are tandem bikes with both riders in recumbent-style seats. Tandem recumbent bikes can be rear-wheel drive only (10.12) or front- and rear-wheel drive (10.13, 10.14). Most front- and rear-wheel-drive tandems use a twisting chain/fixed bottom bracket drive at the front and a more conventional drive at the back. They have independent gearing and pedalling. Like their single-seater cousins, front-wheel-drive tandems can be separated without complex disruption of chains and gear cables. Zoxbikes from Germany have a range of seven front- and rear-wheel-drive recumbent tandems. They all split for easy transport, and some are modular, allowing a single bike to be built from the front and back of the tandem.

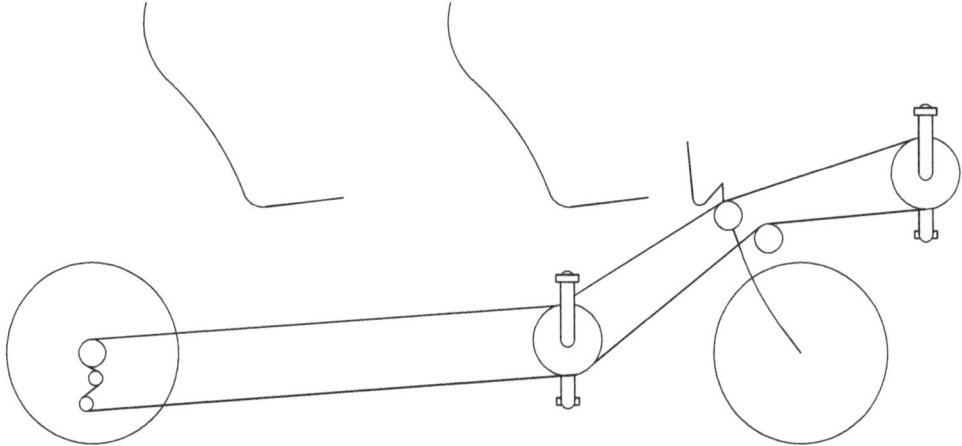

10.12   Recumbent tandem.

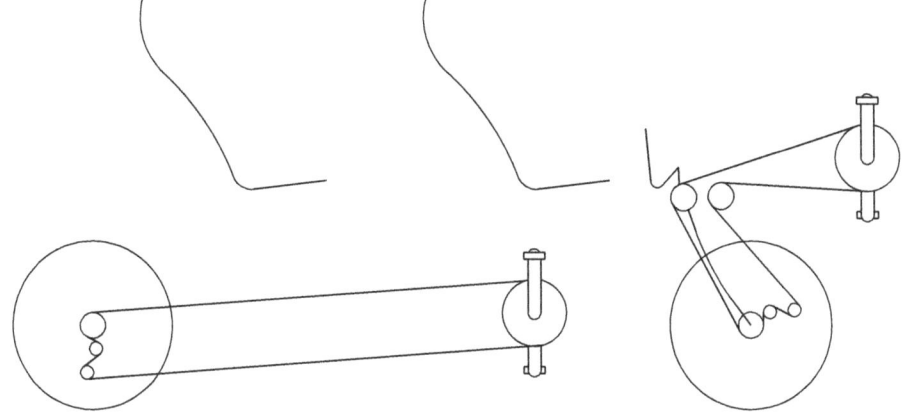

10.13 Recumbent tandem independent drive.

10.14 Jana and Robert with separating independent drive tandem. Photos Robert Waryszak.

One of the classic recumbent tandems is the Flevobike rug-aan-rug (back-to-back) tandem, which has been nicknamed the PushmePullyou after the fictional creature devised by Hugo Lofting. It was sold in the form of plans or as a kit (10.15, 10.16). The bike is aerodynamic. Both riders have a fine view and the riders' heads are close together allowing easy conversation. However, the stoker gets to see the world receding from them! This bike has the rear drive from the 'wrong' side of the chainring and allows the rear-facing stoker to pedal in the normal direction.

My friend Damian Harkin owned a Flevobike rug-aan-rug and enjoyed it immensely, riding it with his family and on organised HPV group rides. He made a variation of this bike that has the stoker pedalling backwards (unpedalling) using a simpler drive train than the rug-aan-rug (10.17). In this case, the rear drive train is on the non-standard left-hand side.

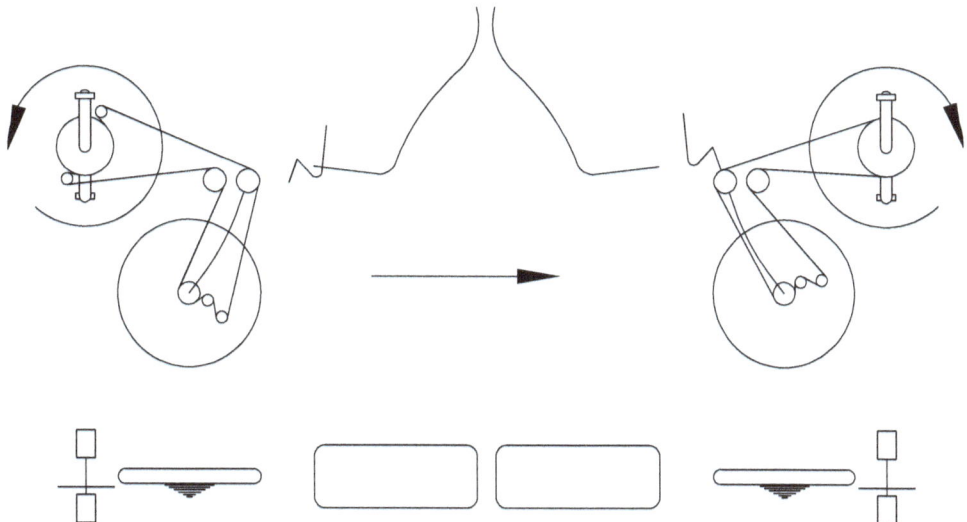

10.15 Rug-aan-rug. Tandem with forward-pedalling rear drive.

10.16 Flevobike rug-aan-rug.

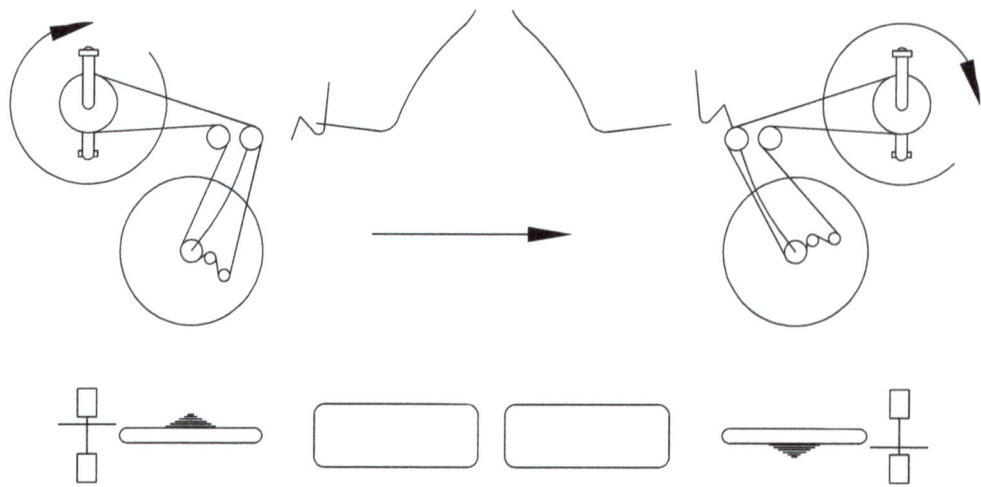

10.17 Rug-aan-rug tandem with reverse-pedalling rear drive.

10.18 Damian Harkin (right) and his Rug-aan-rug tandem bike.

Tadpole recumbent trikes are made by Greenspeed, Trident and Terratrike and other manufacturers, and Atomic Zombie sells plans for Viking tandem trikes. Layout is shown in 10.19. Like Zox tandems, the Trident tandem splits and converts to a single trike.

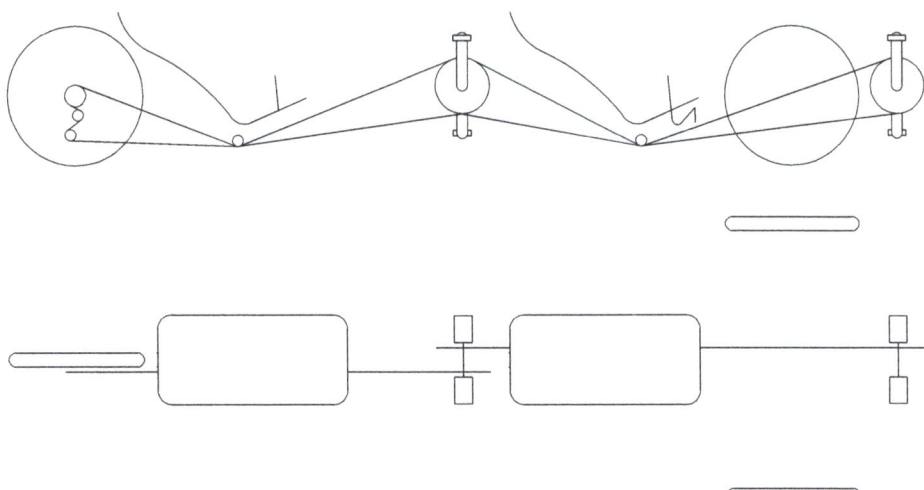

10.19   Tandem tadpole trike.

10.20   Tridenttrikes Chameleon Converto tandem trike changes to a single trike in 15–20 minutes. Photo Kim Aagaard.

Deltas can form modular tandems, with two or more trikes forming a train (10.21, 10.22). The back trike has its front wheel removed and it is attached to and trails the front trike. This form of modularity is available on Greenspeed Anura and Hase delta trikes.

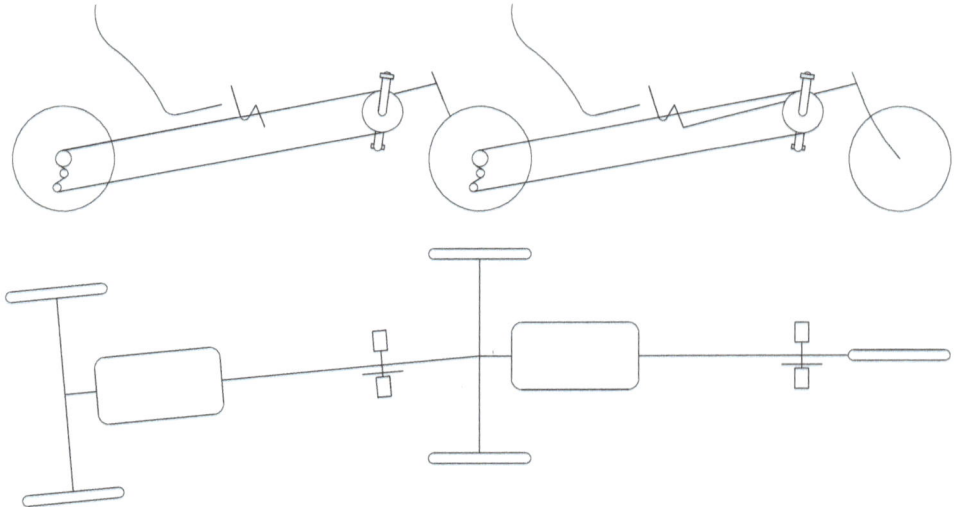

10.21 Delta trike train schematic.

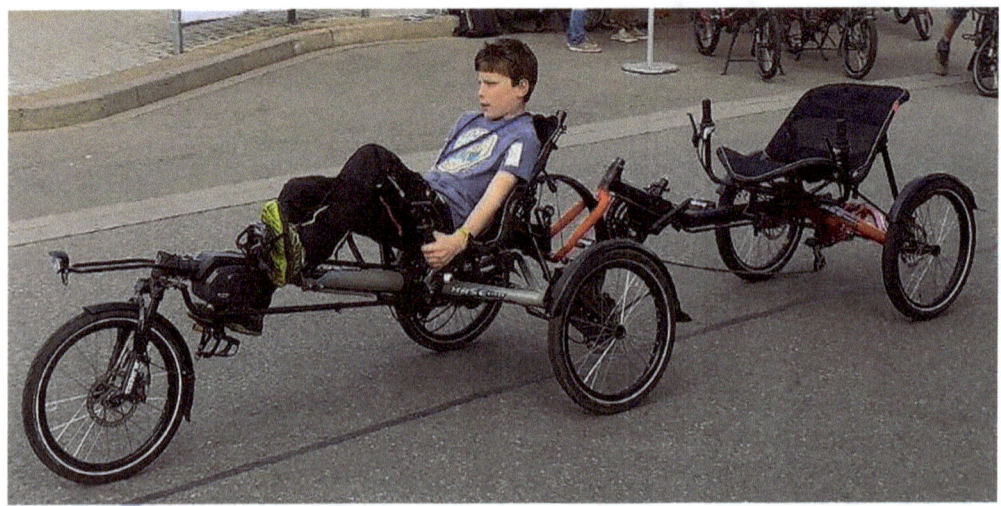

10.22 Delta trike train Photo Kim Aagaard.

This chapter has mainly considered tandems where the riders are in a row in the direction of the bike travel. However, there are many possibilities for side-by-side or 'sociable' tandems. 10.23 is a schematic of an independent drive version, and the Atomic Zombie 'Kyotocruiser' is available as plans. The Van Raam Double Rider is a commercial sociable delta with the same 'no stepover' arrangement as the Trisled Sidestep. The Van Raam is just one of many tandems offering riding for all or adaptive cycling, supporting riders with disability.

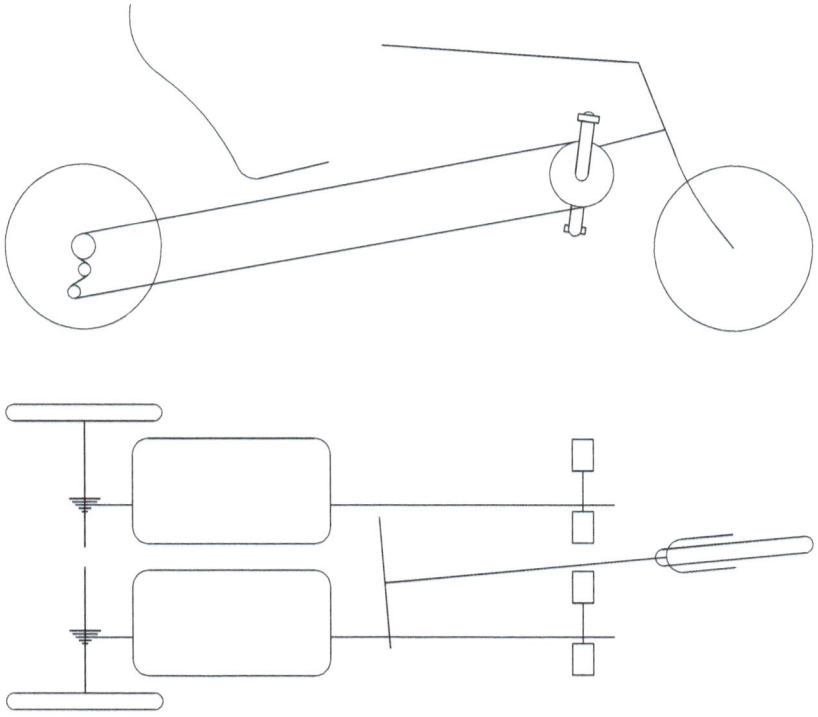

10.23 Above seat steer delta sociable trike.

10.24 Van Raam Double Rider

Larger multi-rider cycles are available, and these include surrey sociable quadracycles for two to four people (10.25) and special purpose multi-rider cycles for events, fairs or carnivals (10.26).

10.25 Four-wheeled sociable surrey.

10.26 Pedalled Cafe in Wierden.

References

Buddybike Steers from behind tandems http://buddybike.com

Cuddlebike Website http://www.cuddlebike.de

Greenspeed Anura modular delta trike http://www.greenspeed-trikes.com/anura.html

Hase modular delta trike https://www.hasebikesusa.com/delta-trikes.html

Hase Pino Bike https://hasebikes.com/95-1-Tandem-PINO-ALLROUND.html

Robert Waryszak's bikes http://comfybikes.blogspot.com

Wikimedia Commons trailerbikes https://commons.wikimedia.org/wiki/Category:Trailer_bikes

Zox modular recumbent tandems https://www.zoxbikes.com/zox-tandems

11 Carrying Loads and Passengers

All cycles need to carry a rider and a load, from a pump, phone, spare tube, water bottle and banana (below 2kg) all the way up to a touring or passenger and freight load (60kg and more). Commuting and shopping loads are up to 20kg and between these extremes. As well as load carrying on bicycles, trikes, trailers, and recumbents, this chapter covers special purpose load- and people-carrying cycles.

11.1   Phil Bissell's touring trike in 1997.

11.2 Chris Hatherly rode round Australia in 1997.

11.3 Delta trike with electric assist.

11.4   Tadpole load trike from xyzcargo.com Photo Kim Aagaard.

11.5   Simple load carrying in Copenhagen Photo Kim Aagaard.

11.6   Rickshaw trike in Bangkok, Thailand.

Load carrying is part of effective cycling, and it makes sense to think through load carrying when purchasing or choosing a cycle. Often it is an afterthought or never considered at all, and riders are expected to come up with their own make-do solutions. So shoppers end up with plastic grocery bags dangling from handlebars and overloaded backpacks, or worse, giving up cycling completely. It's worth checking that bikes you buy or pass on have load carrying. Traditional load carrying on bicycles requires a series of three steps:

- threaded bosses for rack mounting installed in frames
- racks attached to mounting bosses
- panniers or boxes attached to racks.

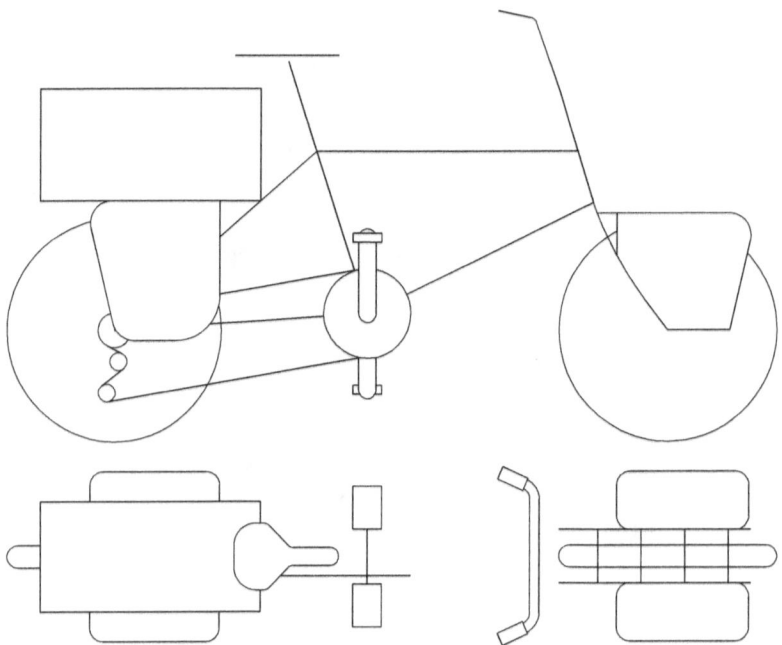

11.7 Traditional bicycle load carrying involves frame bosses, racks, panniers.

This is fine for dedicated cyclists with money to spend on equipment, but for everyone else it could be too hard. Simpler, less expensive solutions are needed. These solutions should cater for volume as well as weight. For example, toilet paper is light, but a package of eight rolls can use half a bicycle's storage capacity. For simple and pragmatic bicycle load carrying:
- Seat post racks don't need extra mounting bosses. They can be purchased separately or as a job lot with pannier bags.
- Child carriers are often attached to the seat post and can provide direct load carrying.
- Front baskets in plastic, cane or wire are available complete with mounting gear.
- Large capacity crates and boxes may be available at little or no cost, and can be attached to racks with cable ties or elastic straps.
- Accessories, including seat post clamps doubling as frame bosses, backpacks, cycle shirts with pockets and frame-attached pouches all help.

If you're considering carrying passengers or more than 40kg regularly:
- Hills have a dramatic effect on power required. In the first instance, this affects gearing and whether a trike should be considered for its stability.

- Consider electric assist or provision for retrofitting electric assist, especially if trips are long and completed daily.

Load carrying should be considered part of any cycle-related *design*. And aerodynamics should be considered as well: on the flat aerodynamics are still a major force on load-carrying cycles.

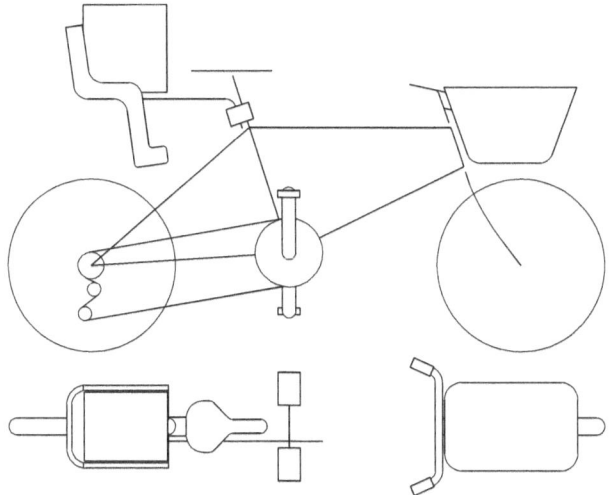

11.8 Direct load carrying with child seat and front basket.

Stability and good practice

The priority of load carrying is stability, meaning cycles should accept and carry cargo easily and safely. When you are moving, the cargo should not need attention and it should arrive in good condition, not squished or wet or damaged. Speed should only be considered once loads are secure. On a load bike, a wide, two-pronged stand is important, and on a load trike there should be a park brake. The load should be as low as possible to aid stability. In physics terms, a low load has a smaller moment of inertia (twisting force) relative to the tyres. On a bike this means smaller movements of the upper body can achieve balance. On a trike it means the load contributes less to tipping instability.

Load carrying can be improved if the driving wheel is 20" rather than 28"/700C. The smaller wheel can have a harsher ride than larger ones, but:

- The loaded area can be kept low.
- 20" wheels can be stronger and more triangulated than 26" wheels.

- For the same gearing, a 26" bike will usually have lower chain speed and higher chain tension than a 20" bike, leading to higher frame forces.
- A heavily laden cycle should have no need for high gears. A standard 52-teeth front/11-teeth rear/20" wheel highest gear giving 7.7m development and uses standard gears should be fast enough.
- If electric assist is used, less speed reduction is needed for 20" wheels.

An example is the Yuba Sweet Curry, a longtail cycle described as having 'Low-rider cargo rack with 20" rear wheel for increased stability and load safety'.

To simplify puncture repairs, racks should not be attached using the same mounting as a wheel. Racks should be solid and rigid on the bike, as repeated swaying of a loaded cycle will quickly fatigue and break a wobbly rack. Panniers are usually carried at the side of a rack while (less bikelike) boxes and crates fit on top.

Bikepacking

A new style of load carrying on cycles is called bikepacking. The World Biking Info website has some good information, and based on their descriptions:

- Bikepacking is a style of lightly loaded bicycle touring.
- Set-ups can include a frame bag, metal baskets, cockpit bags, handlebar roll, seat pack and fork mounted cages.
- Bikepacking involves lighter loads, so steep inclines and other difficult terrain is easier.
- Bags are better for aerodynamics, so you'll be faster than someone with a pannier set-up carrying the same weight.
- Set-ups are smoother and less noisy than racks and panniers, which tend to rattle and shake on rough roads.
- Bikepacking involves more regular resupply compared to more traditional four-pannier touring. For example, food or cafe stops are more frequent, as less food and equipment is carried.
- The improved aerodynamics of bikepacking gear means it is favoured for long-distance, unsupported cycle rides such as the Indian Pacific Wheel Race or the Trans Am Bike Race.

A good example of bikepacking gear is the Tailfin aerodynamic range of racks with matching pannier and top bags. Weight, aerodynamics, load capacity and mounting to a range of bikes were all considered in the design, which adds load capacity to racing and off-road bikes. The result is a claimed speed advantage for some set-ups, and a starting price of A$370 for 20 litres. Materials for Tailfin gear include aluminium, carbon fibre and nylon.

11.9   Direct load carrying with Tailfin rack and bikepacking saddle-, frame-, and handlebar-bags

11.10 Bikepacking in Oregon, USA.

Trailers

A trailer is often the best way to carry large or awkward goods if you don't want to carry racks or panniers, or for quick add-on load capacity.

The classic one-wheel trailer is the Bob Yak. The trailer can swivel up and down, or from side to side, but it can't flop from side to side. Approximately half the combined weight of the trailer and its load will be transferred to the back wheel, but the trailer can't tip no matter how rough the ground.

Two-wheel trailers are supported from a single full-swivel point on a bike, and rely on paired wheels for stability. The load on the trailer can be arranged to balance about the trailer wheels, so the bike back wheel doesn't have to 'feel' much extra weight. If one wheel hits a bump, the trailer can tip, especially if it is narrow or lightly loaded, or the hitching point is high. The most natural wheels for this trailer are cantilever wheels, so a good start point for making this type of trailer are old prams, golf buggies or new pneumatic wheels with industrial roller bearings. Two-wheel trailers include fabric-enclosed child trailers, which double as prams.

Trailers can be low and harder to see from cars than the bicycles towing them. When riding in the city it's worth using a flag. I found an interesting way of avoiding this problem (11.13).

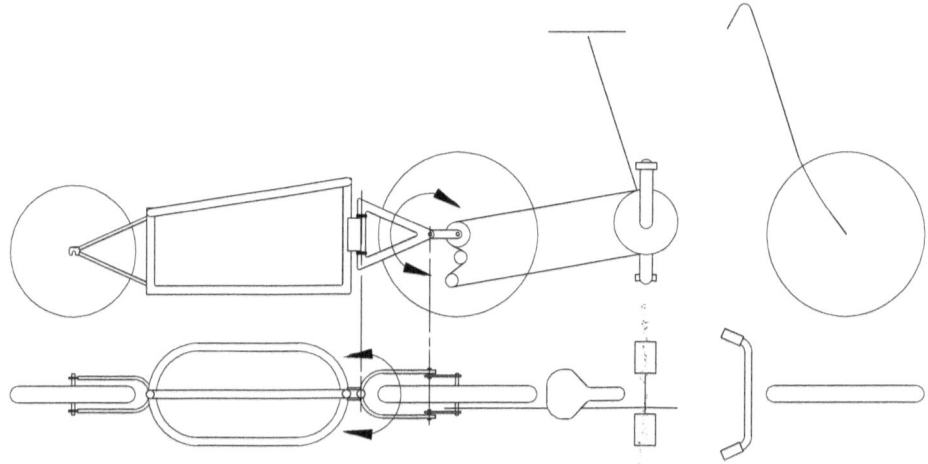

11.11   Single-wheel trailer.

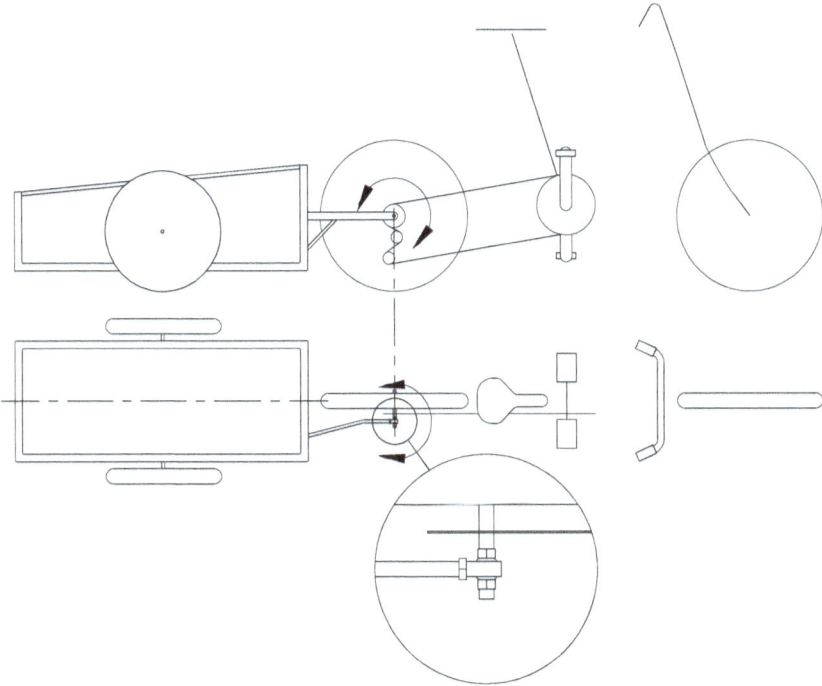

11.12   Two-wheeled trailer.

11.13   Inner trailer.

Load-carrying bikes

For bicycles to carry more than standard accessories allow, changes to frame or forks are required. The resulting cycles are cargo bikes, and their standard forms include butcher's bikes, longjohn bikes and longtail bikes.

Butcher's bikes, or low-gravity cycles, have a smaller wheel at the front and a large load area above it. A DIY option for converting bicycle to butcher's bike is the Clydesdale fork with load-carrying platform.

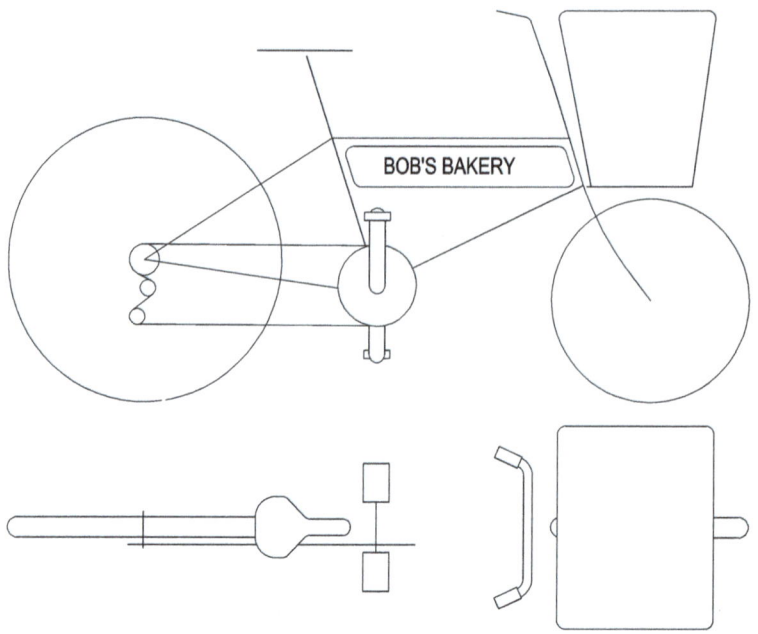

11.14 Butcher's bike schematic.

11.15 Butcher's bike, Benalla.

Longtail bikes have extended chain- and seatstays, and a load-carrying platform above the back wheel. They were developed and documented in the 1970s and 1980s in Adelaide (14.2). The long platform is often used as a child seat. Xtracycle sell a kit to convert a bicycle to a longtail, and Atomic Zombie sell plans to make a 20″ drive-wheel longtail. Tern's GSD models have electric assist and are compact 20″ wheel longtails.

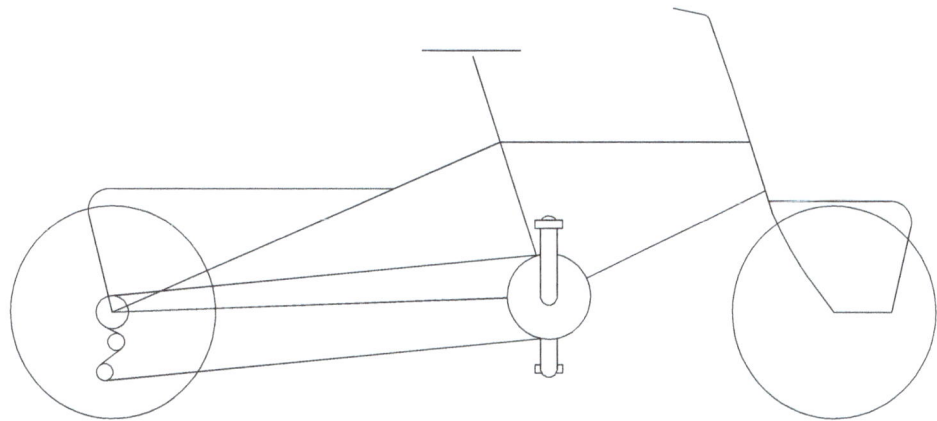

11.16   Longtail schematic.

11.17   Tern GSD compact electric longtail. Photo Kim Aagaard.

Although they originated in Denmark in the 1920s, front-loaders or longjohn bicycles are a relatively recent sight where I live in Melbourne. They have a long, low front tray and a linkage between the steerer and the small front wheel. The front box can be equipped with child seats and a cover. A kit from Argo in the USA converts a bicycle to a longjohn. These bikes are more complex than their longtail cousins — it is easier to extend the chain and frame at the back than to extend steering and provide a front platform.

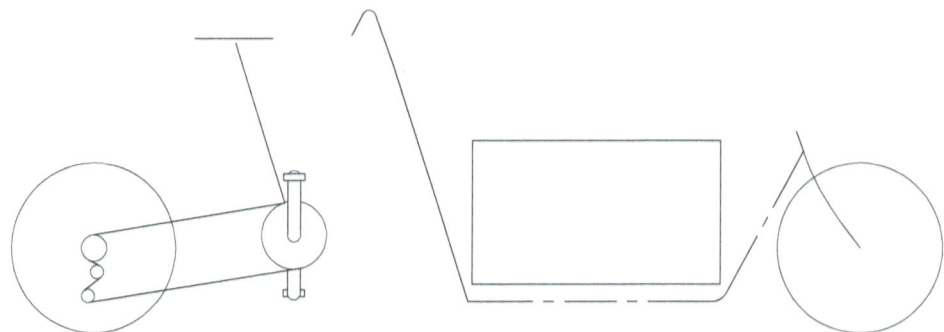

11.18   Longjohn schematic.

11.19   Longjohn . Photo Kim Aagaard.

Upright trikes

Like recumbent trikes, upright load trikes are made in tadpole and delta form. Tadpole uprights are almost always load or passenger carrying. Delta uprights (11.3) can be for stability, or for load and passenger carrying. Sidecar upright load trikes are part of the taxi fleet in Manilla. They are called Trishaws in Singapore and Sai Kaa in Myanmar.

Tadpole trikes with a large front box have been produced by Christiania Bikes in Denmark since 1984, and a range of rickshaw load and passenger tadpole Becak rickshaws have been made in Indonesia since the mid-1930s. Other tadpole load trikes include Vietnamese Cyclos and some Thailand Samlors. Front loading trikes based on the Christiania template our now widely available, and used by families as goods and child transport. Christiania themselves sell an economical bare frame (no box) pedalled version and it's simple but expensive to order fully equipped electric-assist versions from Nihola and Bakfiets.nl. Tadpole samlors in Thailand include food vending trucks, and coffee cart tadpoles are now made in China.

Taga make a range of compact tandem with options for electric assist and conversion to trolley or stroller. Compact tadpole load carriers can be made by adding tilting trike modules to bicycles. An example is the Trego.

Like recumbent tadpoles, the drive on tadpole load carriers in simple, and billycart steering (9.13) is often used, sometimes with some form of damping.

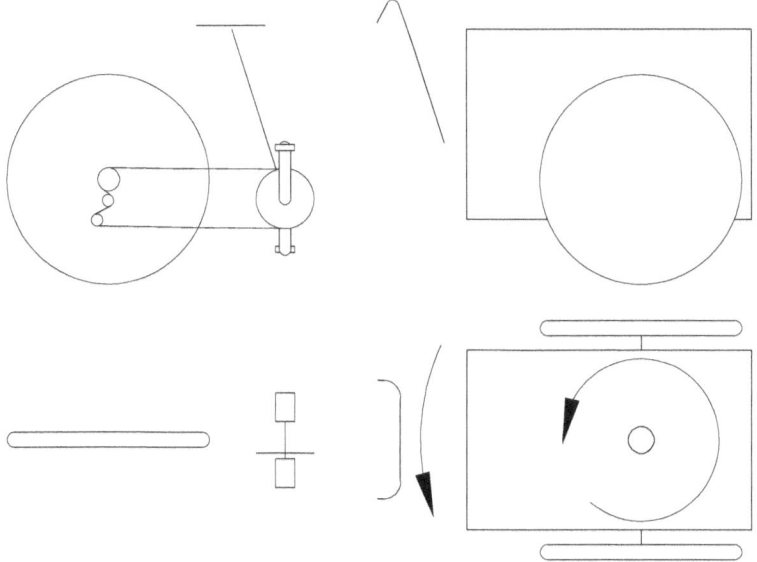

11.20 Tadpole load trike.

11.21   Nihola cargo trike. Photo Kim Aagaard.

11.22   Tadpole samlor, Bangkok, Thailand.

Compact delta trikes are used for stability at low speed but also have good load capacity. Larger deltas are used for passenger and freight, and versions include some samlors in Thailand, rickshaws in Bangladesh, and triciclos in Macau. Delta freight trikes are relatively common but are often part of some form of commercial enterprise. Trisled have developed a modular front-wheel-drive delta trike. This configuration removes the complexity of driving two rear wheels, and means chain length and drive remain the same no matter what freight module is installed.

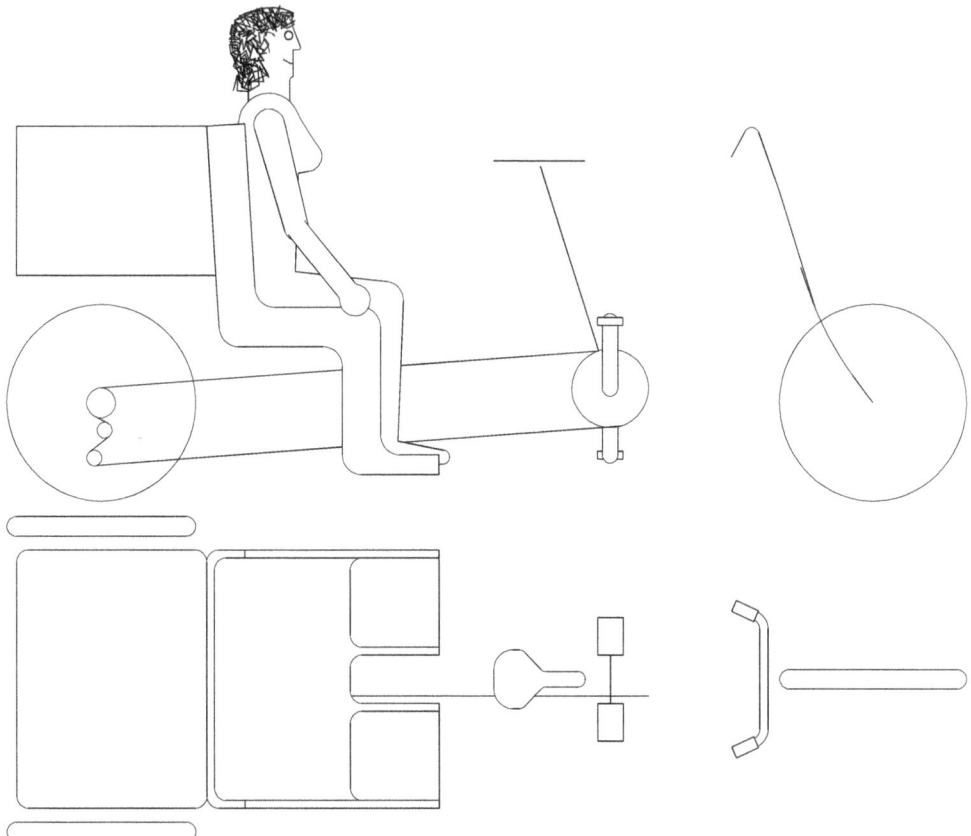

11.23   Delta load trike schematic.

11.24 Front-wheel-drive delta load trike.

Recumbents

The recumbent riding position lets keys, handkerchiefs, money, wallets and phones fall out of jacket and pants pockets, and this is the first thing to note when loading recumbents. Pockets should have zippers and the zippers should be done up for carrying anything on the person while recumbent riding. In lieu of zippered pockets, a bicycle phone case attached to the frame does a good job.

Recumbent riders can't use the pockets on standard cycle shirts, as the pocket area on the back is right where they lie. Aerotechdesigns, Reversegearinc and Benditcycling overcome this by making cycle shirts with front zippered pockets.

Recumbent bikes have their own special load-carrying areas, including tailboxes. If a bike has a small back wheel and a high seat, it becomes relatively easy to make a tailbox that does not interfere with the back wheel and carries a large volume. Tailboxes on bikes and trikes with larger back wheels and low seats are bisected by the back wheel and have less capacity. Bikepacking-style recumbent panniers such as those sold by Radical snuggle in behind the rider and complement or even improve aerodynamics. Dependent on the location of the chain, a large load can be carried down low and between the wheels of recumbent bikes. This loading style is good for front-wheel-drive recumbents where there is no chain to interfere with the load, and the load position increases drive-wheel traction. It's not so aerodynamic though.

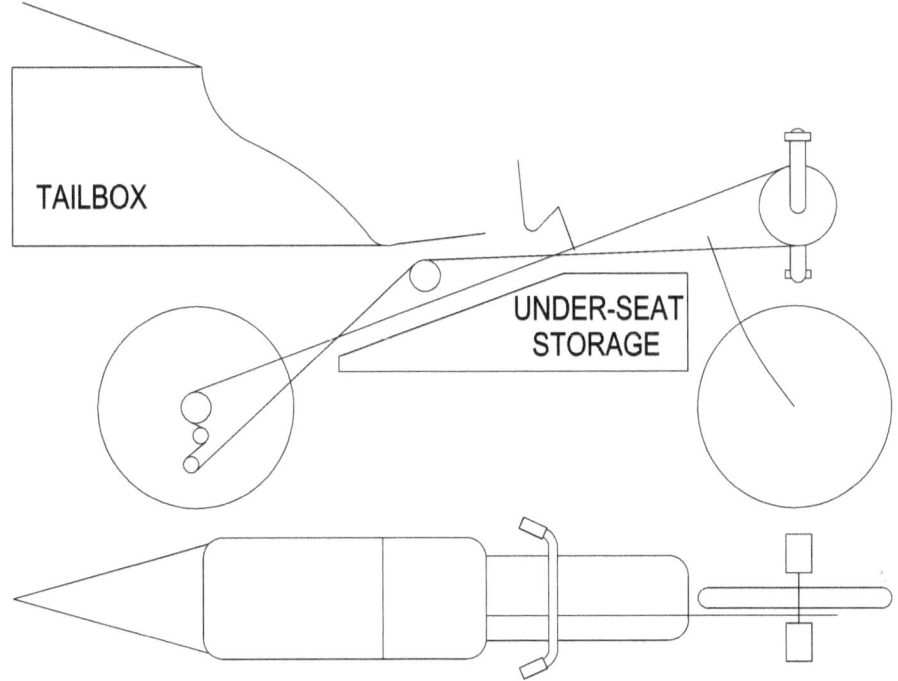

11.25   Recumbent bike storage 1.

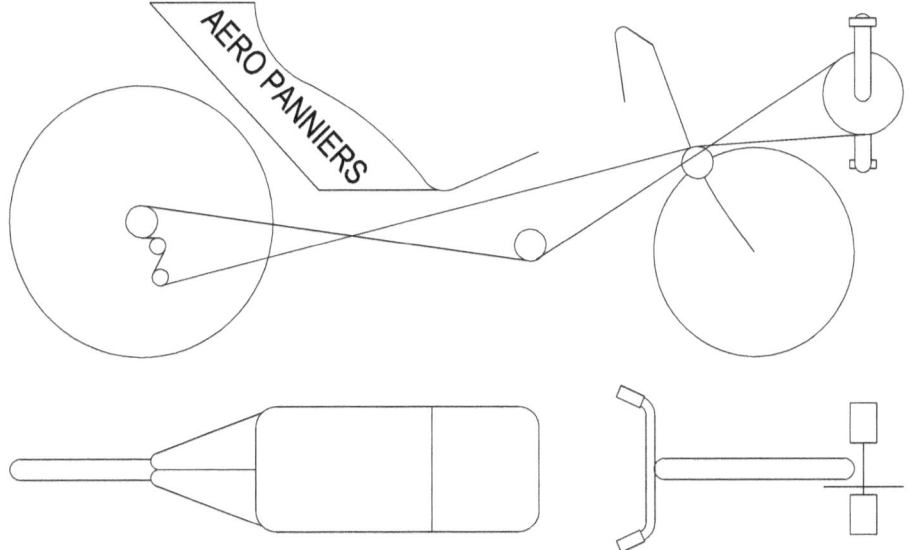

11.26   Recumbent bike storage 2.

The load-carrying area of delta recumbent trikes is shown in 9.20. Loading these trikes between the back wheels increases stability and improves traction.

Tadpole recumbent trikes have completed many long laden tours, and round Australia trike touring was pioneered by Eric Butcher and Val Wright on Greenspeeds. Recumbent touring trikes have additional reasons for having 20" wheels:

More can be placed on top of the rack before the load is above the rider's shoulders affecting aerodynamics by increased frontal area.

Assuming 20" wheels are on the front, keeping all wheel sizes the same means only one size of spare tube is needed.

11.27   Comparison of trikes with 26" and 20" rear wheels.

The recumbent position is sometimes used on cargo trikes and quads for last mile delivery. The sitting position is relaxed and there's no need for the rider to support their back while riding or concentrate on balance. Although large in cycle terms, cargo quads can be small in terms of the vehicles they replace. Bike2 from Denmark are testing sophisticated cargo quads where the rider pedals to run a generator, and drive output is via electric motors and 'electronic differential'.

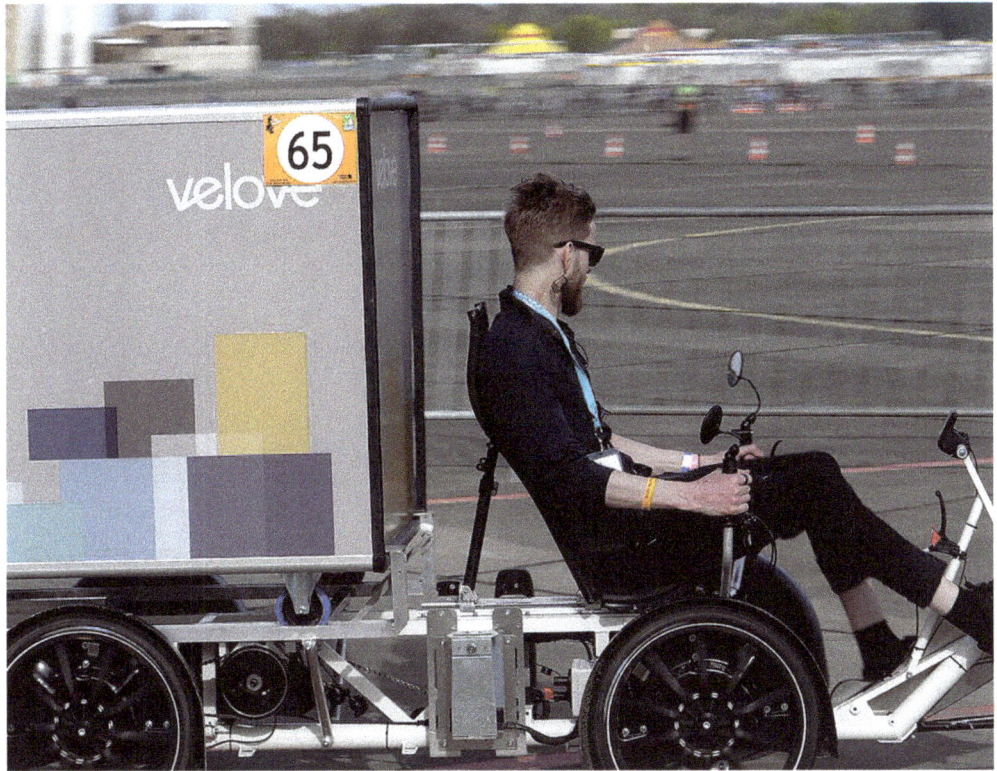

11.28   Electric cargo recumbent quad.

Load carrying is inextricably linked with practical cycling, for the cycle tourist, shopper, bikepacker, parent, professional cycle courier, rickshaw puller and delivery rider.

References

Adelaide Longbikes https://portadbug.org/links-videos-resources/the-adelaide-longbike-an-earlier-cargo-bike-movement

Argobikes Long John Conversion Kit https://argobikes.com

Atomic Zombie Longtail Plan https://www.atomiczombie.com/transporter-carg-bike-diy-plan

Bike2 Website http://bike2.dk/index.html

Cargobike History https://mechaniccycling.com/blogs/blog/a-visual-history-of-the-cargo-bike

Cycle tours by Phil Bissell and Chris Hatherly are mentioned in *Huff* Issue 3 https://www.ozhpv.org.au/HUFF/docs/huff003.pdf

Cycle tour on Greenspeeds https://issuu.com/encycleopedia/docs/enc02_opt/44

Gallagher R., *The rickshaws of Bangladesh*. University Press Dhaka (1992)

Load trike manufacture Jxcycles https://www.jxcycles.com/

Tailfin bikepacking gear website. https://www.tailfin.cc/all-products/ , https://www.tailfin.cc/blog/do-aerodynamics-matter-in-bikepacking

Trego leaning trike module https://trego-trolley.com/home

Wheeler, T. and I'Anson, R., 1998. *Chasing rickshaws*. Lonely Planet.

World biking info bikepacking website http://www.worldbiking.info/wordpress/2017/03/difference-bikepacking-bicycle-touring

Xtracycle Free Radical Kit https://www.xtracycle.com/leap-freeradical/

12   Crate Bikes

Around our Clifton Hill neighbourhood you see a few abandoned bikes, but I don't think any of them stayed in the weather longer than the Dead White Peugeot NS22 of Field Street. One day, I got motivated and put it out of its misery by dragging it home with me. The Field Street residents didn't mind at all, and said that it had been there 2 years or more. Certainly I had passed it many times.

Fixing started when I got it home. The wheels were 22″ and 24″ and steel, and didn't look worth saving. But I happened to have some smaller aluminium 451 mm rim, 20″ wheels salvaged from Byk kids bikes. I've used these for recumbents before, so tried them on the Peugeot. They looked okay, but the different rim size meant I would have to work on the brakes to make rims and brake pads line up.

12.1   White Peugeot before rescue.

12.2 Peugeot front brake rejigged.

With some centre pull brakes from the shed and some brazing and metalwork, I managed to rework the brakes to fit the new wheels and, voila, the bike is already better than before. It's lighter, has better brakes and a wider gear range but is lowered a bit. Some more work and the bike is rideable again with a new crankset with shorter cranks and a cassette bottom bracket bearing. It goes okay, and the shorter cranks mean the pedal clearance to the ground is okay despite the wheel change.

12   Crate Bikes

12.3   Bike with load-carrying crate.

12.4   Neat cable ties hold the crate to the rack.

Then came work on load carrying. The back rack was missing, and first I made a wooden and steel replacement. Milk crates are a favourite local load carrier, and two of them were in the shed holding a large collection of bike tubes. I did a switcheroo of a big black tub for those milk crates. The black tub contained the tubes much better and liberated the milk crates. Since then, I've kept eyes peeled for milk crates, which turn up from time to time at our local recycling depot. Ask nicely and they are free, and so now I have a good supply.

After a few trials and attempts, I had crate carrying sorted on the resuscitated Peugeot and the front set-up is an adaptor between the bike and the crate. The adaptor slots into the rack. Then the crate hooks into the adaptor, leaving only the opposite end to hold down. That is done with an elastic strap pulling the crate down, and the adaptor — sandwiched between bike and crate — is automatically clamped too.

12.5   Home-made rear rack, shapes on top key into a crate. The truncated squares lock into the bottom of a crate.

12.6   Mark 1 front adaptor.

Next I made an adaptor for the back of the Hercules separating bike from Chapter 14, and that works well too. This time the rack doubles as a stand. With the back wheel it props the bike vertically, potentially saving space in flats or garages. Some finishing touches to this adaptor included bogging holes, varnish and a plastic tube over the back to protect the timber.

12.7   Hercules bike rear adaptor.

12.8   Adaptor used as stand on the Hercules bike.

A few days later, the state went into Coronavirus lockdown, and as an isolation project I bought another Peugeot NS folder (Box Hill Purple Peugeot) for $50. This was the complete budget for the project up to that time, as everything else had come from the shed or neighbourhood scrap.

The Dead White Peugeot was missing the back rack, but Box Hill Purple wasn't. However, it was missing a derailleur and was set up with only one gear. I still like riding it though, and have done a 22km round trip on it to collect parts. The gear it has is the middle gear of the standard five-speed set-up, which gives a gear of 52.3 inches (42-tooth front, 18-tooth back, 570mm diameter wheel).

12.9   Box Hill Purple.

This gearing can be restored later, and my work on this bike focused on load carrying and crate adaptors. I have spare 7.8mm plywood and 28 × 15mm reclaimed Mirboo at home, and used that to make a front adaptor, which worked fine.

Up till then, the adaptors had been seat-of-the-pants builds, cutting timber to the right size by measuring racks and crates but not recording anything. But for the back rack adaptor, I decide on an engineering approach, hauling a loose rack inside and using 2d CAD to draw an adaptor plan before making it. This time I didn't use Mirboo and only used plywood.

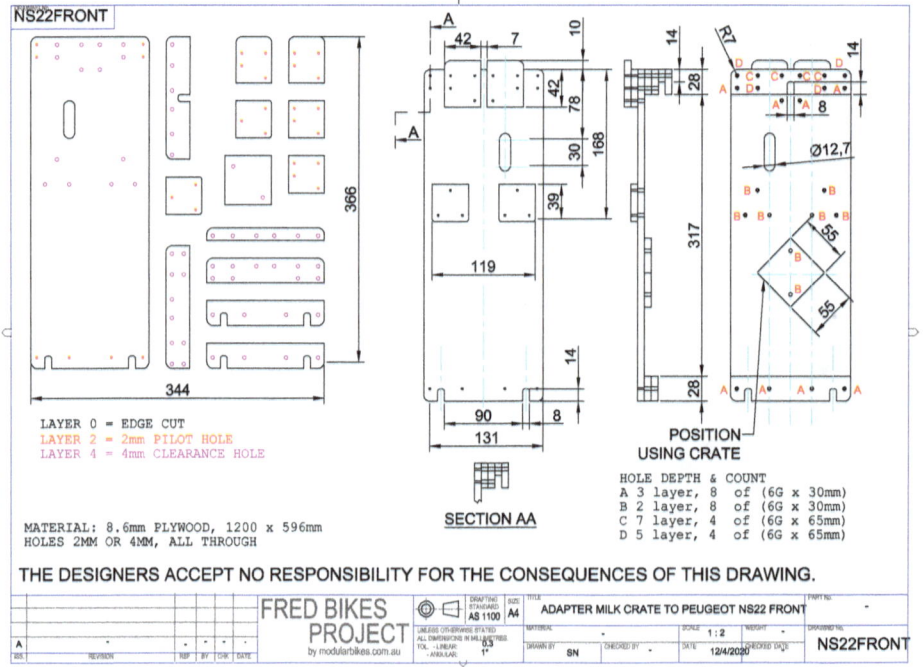

12.10 Drawing of front adaptor

After buying some new plywood from a local store and biking it home, I made CAD plans for front and back adaptors, then sent drawings to a CNC routing contractor for a quote. The contractors (Sean and Horn) are good, and I had worked with them before, making tailboxes for tilting trikes. They itemise all costs and let me do some of the labour to reduce prices. After the price came through and was approved, I delivered the material and talked through the designs with Billy. The different types of cut could be put on different layers to simplify data transfer from CAD to cutting machine, and I did this design change when I got home, then emailed the resulting dxf file through.

A few days later, I had three CNC routed crate adaptor kits with me at home, and started assembling one set. That let me finalise CAD plans down to what screw is used where. The CNC cut set works well. With the kits ready, I have given myself the job of restoring old Peugeot bikes, fitting crate adaptors, and seeing if I can sell them for a profit on eBay. I've had modest success, at least covering costs in the first two sales.

12.11   Adaptors made by CNC routing.

Most of the benefits of these designs come from the adaptor being a separate thing with neither bike nor crate altered to achieve load carrying. This means the bikes are easily switchable from stripped down (racks only) to one crate (front or back) to two crates (front and back), so the rider is not locked in to any set-up as occurs when crates are cable-tied on.

The rider can also swap between crates of different colours. The crate can be removed to carry whatever's in it when stopped (e.g. for bringing groceries into an apartment). Lastly, when released from the bike, the crate is free to become whatever the user wants it to be. The website mymilkcrates.com (https://mymilkcrates.com) subtitles itself 'Portraits of milk crates in their many natural habitats' and shows them as individuals or stacked together, as tables, chairs, steps and artworks, and all of these become possibilities.

In one sense this is a concept design. It shows there are still new cycle load-carrying possibilities, which are not the most expedient — like attaching crates with cable ties, or conventional — like panniers.

This design itself only has a small niche, helping a clunky Peugeot folding bike carry one particular type of crate. I don't even know whether these crates are available in cities besides Melbourne.

That said, this could be a design for the times we are living in (with COVID-19 travel restrictions), enabling simultaneous DIY expression, load-carrying transport and exercise on quiet streets. I hope these cycling conditions come around again post COVID-19.

13   Kids' Bikes

This chapter concerns cycles for children learning to ride. Bikes where children are on board but don't pedal are covered in Chapter 11. Tandems where children pedal are included in Chapter 10.

Background

Until several years ago, few cycles for kids respected that children are smaller, lighter and not as strong as adults, and need cycles designed for them. Instead, common and cheap parts and concepts from BMX and mountain bikes were used on kids' bikes. They were often sold and marketed with crap like multiple chainrings on the front, heavy tread on tyres, colours targeting boys or girls, and football team or Barbie or superhero brandings and attachments.

Thankfully some newer cycle brands respect children and encourage them to be riders for life by being light and simple to ride, mount, handle and control. Well-designed larger kids' bikes also make good, uncomplicated bikes for smaller adults, and well-designed brands market their bikes on their high resale value. Bikes for young children under 40kg are still made with components suitable for heavier adults, or for the abuse of BMX, so should endure easily and be passed on when they are outgrown.

Learning to ride

Learning to ride consists of overlapping steps. Byk bikes generalise these in their bike descriptions as learning to balance, ready to ride, learning to ride, able to ride and developing skills. But the steps can be broken down into individual skills such as:
- propelling by feet on the ground

- balancing by steering
- propelling with pedals
- braking
- use of gears
- locking
- carrying things by bike.

Its only when all of these skills are mastered that children can ride independently. Children are adaptable, and most will end up riding given time and access to any reasonable cycles. My son learnt on a rag-tag bunch (13.5, 13.6, 13.7). He still rides today, and long ago overtook my riding skills by mastering the unicycle. The Sheldon Brown website has a good guide to teaching kids to ride.

13.1 Wishbone 3 in 1 convertible trike.

13.2 A bike with pedals removed becomes a balance bike

13.3   Wooden balance bike.

Cycle types

Initially a pedalless trike can teach seated scootering, or velocipede-style feet-on-the-ground propulsion, and does not require balance. Next comes a balance bike or child velocipede or child bicycle without pedals. Kids are then ready for pedalled bicycles. The smallest of these feature coaster (back-pedal) brakes, which are easier to activate than hand brakes. Scooters and pedalled trikes can be somewhere in the mix as well. Progression is then through bikes of increasing size until adult cycles can be used. Folding bikes make good kids' bikes for ages of about eight and up. They are usually light, have a low stepover height and sequential gearing, and often come with a luggage rack.

13.4 Scooter.

13.5 Pedalled trike.

13   Kids' Bikes

13.6   Small tandem.

A few products convert between learn-to-ride cycle types. The Wishbone 3 in 1 is a trike and a balance bike, and Littlebigbike make bikes designed for conversion to balance bikes. The DIY option for converting bikes to balance bikes involves removing the pedals, and works well. Second-hand or found and competently repaired cycles are also good for kids.

Accessories like detachable push handles and trainer wheels can come with smaller bikes to help children balance. But they are more things added to the cycle. Balance bikes (child bicycles without pedals) have less things on the bicycle and let kids learn in a freer way.

Load carrying should not be ignored on kids' bikes, and some relatively simple accessories like handlebar baskets could lead to some adult–child load-carrying DIY.

Besides individual cycles for kids, a range of other cycling technologies help families travel by bike, and these have the benefit of teaching that bike transport is a good option. Examples are trailers, child seats, tag-alongs, cargo bikes and tandems. Electric motors on these cycles can ensure family cycling fits in with everyday life and is not too exhausting.

Summary

There is still room for improvement in kids' cycles, but they have come a long way in recent years. Mostly the better bikes are expensive, and bikes of poor quality are cheap. I'm an optimist and believe cheaper brands will learn and improve.

13.7   Folding bikes are good for children to ride. This is a vintage Cinzia.

13.8 Family cycling. Photo Kim Aagaard.

13.9 Family cycling. Photo Kim Aagaard.

References

Byk bikes https://www.bykbikes.com.au/collections/kids-bikes

Littlebigbikes https://www.littlebigbikes.com/

Sheldon Brown learn to ride https://www.sheldonbrown.com/teachride.html

Wishbonedesign https://wishbonedesign.com/collections/bikes

14   Modular Cycles

An online dictionary defines modular as 'Constructed out of usually prefabricated units with standardised dimensions, allowing for easy assembly and flexible arrangement: modular furniture; modular homes'.

In this chapter two aspects of modular cycles are discussed:
- Cycles and accessories, which are designed to be versatile.
- The modularity and standard parts making bicycles simple to repair and upgrade. Using bikes' standard features, many designers have made cycle improvements, sometimes creating DIY instructions or kits or new bike types.

Examples away from cycling

Modular design can be a trick where something simple performs better than expected. A Lego set looks like plastic blocks to an adult, but to a child the blocks fit together to become anything in their imagination. Tupperware storage containers can have the same lids but be different sizes. They nest inside each other when not in use and stack to use all the height available on a shelf. And with an appropriate Tupperware set it's easy to find and access things, biscuits stay fresh, unused containers stow away neatly and a pantry can be organised.

Computers are also modular, with some characteristics shared with bikes. Computers, bikes and their standardised parts are made by a number of vendors, which makes for competition, reduced cost and easy repairability. Computers and bikes are modular inside (add more ram to circuit board, fit new pedals) and can be modular outside (using the internet, convert bicycle to longbike). The right model computers and bikes are easy to use for ages 3 to 83 and are relatively easy to configure. The manufacture of computers and bikes is governed by improving standards ensuring parts fit together and devices are simple to operate. They are both available in portable versions.

Several years ago, computers reached a modularity-related tipping point where usefulness and perceived value meant ownership became the norm rather than the exception. Smartphones reached a similar tipping point too. But CD and DVD players are on the way out now. Privately owned cars could be the next thing to go. In comparison to all of these, bikes are enduring.

The aim of many designers is to make their product so useful that everyone starts to buy one, but this requires both luck and skill. A better cycle or part could include:

- improved load or passenger or stoker carrying
- improved comfort, stability, speed, weight and portability
- simple conversions between different bike types.
- reasonable cost.

New and modular cycles

Many efforts to make better bikes are helped by their modular nature. Designers often start by modifying existing bikes, and the end results have varying degrees of success, from one-offs to prototypes to thousand-sellers. A bike that is only ever a one-off is successful if it works for its user, and things get better if designs eventually reach production. There can be a financial side to this, but the results are all improved cycles, which can eventually lead to more cycling and more sustainable transport. Some of these are shown in 14.1 to 14.6. Robert Waryszak and Vi Vuong have made many bikes for the thrill of creating and using them or seeing them used. They don't try to profit from their designs but enjoy showing them on the internet so others can use their ideas.

14   Modular Cycles

14.1   Brompton recumbent conversion kit by Julianne Neuss.

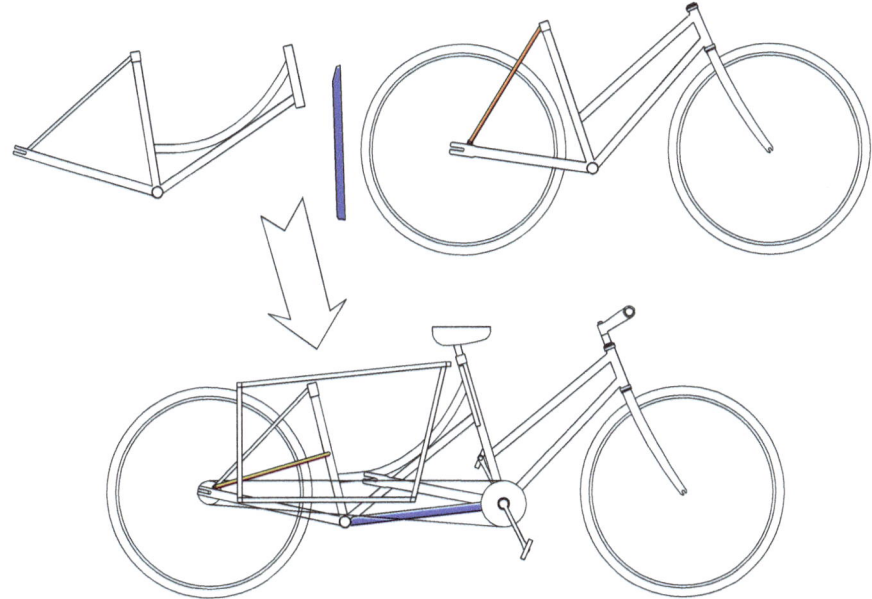

14.2   In the early 1980s, Bruce Steer and Ian Grayson modified bike frames to make Adelaide longbikes. Their how-tos helped longtails become standard.

14.3   Onderwater Tandem, a child in front tandem steered via a linkage from behind. A load-carrying box makes the design versatile and the square main tube simplifies parts attachment.

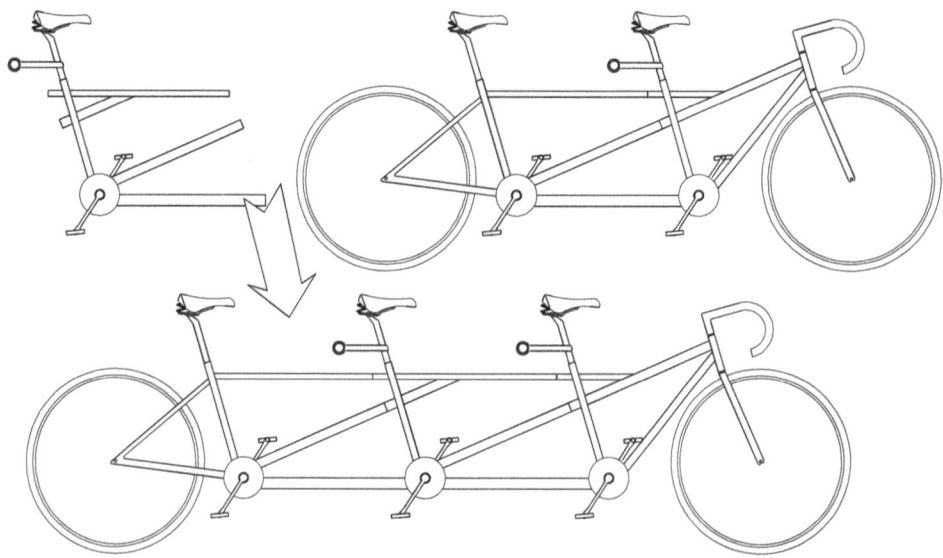

14.4   Santana tandems allow modular switching between two or three seaters.

14.5   Gardner Martin's 1975 recumbent started as a tandem.

14.6 Modifications to make a butchers bike from a 24" mountain bike. Red parts out, blue parts in, including new steel fork blades attached to cropped suspension fork.

Velocino/mule train, two bikes in one

Recently I made two altered bikes by starting with a separating 24" Hercules bike. The first is the Mule Train load bike, made in the style of a Clydesdale fork bike by installing a large 26" fork and swapping in a 20" front wheel. The second bike is a Velocino (simply a very small bicycle) with the front half made from scratch starting with a laser-cut join plate.

The Triset was a Swiss modular bike from the mid-1990s and shares some of my Hercules bike's technology. It has two separable halves with a gravity-assisted join, and the front half can be swapped between shopping trolley, bike front wheel and wheelchair adaptor.

Another bike I have owned, the Peugeot DA40, has the front swappable for an exercise bike attachment. This would be silly but fun.

14.7 Velocino and compacted Velocino front half.

14.8   A plate on the Velocino mimics half of the Hercules bike join.

Convertible bike

An earlier modular bike was built by accident. Inspiration came from a Moulton Tandem described in *Velovision* magazine. The tandem had three sections, with the ends just the separated front and back parts of a Moulton and the centre a specially made insert including handlebars, seat and pedals. The insert piece converts the single bike into a tandem. The Bike Friday Traveller Q is a commercial bike built in a similar way, and Zox Tandem recumbents use the same principles too.

An opportunity to build a bike like this came with a find of two Malvern Star folding bike frames. The resulting HPV (14.9, 14.10) was enjoyable, useful, and combined folding, tandem, load-carrying and chopper bike styles. It was possible to carry large awkward loads — like bike frames — strapped to the handlebars. It still folded, so could be carried in the back seat of our Toyota Corolla.

14.9 Creation of convertible bike.

14.10 Convertible tandem as chopper, tandem, load bike. Note second bell on handlebars.

Modular bikes

The success of the convertible bike prompted me to make three more sets of modular bikes from scratch. They slowly improved and became good proof of concept designs. The most recent were braze-welded from laser-cut round tube. They were versatile, worked well and looked good. However, they were made from heavy 50 × 1.6mm steel tube, and some form of weight loss was needed. 14.11 to 14.13 show this bike in various forms.

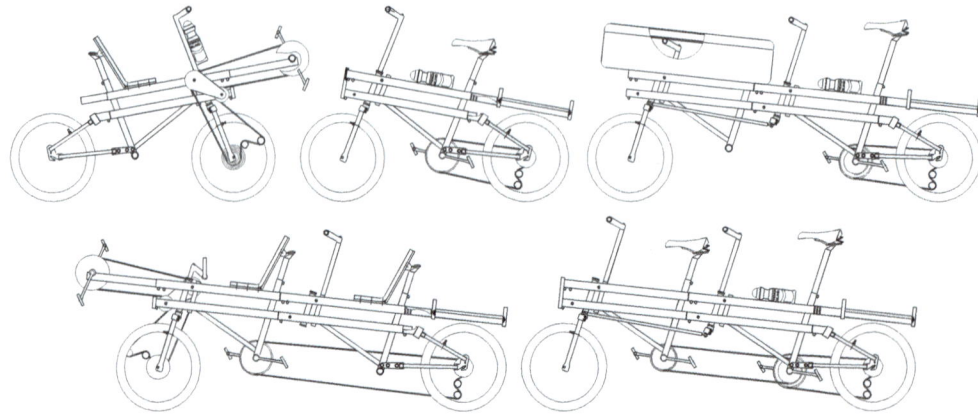

14.11 The most successful version of my modular bike, these (front wheel drive recumbent, bicycle, load bike, all-wheel-drive recumbent tandem, tandem with steering linkage) are some of the configurations that were made. There was frame redundancy with sites for static or steering handlebars.

14.12   Bicycle and counterpoint tandem versions of modular bike.

14.13   Back-to-back tandem and load-carrying versions of modular bike.

Conclusion

Bicycles are great, but if you think they can be improved then go for it. The hurdles might not be that high, and the simplest way to start is to use or adapt existing plans and bikes. Have fun!

References

Adelaide Longbikes https://portadbug.org/links-videos-resources/the-adelaide-longbike-an-earlier-cargo-bike-movement

Brompton Recumbent conversion kit, *Encycleopedia 2001*, p.112 https://issuu.com/encycleopedia/docs/enc2001_complete_lr_opt/142

Free Dictionary Definition of Modular, see https://www.thefreedictionary.com/modular

Gardner Martin Recumbent, *Human Power 9*, 1983 http://www.ihpva.org/HParchive/PDF/09-v2n2-1983.pdf

Kater, M. *Two from one: Moulton tandems, Bike Culture 18*, July 1999.

Nurse S, *Modular Bikes* Velovision 17, Mar 2005, p.18

Onderwater Tandem https://www.onderwaterfiets.nl

Peugeot DA40 http://modularbikes.blogspot.com/2016/08/peugeot-da40.html

Triset trike from Schramm, *Encycleopedia 96*, pp.98-99 retrieved from https://issuu.com/encycleopedia/docs/enc03_opt2

Vuong. Vi *Ilean trikes* http://en.openbike.org/wiki/~iLean

Waryszak R. website http://comfybikes.blogspot.com

15 Cycle Stability

This chapter describes limits set by cycle construction on braking and cornering. These handling limits include skidding and tipping under braking for bikes and trikes, and sideways tipping for trikes. This excludes tilting trikes, which are described in Chapter 16.

Two- and three-wheel HPVs differ fundamentally in stability. Trikes are stable under most conditions, while bikes need active balancing. Unlike bicycles, trikes cannot be leaned into corners, and the speed at which trikes can corner is limited by the tendency to roll over sideways or tip. Trike riders can avoid tipping by leaning their bodies into a turn when cornering, giving an exciting feeling of speed. Tipping under braking is rotation forward over the front wheel or wheels. Bike leaning is rotation around the line between tyre contact points. Trike tipping is rotation about the outside and front wheels on deltas, and outside and back wheels on tadpoles.

Assumptions

Static gravity forces and dynamic motion forces are both related to acceleration via the equation:

Force = Mass × Acceleration (F = ma).

Without support, we, and everything on Earth accelerate down with the force of gravity at $g = 9.8(m/s)/s$. This acceleration acts when we stick to the ground, and downhill and uphill on bikes and trikes. Gravity combines with cornering or starting/stopping acceleration to determine handling. Most of this discussion assumes riding is on smooth level ground. Acceleration due to gravity can be converted to everyday units: it is 35(km/h)/s.

Centre of gravity

Some simplifications help to understand cycle dynamics. The first is centre of gravity. Bikes, trikes, and their riders aren't concentrated masses at a point, but can be treated as if they are to simplify equations. The relevant mass is that of load, cycle and rider — unchanging and easy to quantify. The point of balance or centre of mass is harder to quantify, and changes with rider posture and motion.

Static centre of gravity is an imaginary point in three-dimensional space — if suspended by a CG, an object is free to rotate in all directions and will not pendulum or swing due to gravity. 15.1 shows how the centre of gravity of a bike and rider is an average of the rider's and bike's centres, and how the x position of centres can be calculated. The y positions are on the line between the wheels and z positions can be estimated from a picture. Riders' postures vary while riding, and CG positions vary also. Tilting on a line between the wheels is absolutely standard. Less frequently, the whole bike frame rotates around wheel contact points under hard braking or acceleration.

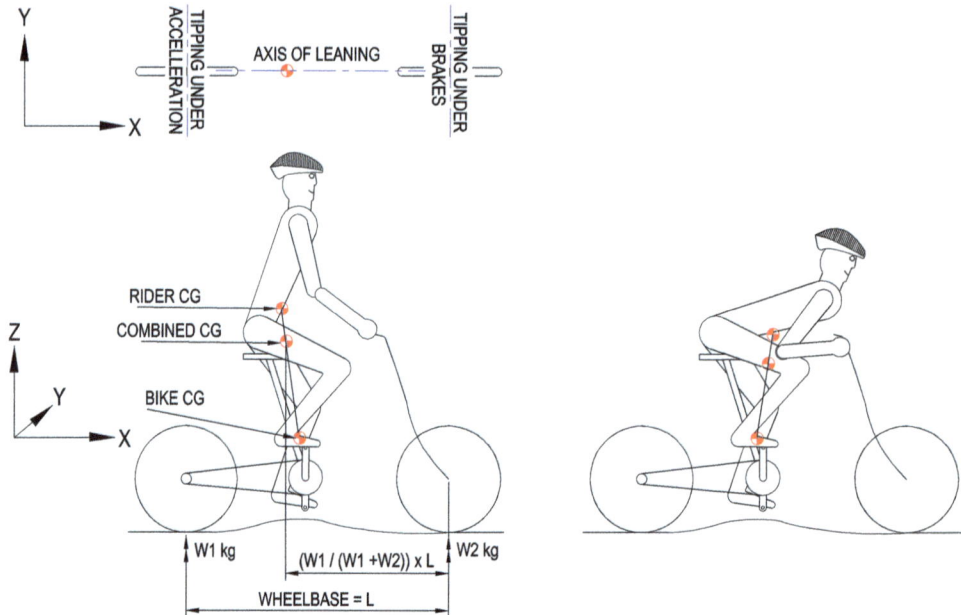

15.1   Bike riders with centres of gravity and tilt/tip axes.

Tipping around the axis line between the tyres occurs during cornering, and the tilt angle can be calculated with the equation in 15.2. The faster a rider travels, the greater the lean angle for a given radius.

A consequence of tilting during cornering is that pedalling can be dangerous when leaning significantly in turns as shown in 15.3. The workaround is to not pedal when cornering. The workaround for avoiding pedal strike in rough terrain is also shown. Pedalstrike is an issue specific to bicycles and determined by geometry. Other cycle types have different geometric specific issues such as wheels scrubbing legs in tadpole trikes, limited steering with tiller steer, and tipping in trikes.

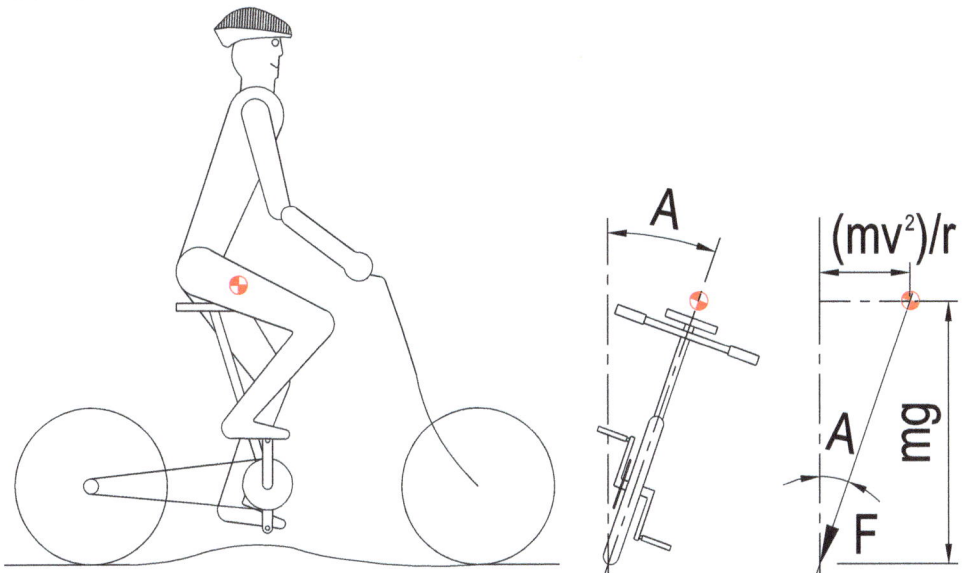

15.2   Bicycle tip angle A can be calculated from speed v and turn radius r. They both contribute to the total downwards force F, and $A = \tan^{-1}(v^2/gr)$.

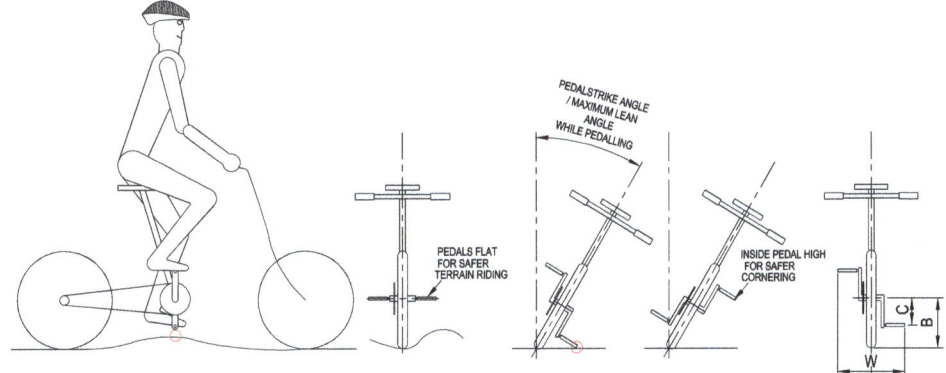

15.3   Avoiding pedal strike. Pedal strike angle is a function of pedal width, crank length and bottom bracket height.

Tipping in recumbent trikes and quads

Recumbent trike geometry differs from bikes, and the tipping layouts of delta and tadpole trikes are shown in 15.4 and 15.5. For these calculations the CG is the top point of a tetrahedron with a base defined by wheel contact points. Whether a trike is stable under gravity and acceleration/braking/cornering depends on whether resultant forces acting through the CG reaches the ground within wheel contact points (15.4).

Under cornering and gravity alone, a tipping speed can be calculated for a given cornering radius (15.5). For example, if the trike shown is cornering on a 6m radius the critical velocity for tipping can be calculated from the expression used before, and $A = \tan^{-1}(v^2/gr)$.

$26 = \tan^{-1}(v^2/(g \times 6m$, so
$\tan 26 = 0.4877 = v^2/g \times 6m$, so
$v^2 = 0.4877 \times 9.8 \times 6 = 28.67$, so
$v = 5.35$ m/s $= 19.3$ km/h

This critical velocity can be increased and tipping avoided if the rider moves in the direction of the turn, moving CG off centre to keep resultant forces within wheel contact points.

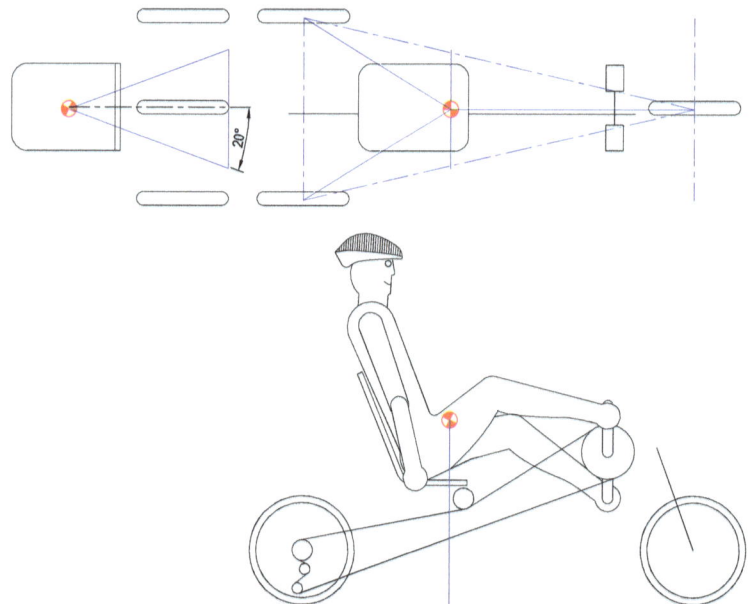

15.4   Delta trike with CG and tilt axes shown as dotted lines.

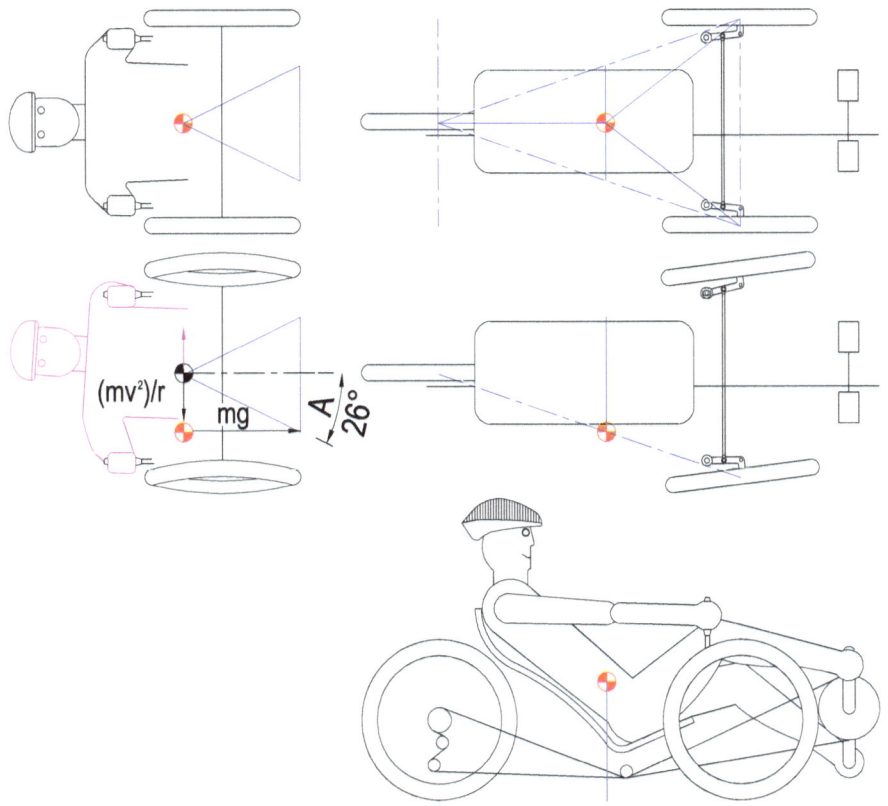

15.5   Tadpole trike and shifted CG at critical cornering speed. By moving right, the rider moves CG to forestall tipping.

15.6 shows the stability diagram for a quad based on the delta trike shown in 15.4. The tip lines at the sides no longer converge at the front or back. The resistance to tipping is increased and is not sensitive to the x position of the CG. The critical tip speed calculations for a 6m radius can be repeated for the delta and quad:

- 15.4, Delta, Angle = 20°, v = 4.63 m/s = 16.7km/h
- 15.6, Quad, Angle = 29°, v = 5.71 m/s = 20.6km/h

There is extra complexity and weight in the quad, although it is more stable.

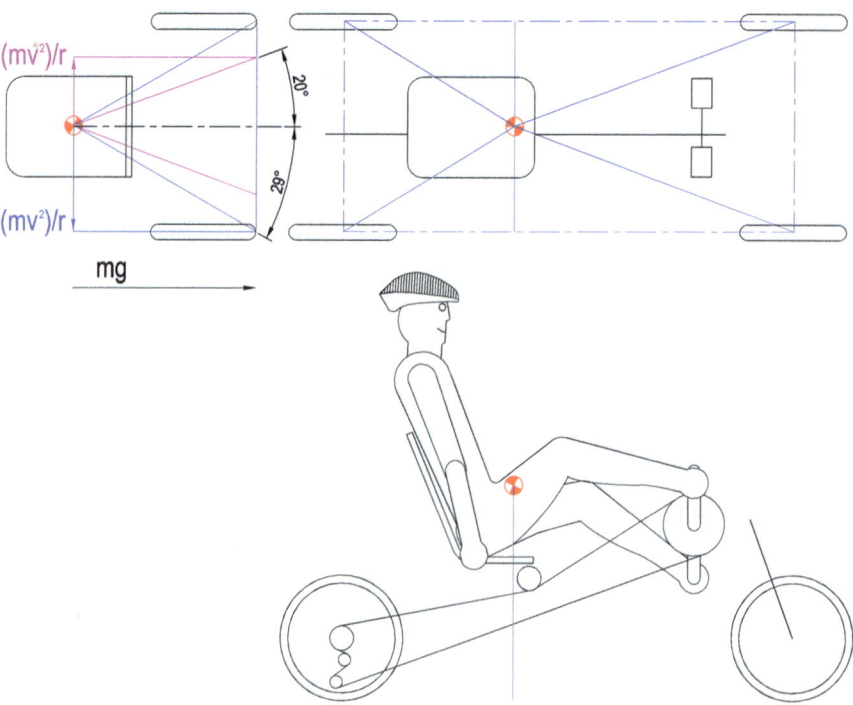

15.6　Quad with dotted tip lines. The tip triangle for the equivalent delta has a smaller top angle, so the delta reaches a tip point sooner under cornering.

Tipping under braking

Tipping of cornering trikes must be calculated by considering 3 dimensional geometry, but braking calculations can be confined to a single plane and use 2 dimensional geometry. Tipping occurs if the front wheel does not skid, and the resultant of braking and gravitational forces falls outside the wheelbase (15.7).

Braking forces involve the same elements as cornering, but pose a simpler problem. The top row of 15.7 shows that if the retarding brake force is more than 86% of gravity, the rear wheel will lose contact with the ground, and unless the rider acts quickly the bicycle will cartwheel and the rider will take a header over the handlebars. Since the mass of rider and machine is common to gravity and braking forces, we can eliminate it, leading to the conclusion that on this bicycle, regardless of masses, the maximum braking acceleration/deceleration without cartwheeling is 0.86g, where g is the acceleration due to gravity.

The formula is a(max) = g × (CG)/h(CG) = g/tanA, where

a(max)   is maximum braking acceleration

x(CG)   is the horizontal component of the distance from the front axle to the CG

h(CG)   is the height of the CG above the ground (in the same units as r(CG))

g   is the acceleration due to gravity, i.e. 9.8 m/s/s or 35(km/h)/s

A   is the (angular) elevation of the CG, measured at the front-wheel contact patch of the (bikes or delta trikes) or midway between front wheels (tadpole trikes).

The value calculated from this formula is a maximum, only achievable if tyres are capable of generating enough braking force. If the tyres hold less than 0.86g deceleration, the bike will not cartwheel on application of the brakes, but under hard braking it will slide and probably swerve.

This formula applies to any cycle, and shows that the maximum deceleration for stable cycling depends on wheelbase and weight distribution of machine and rider. The longer the wheelbase and the lower and further back the CoG, the higher the maximum safe braking acceleration.

The long-wheelbase recumbent shown is in theory capable of undergoing 2g braking acceleration without cartwheeling, well in excess of grip available with current tyres.

The ordinary or penny farthing bicycle shown may be able to withstand only 0.2g before cartwheeling, which even the spoon brakes and solid tyres of the 1870s could create.

A typical touring tadpole trike has equal weight on each wheel, meaning that the centre of gravity is behind the front axle line by one-third of the wheelbase. If such a trike has 1m wheelbase, and a CG 35cm above the road, it may be stable under nearly 1g braking acceleration. While this is near the limit of what current tyres will generate, most current trikes on good quality tyres will lift the rear wheel under hard braking. With a slightly longer wheelbase or the CG slightly lower or further back (or cheaper tyres), these trikes would remain stable under brakes up to the limit of tyre adhesion.

Partly because it is designed to generate high cornering forces, a sporting delta trike commonly has its centre of gravity closer to the rear wheels than does a tadpole trike. Estimated from published specifications, a Greenspeed

Anura has the centre of gravity 0.5m high and 1.05m behind the front wheel leading to a theoretical maximum stopping acceleration of 75km/h per second. Theoretical, because the tyres will not have sufficient grip; beyond their limit, the machine will slide instead of tipping up.

The value of A is critical, and can often be easily calculated. If A for a given machine is 45°, the machine will be stable under braking acceleration on level ground at 1g, which is about the limit of adhesion of modern tyres on dry tarmac. If A is more than 45°, the cycle can lift a rear wheel or even cartwheel under brakes. If A is less than 45°, braking acceleration on level ground will be no greater than if A was equal to 45°, since in both cases, it will be limited by the tyres to about 1g, but the machine will have a reserve of braking capacity for downhills.

For any given initial speed, the distance travelled by a cycle under brakes can be calculated from the braking acceleration. Using the examples above, from the same initial speed, the minimum distance in which the penny farthing can stop without cartwheeling would be 4.3 times that of the safety bicycle and 10 times as great as that of the long-wheelbase recumbent. In fact, the stopping distance of the recumbent would be limited by the tyre grip. The table gives theoretical stopping distances from a fast cruising speed of 40km/h.

In order to achieve braking acceleration close to its theoretical limit, a cycle must have an effective brake working on the front wheel. The actual braking acceleration of a cycle depends on whether it has front brakes, rear brakes or both, and on brake effectiveness. But the limit on braking acceleration is not avoided by using only rear brakes: that may overcome the risk of cartwheeling, but it does so by reducing braking acceleration, which is limited by loss of rear traction and swerving of the rear wheel.

Parameters of the upright bike mentioned above assumed the rider is fairly upright. If the rider leans forward for better aerodynamics as in 15.1, the CG of the laden bike moves forward and slightly down, making stability worse. A rider on tri-bars has the CG shifted even further forward.

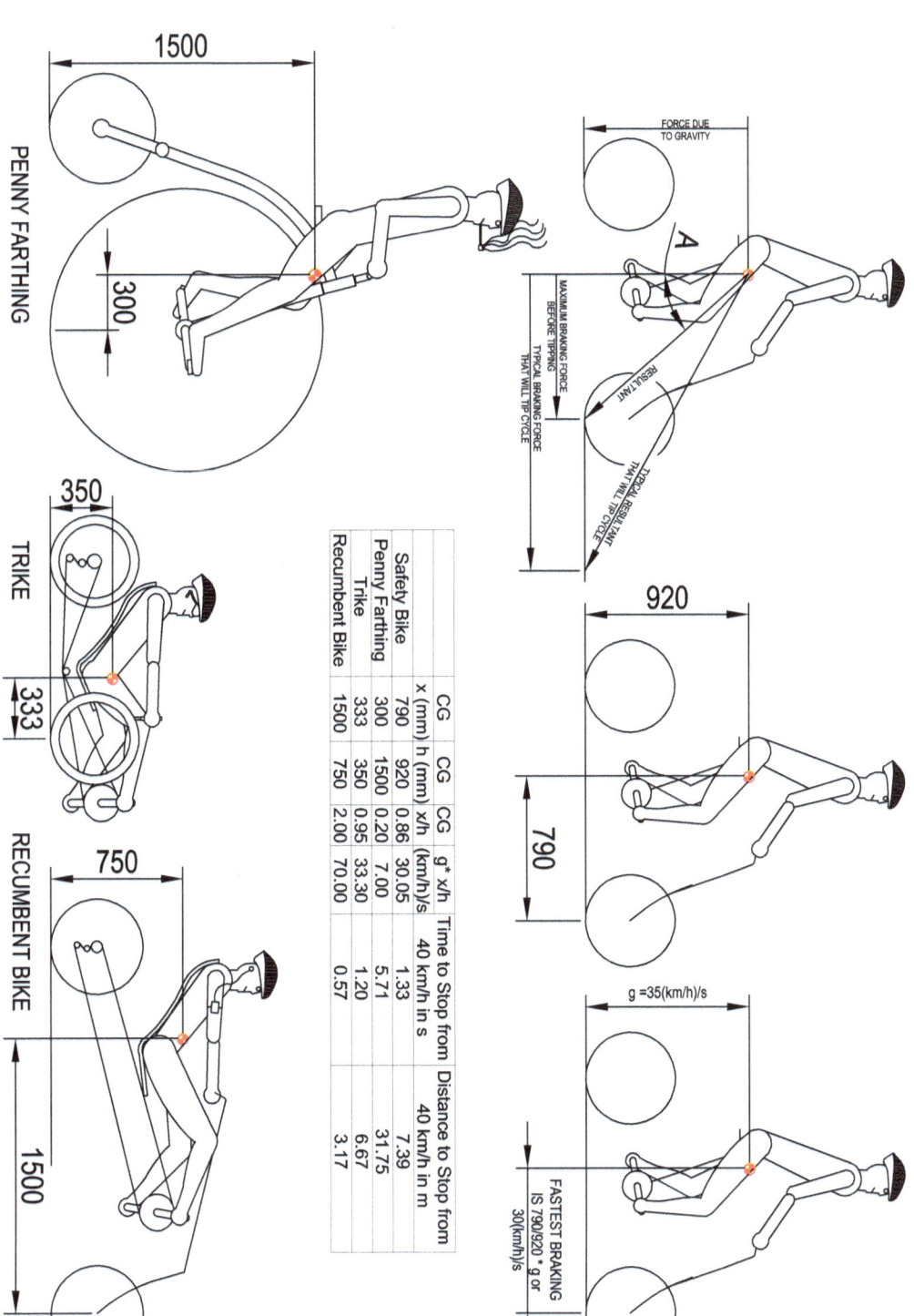

15.7 Minimum stopping times and distances for various human powered vehicles. CG is shown in each case.

	CG x (mm)	CG h (mm)	CG x/h	CG g* x/h (km/h)/s	Time to Stop from 40 km/h in s	Distance to Stop from 40 km/h in m
Safety Bike	790	920	0.86	30.05	1.33	7.39
Penny Farthing	300	1500	0.20	7.00	5.71	31.75
Trike	333	350	0.95	33.30	1.20	6.67
Recumbent Bike	1500	750	2.00	70.00	0.57	3.17

16 Tilting Trikes

The last chapter discussed trikes that tip and bikes that tilt. Tilting trikes are three-wheel vehicles with bikelike tilting. They can be divided into groups including recumbent and upright, delta and tadpole, faired and unfaired, motorised and unmotorised. They can also be classified by the leaning mechanism. Leaning trikes can relieve cornering stresses on wheels through tilting, and remain upright when stopped. There are only a few 4 wheel (quads) tilting human powered vehicles listed on the tilting vehicle blogspot page. Quads and tilting trikes both allow machines with a high centre of gravity to remain stable during cornering. Having both on the same vehicle is overkill.

A wheel and tilting code for trikes takes the form XFYT where X is the number of front wheels and Y is the number of wheels that tilt. From the second number, it's always possible to work out which wheels tilt. That code can be extended to include four wheels and a car's code is 40T (4 zero T — four wheels, none of which tilt).

Tilting wheels are not subject to side loads making it desirable for all trike wheels to tilt.

A tilting code example is the 1F1T Maruishi leaning trike, which has one front wheel, which leans with the frame and two non-leaning back wheels. The single wheel on a tilting trike always tilts, so 3 or 1T denotes a tilter, 0T a non-tilter and 2T does not exist.

16 Tilting Trikes

16.1   Maruishi trike.

16.2   Maruishi leaning mechanism.

Why a tilting trike?

On some cycles, using tilting is just a reasonable construction method. These include skateboard-based tilters for short distance travel and fun, and front-wheel-drive machines with Vuong-style tilting. These machines don't have entanglement of braking, steering, tilting, suspension or drive, making simple DIY versions possible.

16.3   Pushing a skateboard.

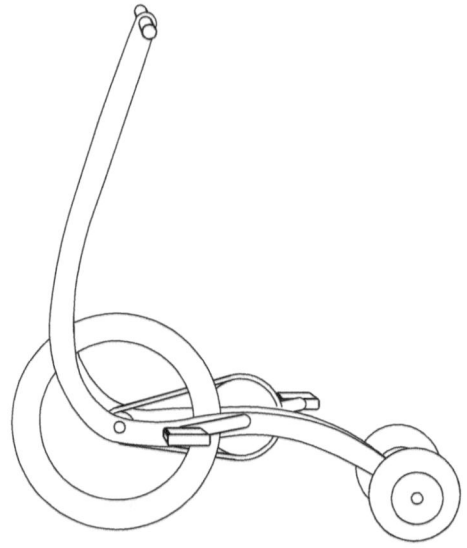

16.4   Front drive Half Bike tilter with rear trucks.

16.5 Skatebike tilter on left, unicycle on right.

16.6 A Vuong tilter. Photo Vi Vuong

For more complex tilters, DIY becomes harder and design justifications become necessary. The following paragraph is based on descriptions of the Tripendo tilter and its prototypes.

Turning a bicycle means leaning, and weight and centrifugal force combine along the line of the bicycle. However, tricycles cannot normally lean. Centrifugal forces must be resisted by wheels and frame, which must be made strong and heavy. Small wheels may be needed to resist these forces, although larger wheels help with comfort and better rolling resistance. The rider must be low to stop tipping, although more height is preferred in traffic to bring rider's eye level up to car drivers' eye level. If a full fairing for weather protection and speed is required, two-wheelers are too unstable in side winds and a leaning trike design is the answer.

So tilting can solve some trike issues, allowing less stress in the frame, larger wheels and a high ride with potential for static stability. This sounds good, but tilting trikes require an articulated frame, potentially adding to weight, cost and wind resistance. For prototypes this is okay, but eventually manufacturers need to make money on their trikes. Nevertheless, tilting trikes are coming onto the market. Other designs are simple and open source.

Lean-to-steer quads and trikes

Lean-to-steer quads include the street skateboards sometimes called longboards. They are a common tilting human powered vehicle, but off-topic for this book. But it's worth examining them and their tilting and steering, which can be applied to cycles.

Longboard steering works through a pair of swivelling trucks mounted on elastomers. When the deck is angled to the road, the trucks are turned, with the lowest part of the deck facing into the turning circle. This turning occurs because truck tilt axes are angled to the road and intersect below the skateboard. This turning can be replicated in solid-axle cycles as shown in 16.20.

Riders have two ways of steering longboards, and after practice both become intuitive:
- With the front foot pointing forward on the board and the other pushing

off the ground, longboards can be used as transport. The front foot is twisted to keep the deck parallel to cambered streets and moving straight ahead. On top of this twist a small amount of steering can be achieved (16.3).

- With two feet on the board and toes pointed sideways, there's more torque available for steering control than with one foot on the board. Turning is easier, and riders can carve a path downhill but not push directly.

Longboards have been scaled up to become mountain boards for riding on grass instead of streets. The propulsion has also been scaled up, and in the 2F1T skatebike (16.5), the front truck is retained and grafted onto a small cycle seat, frame and drive. In the newer 1F1T Halfbike, the rear truck is retained for steering, and there are pedals, a drive-wheel and non-steering hand supports at the front (16.4).

Lean-to-steer vehicles don't absorb road camber, so for straight-line motion skateboard decks are parallel to the street. For straight-line motion skatebike and half bike frames are perpendicular to the street. Lean-to-steer cycles can be adjusted to make leaning simpler. This is done by compressing elastomers for stiff trucks on smooth surfaces or loosening them for carving on streets. Like adjustment of seat height on bicycles, this adjustment can't be done on the fly.

There are some lean-to-steer recumbent cycles. I made an unsafe at any speed lean-to-steer 2F1T recumbent trike years ago. It couldn't absorb street camber, was hard to steer, and I rode about 4km away from home and then rang my wife Christine to come and pick me up. I didn't feel safe riding it any more. The 'Fun Bike' is a lean-to-steer recumbent with one gear made by Trailmate in the USA, and Jouta make a multispeed lean to steer in Holland. Commercial, custom and homebuilt multi-gear lean-to-steer recumbents have also been made, one with the brand name Baccura.

16.7   My first trike, a lean-to-steer tadpole 2F1T — not a success.

16.8   Jouta VX, a lean-to-steer delta 1F1T.

Virtual bike wheel tilters

Less common than skateboards are tilters simulating bicycle leaning. Thankfully, these trikes absorb street camber. They simulate a single wheel between the paired front wheels of a tadpole, or rear wheels of a delta, and like bicycles have a roll axis. Tilting uses mechanisms on paired front or back wheels. Tilt controls range from active control, to on-the-fly adjustment, to tilt locks, to adjustments available when stopped, to no controls. No controls on tilting implies free to lean. An example of a free-to-lean trike is the Ev4 electric trike, which has a kickstand even though it has three wheels.

16.9   EV4 trike with kickstand. Photo www.ev4.pl/en/bike.html

16.10   Trego tilting cargo attachment. Photo trego-trolley.com/home

Tilt lock simplifies tilter parking, starting and stopping. It's of particular use when the vehicle is enclosed in an aerodynamic shell, as riders may need to climb in and then start without feet touching the ground.

Almost always, leaning mechanisms add suspension when compared to a single wheel. Even without extra springing, the virtual wheel contact point rises only half as much as either of the actual wheels. Additional suspension can include springs, dampers and beam flex.

Sometimes leaning mechanisms will cause the rider to rise during tilts, creating a different feel, reluctance to turn, and feeling of static stability. This characteristic is adjustable in the Panthertrike (16.17). In Vuong trikes (16.6) it occurs when cranks are set in the 90° spaced 10:30/1:30 positions instead of the more usual, 180° spaced 3 o'clock 9 o'clock position (see appendix).

Maruishi (16.1, 16.2) and Varna have developed solid-axle tilting deltas with the rear wheels parallel and coaxial. The pedal drive is to one rear wheel, and in addition the Varna has electric front wheel drive. Both trikes have luggage storage between the rear wheels, and the Maruishi is upright while the Varna is semi-recumbent. Another tilting trike similar to the Maruishi is the Bridgestone Picnica. A Picnica was rescued and lovingly restored by Mark Rehder, and the process is described in his Drumbent blog.

In solid-axle tilting deltas, keeping the rear wheel tilt axis close to the neutral axis means rear wheels absorb camber and don't lean to steer (16.20).

An early commercial tilting trike was the Flevobike delta trike developed by Johan Vrielink. The design morphed from a bike design originally built by students in Vrielink's school. The trikes were first built in 1989.

16.11   Flevotrike. Photo David Nurse.

Frank Schleiwert from Germany wrote about his tilting 2F3T faired tilting tadpole trike in *Bike Culture Quarterly* in 1996 and went on to manufacture the Tripendo unfaired tilter. Included were full suspension, mid-drive transmission, parallelogram linkage-articulated front wheels and a tensioner to absorb extra chain length when adjusting seat position.

It came in fibreglass and carbon fibre versions, but even the lighter carbon version weighed 29kg. A right-hand lever controlled tilting and a left-hand lever controlled steering. The Tripendo is an iconic machine, and the website offers maintenance, repair, spare parts, accessories and electric drives for existing machines. It also shows a modern velomobile. A successful modern tilter with the Tripendo's basic layout is the Drymer Business. It is an electric-assist leaning trike with seven gears, lockable luggage compartment, a canopy, front hydraulic disc brakes and a cantilever mounted rear wheel, selling for 9,000 euros.

CYCLE ZOO

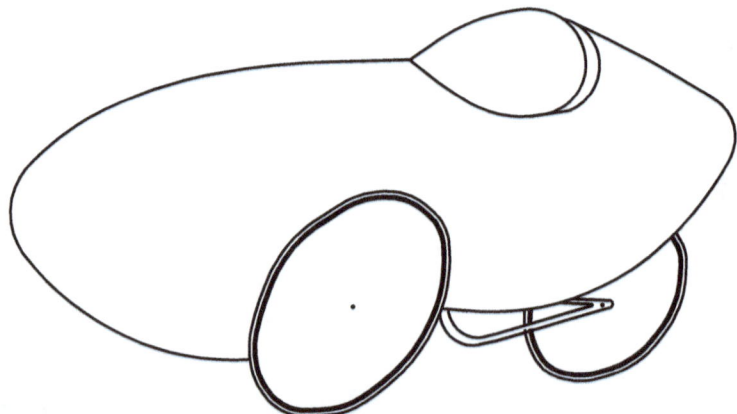

16.12 Frank Schleiwert's leaning velomobile, 1996.

16.13 Tripendo leaning tadpole trike.

Parallelogram tilters

In 2000, Paul Sims from Greenspeed built and documented a front-wheel-drive tilter with a parallelogram linkage. Versions were made by Robert Wood, Dennis Grelk and Tim Hicks in the USA, and Peter Heal in Australia. Braking both back wheels has no tilt lock effect, so an extra tilt lock brake is required.

An example of an upright parallelogram tadpole is the Trego (16.10) add-on cargo module for bicycles, which tilts and converts into a trolley when off the bike. Butchers and Bakers make expensive electric tadpole cargo trikes with parallelogram tilting. Alex Du Pre of Metal Machine Shop has made a series of excellent videos concerning the design of parallelogram velomobile tilters

16.14   Paul Sims leaning trike. Photo Paul Sims

16.15   Peter Heal's Eileen. Photo Peter Heal

Swingarm tilters

Bram Smit from Fastfwd.nl in Holland developed and sold two FWD tilting trike models inspired by a motorcycle patent by Carlos Calleja Vidal. The patent shows the rear wheels on the end of swingarms joined by a linkage. As one wheel rises the other falls.

Smit's first Calleja-style trike was the Leano, and a version with narrower back wheels is called the Munzo TT. Bram's leaning trikes were openly documented and copied by others, and Bram went on to develop the Velotilt front-wheel-drive velomobile tilter.

The rear wheels of the Leano are connected to suspension and damping. Locking a rear wheel to its swingarm brakes the trike. Locking both rear wheels to their swingarms brakes the tilt mechanism, creating a built-in tilt lock.

Peter Heal made a tilting trike called MMaXX in January 2020, using ideas from Chinese and Japanese delivery trikes and Daniele Go's Raptobike solar leaning trike conversion. Like Peter's first leaning trike, it uses fixed bottom bracket front wheel drive. It has a carbon fibre body and weighs only 10kg unfaired. Peter plans to install a fairing later.

The Panthertrike from the University of Milwaukee, Wisconsin is another trike using swingarms to tilt. It is based on a Cruzbike moving bottom bracket front-wheel-drive bike, and has a lever for engaging a tilt lock and adjusting ride characteristic.

16.16 MMaXX with swingarm tilting. Photo Peter Heal

16.17 Panthertrike. Photo panthertrike.com

As shown in 16.22, swingarm trikes cause rear wheel scrub as they tilt, because the distance between the wheels expands as tilting occurs. The scrub distance is proportional to rear wheel trackwidth.

Vuong tilters

Vi Vuong from the USA built and pioneered a leaning trike mechanism on his home-made Ilean (I lean) Python-style recumbents. The tilt mechanism is a pair of wheels mounted in place of pedals on a bicycle crank. Vi filmed his creations, and copies were made by HPV enthusiasts. Cruzbike and Kervelo have both made versions, and Performer recumbents have been converted to Vuong tilting trikes.

16.18 Load-carrying Vuong tilter. Photo Vi Vuong

I combined Vi's tilting mechanism with front wheel drive to make a simple leaning trike. The first of these had a solid wooden frame, and they have gradually improved. The frames of these trikes can be as simple as a beam with holes. The seat is combined with load storage, and provides an aerodynamic fairing behind the rider. Plans for a version of this trike can be downloaded from Thingiverse.

16.19 My leaning trike during an Audax ride.

Like Calleja swingarm trikes, Vuong trikes have wheel scrub while leaning because of expanding rear track width. As well, the non-aligned back wheels must pivot during turning, causing additional scrub (16.23). With 170mm cranks my machines juddered, shook and broke traction due to wheel scrub, but short, 75mm unicycle cranks make the scrub unnoticeable.

Victor Angelo started a discussion at Bentrideronline concerning his conversion of a Performer bike to a Vuong trike with tilt lock. His motivation was to help his friend Rob learn to ride a recumbent bike, and he varied the rear track width and angle between rear cranks. The discussion is informative and includes comments and input from Rob. A 135° angle was made possible by using a combination of diamond and square holed cranks (See Appendix). Victor concluded that:

'The turning point in this exercise was the inverted 90° V crank arrangement. The effect of this was to slow the tilt in a way that allowed Rob to control and ride the bike. As he gained the skill and confidence, the V-angle was reduced to 135°, then 180°. This was over a two-month period. The track width and crank arms were also reduced until it was effectively riding like a two-wheeler.'

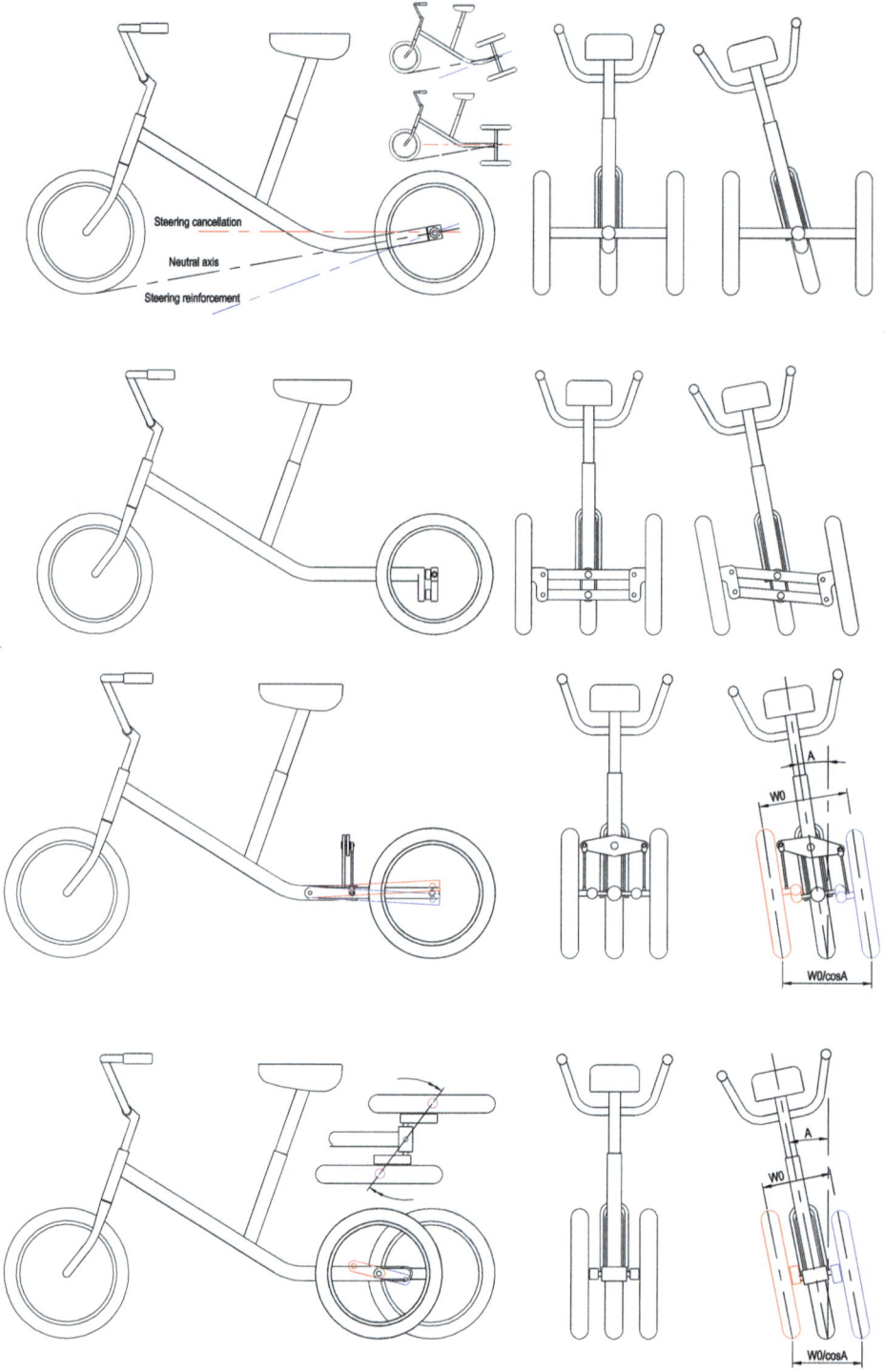

16.20, 21, 22, 23 Solid-axle, parallelogram, Swingarm and Vuong tilt mechanisms

Discussion

Paired wheels are what gives trikes stability, and tilters their ability to tilt. These wheels are the front/steered wheels on tadpoles and the rear/non-steered wheels on deltas. This means tadpole leaners have steering/leaning entanglement, while delta tilters do not.

With the drive-wheel at the back, tadpole tilters don't have drive/leaning entanglement, while rear-wheel-drive deltas do. But front-wheel-drive recumbent delta bikes been available commercially for several years. This means front-wheel-drive recumbent bikes can be converted to tilters relatively easily, with steering/drive entanglement sorted and no steering/leaning entanglement. Commercial FWD recumbent bikes such as the moving bottom bracket Cruzbike and fixed bottom bracket Munzo, Raptobike and Performer have all been used as the basis for tilters.

Motorbike delta tilters are less common than motorbike tadpole tilter trikes. This may be because delta motorbike tilters must have front drive, or rear drive entangled with rear wheel tilting. However, tadpole motorbike tilters are relatively common, with the Yamaha Niken touring motorbike providing support for grand tour cycling events such as the Tour de France.

16.24 Yamaha Niken motorbike.

The TiltDragonFly from Ecosunrider is a prototype delta tilter, and is discussed in Chapter 4. It has motorbike and bicycle elements. The only drive is electric and on the front wheel, but it has electrical inputs from solar panels and a pedalled generator. Ezeebikes sponsor Ecosunrider and make the Longabike, a commercial delta tilting trike with one rear wheel driven by electric motor, and the other by pedal power.

16.25   Ecosunriders series hybrid tilting trike. Photo www.sunrider.fr

Tilting trikes have great potential, and hopefully this information will help designers and customers choose. Interesting designs are possible — for example, a delta trike with solid axle tilting could have a small amount of beneficial rear steer if the tilt axis is oriented correctly.

Tilting trike code examples

1F0T: Greenspeed Anura Delta Trike
2F0T: Greenspeed Magnum, Trisled Gizmo tadpoles, the most common unmotorised recumbent trike.
2F1T: Skatebike
1F3T: Racing trikes and Voung trikes, often front wheel drive. Includes Velotilt.
1F1T: Maruishi, Varna, Halfbike
2F3T: Drymer, Tripendo, Yamaha Nixen, Trego conversion kit.
44T: EV4 City Quad Electric (https://www.ev4.pl/en/city-quad.html).
40T   Skateboard, mountain board.

References

Angelo V. Bentrider Ilean trike thread http://www.bentrideronline.com/messageboard/showthread.php?t=146083

Baccura trike http://alternativevehicles.blogspot.com/2010/11/baccura-tilting-trike.html

Baccura trike thread on recumbents.com http://recumbents.com/forums/topic.asp?TOPIC_ID=4564

Bridgestone Picnica trike restoration: http://drumbent.blogspot.com/2008/08/tiny-trike.html

Butchers and Bicycles tilting trike review by Rideon https://rideonmagazine.com.au/butchers-and-bicycles-review/

Drymer Business Webpage. https://www.drymer.nl/en/models/drymer-business

Ecosunriders tilting trike https://www.ecosunriders.com/category/pressbook , www.sunrider.fr

EV4 Poland http://ev4.pl/en/bike.html

Ezeebike Longabike http://ezeebike.com/gallery/longabike-2

Fastfwd.nl webpage http://www.fastfwd.nl/en/bike/index.html

Flevobike tilting trike https://flevofanclub.ligfiets.net/?doc=ch1&lang=en

Go D. Tilting Solar Trike http://gonano.eu

Halfbike DIY Webpage https://halfbikes.com/diy-halfbikes

Heal, P. Eileen https://www.ozhpv.org.au/HUFF/docs/huff072.pdf

Heal. P. MMaXX OzHpv *Huff*, July 2020

Jouta trikes https://joutaligfietsen.eu/?page_id=10

Metal machine shop videos https://www.youtube.com/watch?v=4vtOcou_qXQ

Nurse, S. Maruishi trike repair https://modularbikes.blogspot.com/2017/11/maruishi-leaning-trike.html

Nurse, S. Leaning Trike http://modularbikes.com.au/bigatthefront.html

Panthertrike Website https://panthertrike.com

Schleiwert, F. Lightweight Leanings, *Bike Culture 10*, July 1996

Schleiwert, F. Tripendo, *Encycleopedia 1999*, Open Road

Schleiwert, F. Tripendo Website http://www.tripendo.de

Sims P. Leaning Trike, OzHpv *Huff*, April 2000 https://www.ozhpv.org.au/HUFF/docs/huff015.pdf

Skatebike Restoration, Rich Helms https://richhelms.net/rich/category/skatebike-restoration

Tilting vehicles blog http://tiltingvehicles.blogspot.com

Trailmate Fun Cycle Video https://www.youtube.com/watch?v=3b4YsZ9-dWU

Trailmate Fun Cycle webpage https://www.trailmate.com/product.cfm?proID=41

Trego leaning trike module https://trego-trolley.com/home

Velotilt Thread on Recumbents.com http://recumbents.com/forums/topic.asp?TOPIC_ID=8543&whichpage=1

Vidal C. Leaning motorcycle patent. https://patents.google.com/patent/EP0606191A1/en

Vuong, V. Ilean cargo trike https://www.youtube.com/watch?v=rxlT1XSvWoU

Vuong, V. Openbike webpage http://fr.openbike.org/wiki/~iLean

Wood, R. leaning delta http://www.wisil.recumbents.com/wisil/Wood/delta_trike.htm

Yamaha Niken Review https://www.bennetts.co.uk/bikesocial/reviews/bikes/long-term-test-bikes/yamaha-long-term-test-bikes/yamaha-niken-long-term-review-final-report

17 Some Long-wheelbase front-wheel drives

This cycle series started 15 years ago as an experiment, trying to make a bike like a front-wheel-drive Bevo (7.14) with direct drive and a fixed bottom bracket. Since then I've made about 12 of them, trying new techniques and progressing ideas and build quality. This chapter describes most of them. Thankfully, some research was sponsored during a Monash University industrial design masters degree supervised by Robbie Napper and Mark Richardson. More details of the bikes and trikes are available free online including my masters degree writeup (exegesis), the blog I've kept since 2010, journal and conference articles, and plans for aluminium- and plywood-frame trikes on Thingiverse.

Proof of concept

The proof of concept bike was a suspended six-speed 20″ child's bike. The existing bike was drawn on 2d CAD, and then a main beam and driven front wheel added in.

Then the donor bike's back half was removed, and from the CAD drawing and sketching I worked out how to start building. A tube mitring program was used to get the profile for cutting through the main tube for the steerer and pedals, and parts were brazed on. The front wheel is big and out front, so going over bumps doesn't affect the rider much. Although the rear wheel is small, it is suspended, and again, the rider doesn't feel many bumps. Steering was 'ape hanger' bars fitted to an extended stem, giving a big tiller effect. Altogether it has a likeable 'rangy' look and feel.

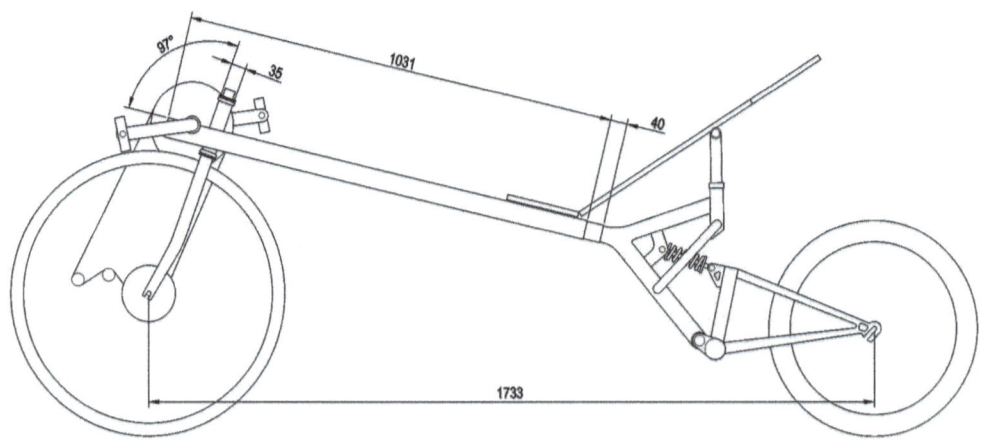

17.1   Plan for proof of concept bike.

17.2   Building it.

As with all of the bikes and trikes described in this chapter, steering was restricted. Pedalling includes the knees rising up inside the handlebars. This assists the drive mechanism: it is entangled with steering and the chain derails with steering at large angles. Turning sharply is possible — just not while pedalling.

Before long, the back part of the bike had bent. I had been over-zealous hacksawing, and had taken away a reinforcing part of the 20″ bike, but had learnt enough.

Steel Mark 1

Using the earlier bike as a template, I started drawing a bike made from scratch with no recycled frame parts. When drawing was finished, I ordered two types of laser-cut flats and one type of laser-cut tube. I bought enough to make four bikes, as four sets cost not that much more than one. I also asked for and got the offcut pieces. Laser-cut parts were supplemented by tube steel.

The laser-cut tubes weren't what I really needed, and I ended up mounting the front tube backwards to get clearances between chain and brakes. With the bike together, I rode it unpainted for several months with the steering assembly from the proof of concept machine. Rides included trips to work, rides from Geelong to Aireys Inlet, and a few trips from Aireys Inlet to Lorne and back. A Corflute fairing/tailbox was made. The tailbox is good for load carrying and speed, and makes the bike more visible in traffic. Another part was a Biopace oval chainring. The combination of a backrest to push against when pedalling, an oval chainring and a short, direct drive made the bike willing and quick to accelerate. Often I beat other bikes when moving away from traffic lights, much to their surprise.

As shown in 17.4, I had started mounting handbrakes in reverse position, and this has worked well. The handlebars support and accept guidance from the hands, but there's normally no pressure of hands on steerer or vice versa. However, hand pressure is created during deceleration as the body moves forward, and this energy helps brake actuation.

Eventually this bike's main tube started to bend, and it was back to the drawing board.

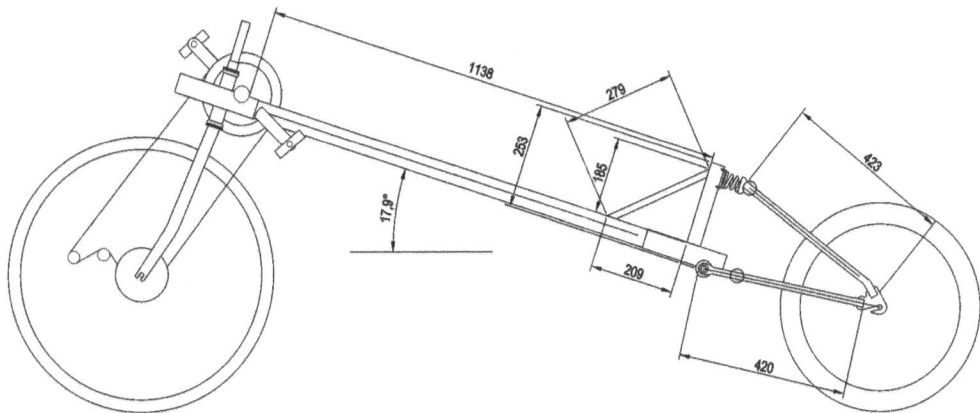

17.3   Steel Mark 1 plan.

17.4   Steel Mark 1.

Steel Mark 2

So I started again and specified mild steel frame material again. Although lighter than the (41.8 OD × 1.6 thick) tube used for Mark 1, the new (51 OD × 1.2 thick) tube was slightly stronger. The numbers to compare are OD × OD × thickness.

I ordered new design laser-cut parts and took the completed bike to the 2007 OzHPV Challenge. It went well. If your home-made bike finishes the races without causing incident or injury, it's a good result. On top of this, I kept up with Michael Kater on a Moulton and Axel Allgaier on a commercially made Toxy Recumbent for most of the road race.

Problems with bending the main tube continued, so I bought a stronger cro-mo steel main tube from Greenspeed and remade the frame. An offcut was used as reinforcement. Since then, my metal bike frames have been strong enough and haven't bent. Eventually this bike was retired and consumed for parts, but the frame is still in the shed.

17.5   Steel Mark 2 bike at a Myrtleford OzHpv rally.

Timber Mark 3

While building the steel bikes I realised the main beam could be wooden. I drew up and ordered a few laser-cut steel flats to disperse bearing stresses into the frame. The parts arrived, but it took a few weeks for me to get enough shed time to build it.

And then one Saturday I woke up and told my wife Christine I was going out to get a new bed so I could turn the one we were sleeping in into a bike. I proceeded to do just that, using part of the old wooden bed as the main beam. A few weeks later, the bike was rideable. It shared geometry with the steel bikes with the head tube at 90° to the main beam, but this time the front wheel was 24", the rear 20" and the lower rear wheel struts horizontal. This lowers the seat, reduces aerodynamic drag and makes the bike faster. Maybe the backrest is a bit more reclined, but it seemed comfortable.

The bike was finished and I took it on an 80km flat ride to Altona with friends. It was unusual and certainly attracted attention. The geometry worked well and I used 24"/20" wheels for later bikes. The whole bike was proof of concept for later timber frame bikes.

A consistent modification for these bikes is adapting forks to accept a rear wheel for front wheel drive. I've become used to this, and eventually designed and commissioned laser-cut dropouts just for the job. They are brazed in to replace standard dropouts and offset the derailleur to cope with wide-range 11–40 cog clusters. Other standard modifications are widening the forks and brazing on additional V-brake bosses. All my fork mods have been DIY, but commercial front-wheel-drive forks are available from Performer Cycles in Taiwan.

17.6   Timber Mark 3 bike.

Mark 4 with aluminium castings

The most sophisticated parts made for my bikes had been rotary laser-cut tubes. But maybe a casting for this would be good, or a custom-made lug for that — such are the dreams of bike building cyclists.

I worked out that one casting could be used twice at the front and twice at the back to work as steerer tube, bottom bracket, suspension pivot and seat tube support, and I began to shape this using 3d CAD. After several attempts I had a casting solid model and drawing.

The drawing process included making a solid model of two parts assembled as a pair, complete with nuts and bolts. This helped work out how parts would fit together. The assembly does the same as the custom laser-cut steel tubes, but it's lighter and prettier, and the steerer tube and bottom bracket are included.

I sent out some files for quotes on the parts, but it was too expensive for me to go ahead, so I thought about getting sponsorship. After more drawing, I had a set of images of bikes complete with my 'target company's' logos. I went to see my company's marketing manager about my sponsorship ideas, armed with a draft letter and images. Steve F. was helpful and rewrote my letter and picked out images to send. A day or two later, I sent an email to my prospective sponsor, and a week later gained sponsorship for half the cost of lost-wax method, heat-treated aluminium castings for two bikes. My order to the rapid prototype manufacturer followed after some last-minute CAD tweaking. Initial manufacture would sometimes be just the start. It is expensive but shows what can be made from diecasting.

In order to proceed further and make the part cheaply using diecasting:
- a casting die costing about A$10,000 would be made and commissioned.
- demand would need to be established. For economic diecasting, hundreds of parts are made in one run, and designers would hope for many runs from the die.

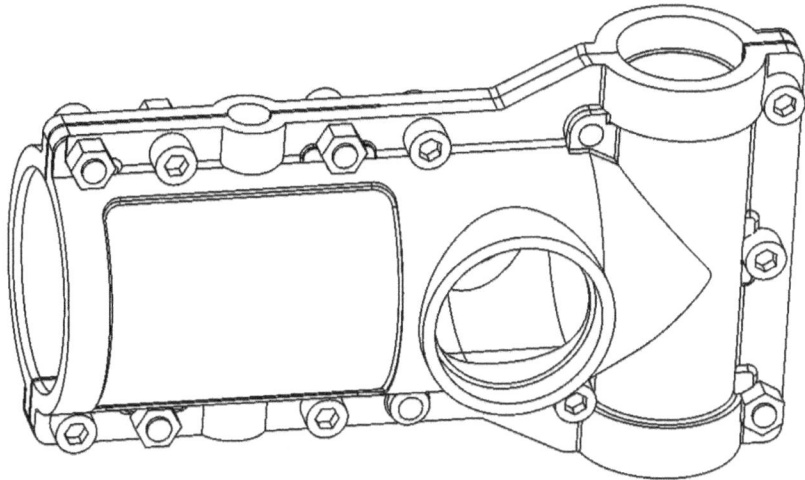

17.7   3d CAD image of casting assembly.

The castings bike has a cro-mo steel main beam, and tube instead of solid bolts where possible. The aluminium parts needed filing and trimming, and bottom brackets threads were pressed in. The bike is low and disinclined to tip when braking, so the back-wheel brake was eliminated and replaced by one on the rear of the front fork. I used a round 48-tooth chainring with chainguides on both sides to keep the chain on. The screw-on cluster it drives was eight-speed with 11–34 tooth sprockets. Works a treat!

All the bike controls are now concentrated around the front wheel, simplifying separating the front of the bike from the rest for transporting inside a car. All controls remain in place.

17.8   Assembly of casting in Mark 4.

Brad at work painted the bike with flecked purple metallic paint. There were stripes in blue and red, and a strip where the aluminium from the steerer shows through. In short it looked great. Thanks, Brad. Originally the seat had been a cut-up skateboard. This worked, but didn't look that good, so I ordered a fibreglass seat from TW Bents. When the seat was fitted, I added padding and a new Corflute tailbox. It was a great relief to have the tailbox again so I could carry luggage without resorting to tying bags to the seat. The combination of seat, padding and tailbox are good. There is a bend in the seat that presses the lower part of the back forwards. This slight change in angle gives something solid for the legs to press against when starting.

Early in 2008, I started making a front fairing with two small steel frames inside. There is reasonable clearance between my pedalling legs and the fairing. When I first rode home from work on the bike with the fairing, my time was cut by 5 minutes over 1½ hours, and on a roll-down test times were slightly better with the fairing on. The fairing weighs only 800g, so is worth having on the bike for most riding. Materials cost about $10, which was for 100 cable ties. The Corflute was free and the frame material was left over from Ikea furniture.

The next and last step for the bike was a lycra body-sock for the whole of the bike. For a long time I had seen pictures of recumbents with socks to improve aerodynamics, and several upcoming races would allow me to try it out.

I bought 2.5 metres by 1.5 metres of bright yellow lycra from a fabric shop along with elasticised thread, velcro dots and some big needles. The lycra was laid out and marked, then cut into two 75cm strips. The strips were sewn together at one end and the resulting long strip wrapped around the bike to check for size. When fitted on the bike, this finished size would stretch the lycra slightly. The lycra was cut to size and the 75cm ends of the material sewn together. All the edges were hemmed. The sock was now the shape of a headband for a giant.

There followed a series of fittings on the bike, then sewing, then fitting again. I used velcro dots sewn to the fabric to help secure the sock to the fairings but now use bulldog clips.

Initially I didn't keep the body-sock on when riding in the city, but did later. The inconvenience of getting in and out means it's not worth riding the bike for short distances, and I choose another bike. For my longish commutes it was really good.

Because of the good aerodynamics, it's a bit faster than most other bike traffic on the road, especially on the flat. It has been called 'The Yellow Peril' and described as resembling a tissue box with my head sticking out as the tissue, or a giant banana and a block of cheese. I don't care! People take photos of me from their cars and I get to wave to all and sundry who are staring at me. To have a car that attracts as much attention you need to spend $100,000 or more, but this bike will do me.

17.9   Ready to race in Wodonga, 2008. Matt Heal in foreground. Photo Yi-Ting Wu.

So far I've used it a couple of times in races or trials. The bike was fourth-fastest in the 2008 OzHpv 200m sprint with a speed of 53km/h. It came second (recumbent bikes were 1st, 2nd and 3rd) in a half-hour 'Go for Your Life' ride in Albert Park in April 2008. In a ride along the Eastlink freeway in June 2008, I averaged 35km/h over 65km and it completed the 210km 2008 Round the Bay in a Day ride at an average speed of 23km including stops.

Later I sold the bike to Aki Kubota, who has since become a friend. I needed to cut down the frame length for him, but after that he was very happy. He rode the bike in the 2014 OzHPV Challenge, and I still have a set of the castings.

17.10   Aki Kubota, Corryong, 2014.

Aluminium bike Murray Tour

Some of my cycling has been with the Audax long-distance cycling club. I had finished some of their 200km rides, but wanted to try their longer rides with a good light bike in the style I was making. These were 1,000 and 1,200km rides over 4 days. Part of the problem with my bikes had been the lack of ability to adjust for riders of different sizes, and I also realised that the frame's main stress was from rider weight. Chain stress was in the front of the frame and in the front forks. That freed up the design, and I sought out an aluminium section that had the same vertical 'Z' strength as the cro-mo steel I'd used with 'X' strength not so important. When I'd found one, (82.3 × 28.3 × 2.2mm) I designed and ordered some frames using it through Michael Rogan of MR Recumbent trikes.

The rear triangle for this bike was worked out on the fly after I'd received the frames, and I put some good kit on it to finish it off. This included a Schlumpf mountain drive speed reducing gearbox. The seat was NC routed timber surrounded by Corflute, which made up the tailbox. This was clamped to the frame and could slide up and down for different leg lengths or be removed for transporting in a car or train.

With this set-up I tried the 2008 Great Southern Randonnée 1,000km ride, but didn't finish. It was hot, hard to ride, and there were navigation problems. The Schlumpf didn't perform well, but that was more about the application than the gearbox itself. With low gear engaged for hillclimbing, the chain was halfway along the cluster causing pedal steer. This combined with low speeds and challenging hills to make the bike hard to ride.

In 2014, I used this bike again and managed to finish the much flatter Murray Tour 1,200km ride organised by my friend Simon Watt. This time I had a Shutter Precision dynamo to power lighting and fell in with experienced riders who provided good company and helped me throughout. A highlight was the last day of riding. Peter Donnan wanted to start at 2 a.m., and myself, Peter Donnan and Melvyn Yap did this, and were treated to the sight, smells and sounds of farmers burning recently harvested wheatfields in the middle of the night. We finished in plenty of time despite heat and wind, but the early start had shattered my already sleep-deprived body clock, and I was chronically tired for days to come.

17.11   Early morning, Murray Tour 2014. Photo Melvyn Yap.

All-timber frame bike

The first timber framed bike I'd made used a steel rear triangle and I decided to make an all-timber framed bike. Everything was done on the fly with parts from the shed, including a front wheel hub for the rear suspension pivot. The bike rode okay and I took it on a few short rides around town. It was proof of concept for later all-timber machines.

17.12   At St Kilda.

17.13   Ewan Nurse.

Timber leaning trike

Early in 2013, I saw videos of Vi Vuong's leaning trikes. They had bike cranks holding the back wheels, and I was amazed. One clip was popular, and even non-cycling friends had seen it and pointed it out to me. It took a while for it to get under my skin, but a few months later in August I started rummaging for parts to replicate the wheels-with-pedal-threads shown in the video. For me, this was messy, requiring pedal shafts to be fitted to 20" wheels.

It is hard to get matching front wheels from junk without respoking because the wheels mostly come from the front-and-back-wheel pairs of discarded bikes. So making the wheels was the hardest part. I had already made two bikes with wooden frames including bottom brackets attached to frames, and mounting the back wheels now just required mounting another bottom bracket. I also had seats fitting wooden frames, so finishing this proof of concept trike was easy. It worked almost straight away and was a revelation. With the Vuong wheelset, the frame became a single piece of wood with holes and reinforcements. This was simpler than wooden bikes I had made, which needed extra custom rear wheel stays and suspension.

17.14   Leaning trike #1, Federation Square, Melbourne.

Later in the year, I completed a 200km Audax permanent ride on this leaning trike. As well I took it to Wodonga for the 2013 OzHPV Challenge, and won a shopping race on it at the 2014 Corryong event.

Although I can get down and dirty with bike parts and make things quickly with immediately available parts, it's not my preference. As an engineer, I was used to getting parts I'd designed made on CNC lathes and other professional equipment. Having rough parts is okay temporarily, but something a bit better has to be made if you are serious. So I had some small shafts made to adapt 15mm thru-axle wheels to pedal cranks. I have been using these with Pedal Prix trike wheels from Trisled and MR components ever since.

Chambered frame wooden bike

Although I'd already built three direct-drive front-wheel-drive wooden frame cycles and used laser-cut parts, I'd never fully designed a wooden frame, as things were mostly made on the fly. So I had two frames made using chambering or hollowing out, a technique used for making wooden surfboards. This design had four main components, a frame, two rear wheel stays and the seat. The wheel stays and frame were hollowed out using CNC routing and then capped with routed plywood. The seat was routed plywood. There was laser-cut steel for bearing housing adaptors and rear dropouts. Although the frame was hollowed out, timber was left solid where there were frame stresses.

17.15   Chambered bike frame with Schlumpf Mountain drive two-speed gearbox.

I took the bike on several trips to north-east Victoria near Corryong, where the 2014 OzHPV Challenge was held. Some of these trips were to organise the Challenge but I started coming back for rides because I liked the country and the people. It is quiet and there are small towns, rolling hills, winding roads and views across the upper Murray into New South Wales.

17.16   Lloyd Charter with chambered bike near Corryong.

NC routed timber trikes

After making several timber cycles, I realised it had problems as a frame material. It has grain, and will split along the grain especially when screws are forced in. As well, the only engineered timber frame I'd made had plywood as well as timber, and I thought frames could be made completely from plywood instead. It took three goes to get this right, with the first two trikes made as part of my industrial design masters. The first frame failed because it wasn't solid at the front and crushed under chain stresses. This was fixed for later versions. The second timber frame worked well but the seat and tailbox weren't made to my latest most comfortable design.

17.17   A minor drama about 1km from home.

The third frame is in the timber leaning trike I still have. It has a curved seat made by softening the seat plywood in water before strapping it to parts acting as a bending jig. Panels on the side of the tailbox can be swapped between plywood, Corflute, or any desired cloth covering. The steering stem is plywood and softwood supported by custom aluminium parts.

17.18   Tailbox and seat construction. Most of the cable ties are permanent .

17.19   My current timber trike, Fringe Furniture exhibition, 2017.

As well as the shape of the plywood trike parts, grain direction must be considered. A ply beam is stronger when the outer plywood grains run in the beam direction. This makes for longer, stronger fibres in the direction taking stress. Ply bends better with bends aligned to grain, and this is important in some pieces (20.2).

It's slow and satisfying making an HPV this way. Things can't be done quickly, as that means it's easy to make mistakes, and it takes a while for glue and varnishes to dry. Once it's done, the timber can't be left. It has to be cleaned, varnished and maintained. But unlike most bike seats, it can be recycled, repaired, accessed, refurbished and redecorated.

If I designed trikes like this again, I might try a different construction. Layering the plywood to make the reinforced head tube and rear axle area is painstaking and error-prone. The thickness of the ply isn't always as published, so that can mean one more or one less layer required in reinforced areas. As well, the layers of ply on the top and bottom of the beam are complex. To simplify frame manufacture, 12 × 40mm softwood could be sandwiched between plywood, with layering to make solid timber at the ends.

Aluminium extrusion trike

A few recumbents have custom extrusion frames including Linears (7.7, 7.8), Bike Es and Oke Jas (7.6). The Mindbike is a bicycle from custom extrusions. At one stage I designed and printed an extrusion profile sampler to suit bikes I make, including a top slot matching existing extrusion hardware.

One of my masters supervisors, Robbie, had done his doctoral thesis on bus design, and he still had aluminium bus extrusion and joiners lying around in his office. I thought I could make a bike out of the extrusion profiles. Robbie still had contacts at the busmaker Volgren, and I was able to buy a piece of the most suitable extrusion from them. Among other parts at home there was a recumbent seat from a trade with Cruzbike.

A few laser-cut plates were designed, brazed together and then fitted on to the extrusion. They adapted the seat, steerer/drive and rear wheel assembly to the extrusion. The extrusion remained unaltered.

There is limited space at our house, and after not riding this trike for months, did it up to sell it as a ute. To spice up the sale I threw in a vintage Esky, and the trike now has a home in Gippsland.

17.20   Robbie on a ply trike.

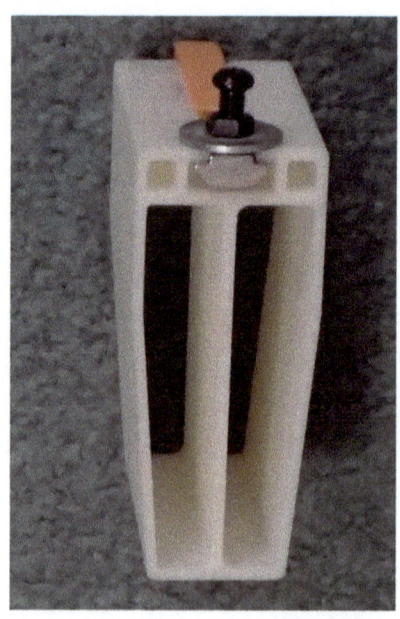

17.21 Extrusion sampler with compatible hardware.

17.22 Bus extrusion with laser-cut parts

17.23   Trike disassembled for cleaning.

17.24   Just add beer and ice.

Murray Tour aluminium trike

In 2008, I'd built an aluminium framed bike for the Great Southern Randonnée, so had experience with aluminium as a frame material. As well, I'd had separating bikes like the Hercules with a gravity-assisted frame join. This experience came together when I made some new aluminium frame leaning trikes. They didn't use welding for the frame and could be made with DIY.

The new trike could have been made from a single piece of 100 × 40 × 3mm rectangular hollow aluminium section. This is just wide enough to fit the 34mm bearing housings that come with some bicycle forks, but overly strong and heavy compared to the 82.3 × 28.3 × 2.2mm section which worked previously.

Making a frame using both these aluminium sizes seemed possible, with the strength and width of the heavy section at the front and the lighter section making up most of the length. Using the two sections could also make the frame separable, a feature of previous machines.

At this stage I had access to some university 3d printers and was able to design, print and try some plastic bushes as part of the mechanism securing frame sections together. My first attempts had four bushes between frames, but I later found that with gravity holding frames together, two bushes and two bolts were enough. Initially I was shy of using 3d printing and had timber inserts inside the smaller frame to hold bushes in place. Now the assembly has been simplified and uses 3d printed bushes and inserts made from PLA material on home printers.

17.25 Front of frame with custom light mount and aluminium bottom bracket support.

17.26   Rear frame section with home 3d printed plastic bushes.

The second frame issue was working out how to support the pedal and back-wheel axle bearings. Previously I'd used Schlumpf geared bottom brackets (17.15), which screwed together and clamped on to frames using a 45°chamfered surface. I found an equivalent ungeared bottom bracket from YST. This fitted in neatly with rubber gaskets and a set of custom aluminium supports. At the start I used four screws and nuts and a timber infill to stop the aluminium crushing. Now the number of parts is reduced. One screw and a fibreglass tube stop rotation and frame crush.

It took several attempts to get the tailbox right. It needed to be strong and light, and fit luggage inside. I am happy with the end result. It is held together by cable ties, glue and bolts, and still takes about a day and a half to put together and varnish. It is waterproof from below to resist splashes from the back wheels, and I have settled on birch ply as a material. This ply is readily available and of consistent quality. Previously I had specified marine ply, but that meant I could end up with just about anything.

A recent development has been to use parts from second-hand Byk 450-7 bikes with 20" wheels and 451 rims. These sell second-hand from about $80, and they provide the front wheel, brakes, brake levers, front forks and front wheel for the bike. As well I am using scooter parts for the steerer.

When Simon Watt decided to rerun his Audax Murray Tour event in 2020, I entered, as it was a challenging ride I thought I could cope with. I had now been riding the latest trike for years, and a recent addition had been an aerodynamic fairing. Peter Heal had found the fairing in a trailer when he'd picked up a recumbent from a Sydney house. He offered it to me and I accepted. It was transferred to me via an Audax ride Ian Boehm had attended, and I picked it up from Ian in Coburg on the Mule Train bike (14.8). It didn't take long to fit, and I noticed improved aerodynamics and faster speeds downhill or on the flat.

This Murray Tour was harder for me than the previous one. I wasn't with a single group of riders throughout, and made a few wrong decisions about when to eat and rest. This meant I always rode late into the night and was sleep-deprived throughout. The first day was quite tough and featured 90km of hot, flat riding in strong headwinds with no towns to stop at. Riding with Alex and Simon at the end of the day helped significantly.

A few punctures at night did not help, but in the end I finished the 4-day ride with 1 hour left before the cut-off time. This time my body clock was not in revolt but my feet were! Constant pressure on my toes caused tingling, and now 6 months later I can still feel it.

17 Some Long-wheelbase front-wheel drives

17.27   Near Wycheproof.

17.28 Morning of day four with Richard Ferris.

This account of my long-wheelbase cycles doesn't include all the developments. Some are in process or not in working bikes and are in the digital tools chapter. Altogether the cycles a body of work, one that I hope will prove useful.

References

Chambering surfboards https://surfinggreen.com.au/pages/how-to-make-a-chambered-hollow-wood-surfboard

Mindbike http://www.mindbike.jp/concept/index_e.html

Nurse, S. Chain forces on recumbent cycles https://hupi.org/HPeJ/0024/ChainForcesRecumbentCycles.pdf

Nurse, S. Ilean trikes on Thingiverse https://www.thingiverse.com/thing:4201871 and https://www.thingiverse.com/thing:4871525

Nurse, S. Leaning Trikes using Rear Axle Pedal Crank Mechanism https://hupi.org/HPeJ/0020/0020.html

Nurse, S. Masters Exegesis https://bridges.monash.edu/articles/thesis/A_Simple_Leaning_Trike/5373910

Volgren Aluminium Technology http://volgren.com.au/why-volgren/aluminium-technology

18 Tools

Tools are needed to fix, maintain and make bikes, and this chapter discusses them.

On the road

No matter what bike or trike you ride, it's satisfying to ride independently with the ability to fix mechanical problems. It depends on the riding you do. For visiting a friend or shopping, fixing can be walking the bike and repairing it at home. Public bike repair stations are another option.

For riding further afield, tools that are with you become more important. You might consider carrying:
- spare tube or tubes if there is more than one wheel size on the cycle
- puncture repair kit
- tyre levers
- pocket knife with needle nose pliers
- small pair of scissors
- small retractable blade knife
- pump with pressure gauge
- spare nuts, bolts, V-brake noodle, derailleur pulley, quick-link chain joiner, cable ties
- multi-tool, including metric Allen keys, Phillips head and standard screwdriver and chainbreaker
- crank remover
- 15mm open-ended spanner (removes pedals)
- 6" shifting spanner

It would almost be heresy to carry this kit on a 9kg racing bike but on an 18kg recumbent, what the hell, I'm ok with it!

18.1　Tools for road trips.

At home

To restore standard cycles at home, you might also need:
- bike stand
- rags
- mineral turpentine for cleaning bearings
- clean containers for cleaning bearings
- oil
- grease
- alligator (adjusting) pliers
- vice grips
- metric nuts and bolts
- metric ring spanners
- metric open-ended spanners
- spoke spanners
- flat and round files
- screwdriver set including Phillips and flat head types
- cable ties

- loctite or other anaerobic adhesive
- bike parts like cotter pins, bottom bracket axles and nuts, bearings
- plastic bags for storing bearings away from grit
- digital calipers for measuring seatposts
- bench and vice
- track pump with pressure gauge
- large spanners for headsets
- cable cutters
- Shimano-type cluster removal tool
- sealed bottom bracket removal tool
- thin spanners for axle nuts

The five items at the end of this list are specialist bike tools, and available in bike tool kits. These kits start at around $50 and are good value. Individual tools for use by professional bike mechanics can cost $50 or more each.

Larger workshop tools

The more you have of these, the more work on bikes you'll be able to do. Some can be used for building bikes.
- hacksaw
- tape measure
- superglue
- two-part epoxy resin, 1-hour cure time
- metric tap and die set for M10, M8, M6, M5, M4
- electric jigsaw
- grinding wheel
- shed
- hammer
- angle grinder
- lathe
- pipe bender
- oxy-acetylene or oxy-LPG welding set
- stock of steel such as 12.7 OD × 1.6mm wall thickness tube
- handheld electric drill and bits

- large right angle with straight edge, 600mm long
- clamps for welding
- drill press
- hole saws
- old soldering iron for Corflute
- heat gun for Corflute
- MIG welder
- appropriate safety equipment such as safety glasses, ear muffs, strong boots

Some of these tools need more elaboration.

Spanners

Ring and open-ended spanners are better for bikes than shifting spanners. They are more likely to loosen stuck bolts — and less likely to damage them — than one-size-fits-all shifting spanners. But it's just not worth the weight of carrying full sets of spanners on the road.

Drill press

A drill press is a mounted electric drill. The workpiece is usually mounted in a vice on a table that can be raised, lowered, swivelled and tilted. The head with the drill mechanism is moved down with a handle. The drill's speed range is important. Drilling or holesawing a material is a cutting process, and every material has an ideal cutting speed. Exceeding the cutting speed wears out cutting tools (For a 40mm holesaw drilling into hard steel, the recommended speed is low and about 130rpm. Recommended speeds are higher for softer materials and smaller diameter tools).

Low-speed drill presses can be expensive, but are usually robust and have strong tables and good tilt mechanisms. A drill press is usually limited to drilling, but with some ingenuity can be adapted to rotate and machine a workpiece, such as a skateboard wheel being made into a chain pulley.

18 Tools

18.2   Drill press running at low speed with holesaw.

Lathes

A lathe is a machine tool where the workpiece rotates in a chuck and is worked on by a solidly mounted cutting tool or by a drill bit mounted on the same axis as the workpiece. The rules about cutting speeds on drill presses apply equally well for lathes, but for lathes it is the tool contact point radius determining cutting speed. Low rpm is important on a lathe, and so is having a chuck assembly that can accommodate a reasonable size tube or bar. Some lathes include automatic feeding allowing thread cutting.

In their trike manufacture, Greenspeed reversed the usual lathe process and used holesaws rotating in a lathe chuck to drill stationary frame tubes. This process exploits the low rotation speeds and solid mounting offered by a well-constructed lathe.

Welding metals

Steel and aluminium are the metals commonly used for bike manufacture. Steel can be joined with braze and fusion welding, both possible in home workshops. Welding aluminium is more complex. It can involve heat treatment and I have always left it to professionals. However, aluminium can easily be sawn, ground and drilled at home to accommodate standard or specialised fasteners. These are used to attach the various mudguards, wheels, handlebars, seats, etc.

Braze welding uses filler rod that melts into the surface of the metals being joined. It is not as strong as fusion welding, and is best used where there is a large, close contact area between parts. Brazing takes place at low temperatures and generally does not damage or weaken steel. It is not harsh and should not blow holes in thin-walled parts.

Traditional bike manufacture uses lugs to provide a socket for the tube ends. In larger bike factories, the brazing only takes place after frames have been heated in ovens. Home brazing done can be done with oxygen and acetylene, or oxygen and LPG (low-pressure gas/barbecue gas) mix. Oxygen and acetylene cylinders must be rented from specialist stores but LPG cylinders can be bought and swapped from hardware stores or service stations. Oxy/LPG is less expensive than oxy-acetylene but produces less heat.

Fusion welding is possible with oxy-acetylene welding kits. Mild steel filler rod is melted into a small molten area of the workpiece. A well-crafted weld of this type is as strong as the surrounding material.

Other fusion welding processes involve electrical current melting steel. Processes include metal inert gas (Mig), tungsten inert gas (Tig) and stick (standard arc) welding. All these types of arc welding have a shielding gas, which can be on the flux wire or welding rod or supplied as a stream of argon. Of all electrical welding types, stick welding is the simplest, as there is no wire feed or gas.

Use of a lathe, welding and brazing can be professional occupations. If you are keen to use them in your bike building it's best to ask advice from someone qualified, or to take a short course before plunging in and buying equipment.

Corflute and timber

These materials can be used to make bike accessories including panniers, frame bags and crate adaptors. Timber can be used to make entire bike frames.

It's worth marking the materials as accurately as possible using squares or protractors. Saw and knife cuts, and creases in Corflute are improved by using straight edge cutting guides clamped to the workpiece.

Corflute can be held together with cable ties, or bolts and washers. It can be holed with a screwdriver, drill or old soldering iron. A soldering iron can also spot weld Corflute. A heatgun can raise the temperature of Corflute enough for bending.

Organising a shed

It is worth keeping your shed clean, tidy and sorted, with tools and parts readily available. It's a waste having (say) a front derailleur in your shed if you can't find it, or two sets of pliers when you only ever use one. Similarly, if you use open-ended spanners every day, it's worth giving them a spot hanging on a wall for quick access. It wastes time if they're stored away somewhere.

Large corporations organise their workplaces on a principle called 5s (sort, set in order, shine, standardise and sustain), which eliminates these sorts of wasted time and resources.

5s can and should be applied in sheds as well. The only argument for having unsorted junk is that it could provide inspiration or alternatives. It happens occasionally!

References

Bike repair stations in Boroondara https://www.boroondara.vic.gov.au/recreation-arts/cycling-and-walking/find-bike-and-skate-repair-station

5s https://www.5stoday.com/what-is-5s

19 Digital and Design Tools

Bicycles have a long history. They were in widespread use before automobiles were affordable, and before aeroplanes flew. Bicycles preceded personal computers by at least a century, but now computers and digital tools influence cycling in many ways. This includes how they are navigated, sold, marketed, used, made and designed.

I have a Garmin cycle computer for navigating longer rides, but don't have a smartphone or use power meters. Generally I ride without onboard computers. This chapter concentrates on what I know better: computer tools that designers and builders use to make bikes.

Designing for people

Design tasks for a new bike can be limited, with just incremental changes and improvements over previous models. For example, to design a cycle I can ride, the length from pedals to seat stays the same, and if this dimension was OK on a previous machine, it need not be redesigned. Most commercial cycle designs need this adjustment of seat to pedal distance. Otherwise they would only suit a very few people of a particular height.

Cycle designers need to consider what range of people their creations will suit, and can refer to published statistics on height and weight of populations to maximise their designs' potential. These statistics include detailed body measurements like hip height and arm reach, and exist for different populations like men, women, children of a certain age, or people from a particular country.

Sketching and scale drawing

Before computers were widespread, sketching, scale drawing and manual drafting were the main ways of conveying designs. Craftspeople interpreted drawings to make parts and bikes, or parts were the designs. We can still use handmade parts, sketches and scale drawings to communicate and develop cycle designs but CAD (computer-aided design/drafting) has advantages.

Scale drawing can be done by just about anyone, with compass, ruler, protractor, graph paper and pencil. Consider using 1:10 or 1:5 full scale and calculate the paper size you before starting. For example, the length of a bike could be estimated at 2–3 times its wheel diameter. If the wheel is 28"/700C or approx. 700mm diameter, then a 1:10 scale means each wheel will be drawn 70mm diameter and the whole bike would take up to 210mm on the paper. This is the width of A4 (210 × 297) paper. One bike I own is 1,730mm long, and this length fits easily on A4 at 1:10 scale. Paper sizes for drawings go up to A0 (841mm × 1,189mm) and larger, so drawing bike parts at 1:1 is possible and advisable.

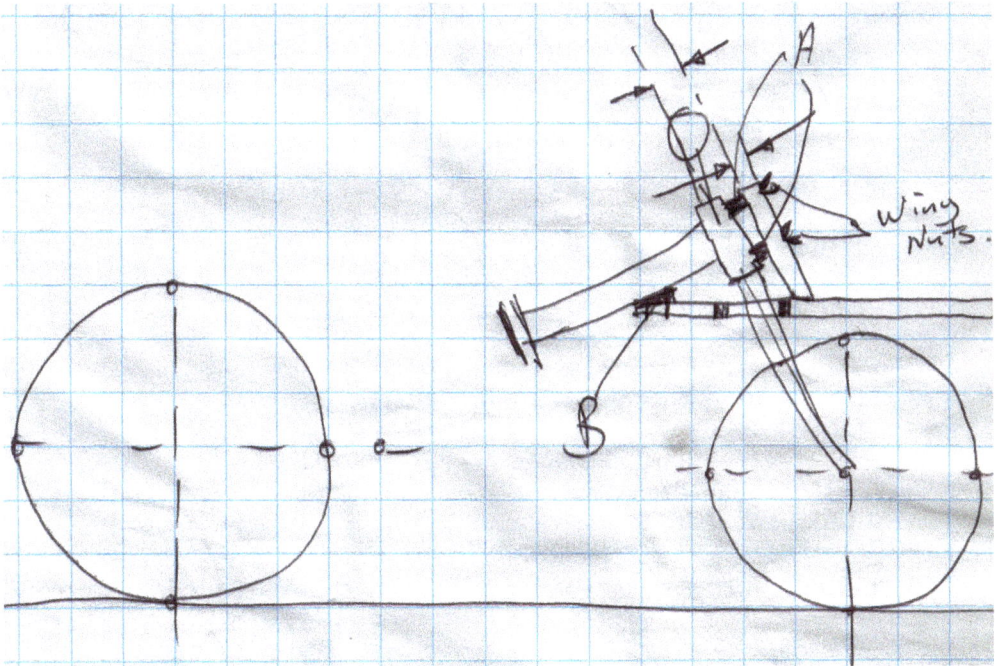

19.1   Sketch of Mule Train bike (Chapter 14) at 1:10 scale on 10mm graph paper. Front wheel is 20"/500mm diameter.

A local bike builder Jamie Friday uses 1:1 scale drawing for his designs: 'It is possible to lie on the drawing and try out the bike before you've even built it, and to lay out the frame tubes on the plan. Also you draw all of the details, which get glossed over at 1:5 scale.'

CAD and ordering parts

CAD takes place on computer. It can:
- use information available from the internet such as parts drawings, pictures and dimensioned sketches
- create files others can use, for transfer using email and cloud storage
- create files machines can use to make parts.

Many machines capable of receiving instructions from CAD process data in the form of G-code. For example, G-code specifies all individual tools used, tool paths, and tool speeds for routed parts. For some CAD-related processes including 3d printing, G-code creation is done automatically by software.

In recent years, both computers and computer-aided design software have improved and come down in price. Useful software is free, so it is worth considering using computers to help design bikes and cycles.

CAD enables ordering parts from outside contractors and basic rules apply whatever the parts:
- The more professional and clear your emails, drawings and CAD files, the more prompt your contractors' responses will be.
- CAD files don't speak for themselves. If possible, a drawing of what you want made should support supplied CAD files. Drawings include tolerances on dimensions, surface finishes, material, company and contact details and other boring but necessary information. You can't argue with your supplier about something you never specified in the first place.
- If you've received advice that will help your order, quote it in your emails, don't attempt to rewrite it. This saves time and improves credibility.
- Follow contractors' advice on file formats and CAD layout. This will save difficulty and extra work.
- It helps to discuss what your cycle project is with your contractor. There's a chance they ride a bike and will be enthused.
- The more parts ordered, the less the price per component and the greater the value you get for the programming/set-up cost.
- Use contractors' facilities. For example, if aluminium extrusions can be

cut by the supplier I order them cut to the lengths required. This saves time and does a better job than can be achieved at home.
- Don't be afraid to stand up for yourself. For example, if a supplier used wrong material despite it being clearly specified, let them know. Insist that parts be remade if you can't use what is supplied. The safest way to get the right material is to buy it yourself after checking it, then deliver it to the contractor yourself.

2d CAD

2d CAD was part of my work for 20 years. I'm familiar with it and enjoy using it. 2d CAD is enough for some bike designs because many bikes can be considered 2d objects for design purposes. Even though fork angle and front-wheel offset affect bike performance, these distances can be selected from a table to achieve desired ride characteristics, and no 3d is required. Trike design and design of specific bike components may be better performed on 3d CAD.

Care must be taken to back up files you are producing, as computers can crash or be hacked. Given that you stick to this precaution, the advantages of 2d over manual scale drawing are:
- 2d CAD drawing can be accurate to thousandths of a millimetre. Even a well-executed manual drawing of a bike could be accurate to only 1 to 10mm depending on scale.
- 2d CAD allows angles and lengths to be taken from a drawing accurately and can act as a geometric calculator.
- Altering designs is simpler with CAD and does not involve manual erasing or restarting.
- Drawings or parts of drawings can be quickly copied and used again without redrawing.
- 2d CAD opens the door to standard manufacturing methods that can simplify HPV building. Here are some examples.

CNC routing and low-powered laser

CNC (computer numerically controlled) routing is a form of milling for cutting sheets of plastic, foam, timber or other soft material. The material is secured by vacuum while a rotating drill, cutter or mill shapes it to a programmed pattern. The cutter moves in three dimensions, but generally only cuts shapes in one horizontal plane at a time. Parts should be laid out with surrounding margins of about 20mm. It's best to ask your machine operator for the minimum margins needed for a particular job before design begins. As an engineer I've designed CNC routed parts for storage boxes for plane engines, telephone, military, hydraulic and medical equipment.

Cut profiles can be transferred to routing machines via a dxf (widely accepted 'drawing exchange format'/2d CAD) file generated using a program. Unlike other forms of manufacture, there is no specific tooling for parts, so relatively small jobs can be done economically.

Several cut types create CNC routed parts:

Thru cuts: The mill cuts while skimming the top of the vacuum board, cutting a part free from surrounding material. Thru cuts are usually done last, so the part only breaks free from the vacuum board at the last moment (Spelling note: It is rare for 'through' to be spelled out fully in engineering drawings and I'm using the engineering spelling here).

Depth cuts/hatching: The mill drills part of the way through, then proceeds to cut out a shape. The shape can be a single cutter pass or hatched out area. Hatched out areas will have a minimum corner radius equal to the tool radius. It is simplest to make depth cuts in only one side of the part. Routing can be done on both sides, but the part must be turned and secured back in exactly the right position. The chambered frame wooden bike discussed in Chapter 17 used depth cuts.

Small parts: Small parts can be clustered and then sawn apart after routing. This adds work, and parts aren't cut quite as accurately, but means parts won't be flicked away by a cutter and lost. Clustered parts don't have margins around every part, which saves material.

Dowel pin or screw holes: Parts thicker than the sheet material can made with layers that are glued, screwed or pinned together. Common sets of dowel pin or screw holes in each layer simplify accurate joining. For a given screw there are two hole types: clearance holes just larger than the screw, or a pilot or tapping hole, which the screw grips on when assembled. I use holes down to 2mm diameter for layering plywood, and these are drilled rather than milled.

Routed cycle parts: I've designed include bike rack ends, crate adaptors and recumbent tailboxes, all the way up to entire leaning trikes. Another application is making a male plug mould for a streamliner from foam layers.

Low-powered lasers do jobs equivalent to CNC routing. The laser beam vaporises the material, and the beam path determines shape. Although they can cut finer detail than routing and need less margin space, low-powered lasers can't do depth cuts. Talk to your machine operator about this.

Firms who have CNC routing and low-powered laser machines include caravan, furniture, cabinet and kitchen-makers, and these firms will often give good prices on CNC cut parts.

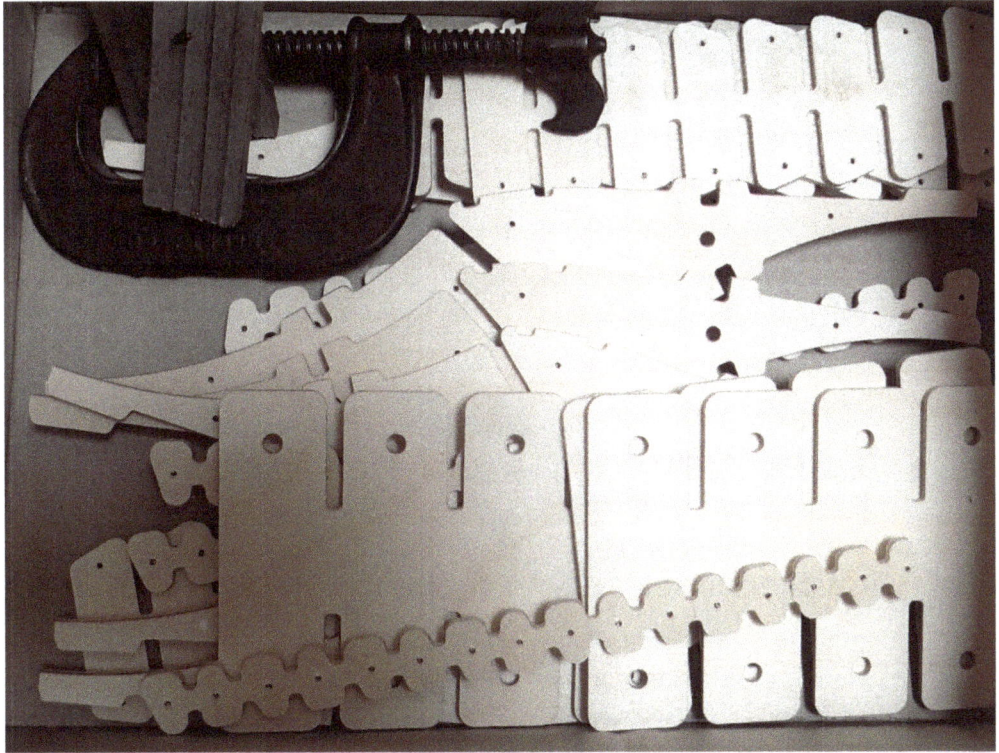

19.2   Clumped routed parts.

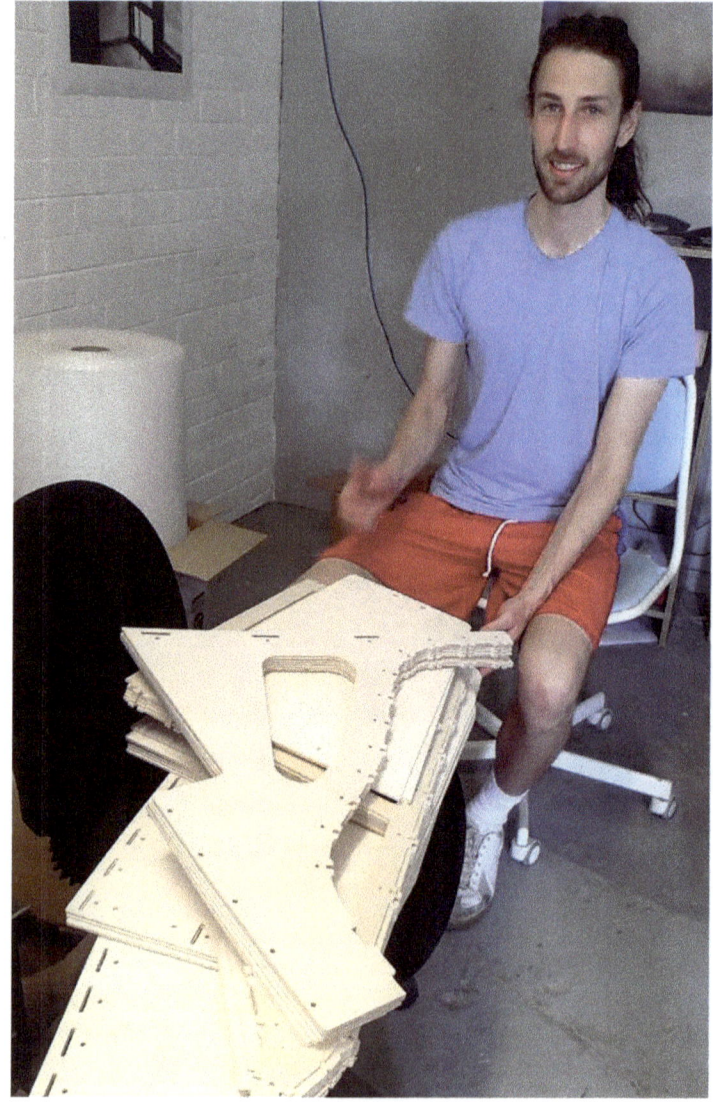

19.3 Billy from Sean and Horn with tailbox parts.

High-powered laser and water-jet

High-powered laser cutting can cut steel as well as timber. Another similar process is water-jet cutting where water containing a grit is sprayed at high pressure onto the material — in this case the material is worn away. Different materials are better suited to the various cutting methods, but both processes are CNC and are programmed using 2d CAD.

Flat-bed laser cutting is 'simple' cutting. Material is laid on a bed and the beam moves above it on a single plane and cuts. Bike parts that can be made with this process include fork dropouts, reinforcing gussets and bottom bracket holders as shown in 17.22. Giles Pucket has automated the process of making cycle spocket dxfs — see the link in the references.

As an engineer for the Cmg motor company I designed laser-cut bases for electric motors. Lasercutters often stock flat mild steel in various thicknesses, so you may not have to source and supply material.

- Laser cuts are only about 0.3mm wide, and actual width depends on the material type and thickness. Most cutting programs automatically compensate for beam thickness.
- Thin material (up to about 4mm) is cut smoothly because it doesn't heat up and distort, but thicker parts can cut rough.
- 3D laser cutting has lasers mounted on a robot, which can point in any direction and cut. This process is often used to trim moulded plastic or pressed metal components.
- Rotary axis laser is for round tubes mounted in a chuck as in a lathe. Parts are cut by a laser passing up and down its length. This isn't complicated machine as lasercutters go, but getting the cut profiles right can be hard because:
  - lasercutters need a developed (flattened) profile of the tube being cut to program their machines.
  - the laser always cuts with a beam at 90° to the material surface. This means that cut profiles must consider the tube thickness.
  - close fits are required for brazing and welding.
- Some 3d CAD packages provide output suitable for rotary laser cutting, for example in Solidworks, the sheet metal module can be used.
- A plot of a profile suitable for rotary lasercutting makes a useful tool for hand-cutting holes in tubes. Giles Puckett has created a tubemitre program that provides plot profiles for tube mitreing. The program exports dxfs that can be used as cut profiles by lasercutting workshops and a link to the program is in the references.

3d CAD

3d CAD is sometimes known as solid modelling, and is used to build computer-visible 3d models of objects and assemblies. These models can later become machine parts. Designers can transfer their ideas to conventional 2d drawings or render them to provide realistic images. Working in 3d provides a good feel for parts. This means receiving parts made from a 3d design should give designers few surprises, having seen them as computer images for several hours. 3d CAD extends to:

- Providing realistic pictures, assembly diagrams, cutaway sections, walk throughs and animations of objects for product proposals, brochures and presentations.
- Allowing a part or working assembly of parts to be viewed from all angles, letting anyone comment on style or function.
- Providing accurate part weights.
- Predicting fatigue and failure points in parts and assemblies. This procedure uses Finite element analysis (FEA) and simplifies complex mathematical processes.
- Predicting, optimising and modelling aerodynamic or hydrodynamic drag characteristics of a proposed design (Fully enclosed HPV styles such as streamliners/velomobiles are easier to model in this way because the shape is unchanging. Unfaired HPVs have a changing shape due to rider's leg motion).
- Predicting flows and residual stresses of plastics and metals during moulding and diecasting.
- Allowing economical rapid prototypes of parts to be made for proof of concept, display or testing from resins, rubber, nylons, aluminium, steel and titanium.
- Allowing dies (for metals) and moulds (for plastics) to be made using CAD data.

Efficient, well used solid modelling allows a team to learn at the design stage what was previously only discovered after expensive prototyping. Solid modelling techniques also allow weight to be removed from plastic and cast parts while maintaining strength using ribs. Extensive use of cast and plastic parts can allow for a lower number of parts to be used for a given structure and less labour to be used putting it together. This is not always a good thing. Older manufactured products can be heavier but more reliable and repairable than modern counterparts. For example, a new, plastic-cased power drill I owned died irreparably after about 2 years of use, but a steel-bodied power drill given me by my aunt is still going — and it's 40 years old or more.

Solid modelling was once only found in large aerospace and automotive industries, where huge workstation and software costs were worth the benefits of better and quicker parts design. 3d CAD has trickled down, firstly to medium and small-sized industries and finally to hobbyists at home. Part of this is due to the rise of 3d printing.

3d printing

Although I'd used 3d CAD for several years in industry, it took some time for me to get the idea of home 3d printing. Some students of my masters supervisor Mark Richardson were building 3d printers in the room I was working in, and gradually it sunk in that it couldn't be that hard. A friend recommended a Cetus printer and I bought one. There are a huge amount of distractions available to the 3d printer owner, with free printable models available online and myriad settings, adjustments, softwares and printer upgrades available. Thankfully, I mostly just make things I design and don't fiddle too much. The standard material for home 3d printing is biodegradable polylactic acid plastic or PLA. Parts printed at home using PLA are shown in orange and white in 17.25, 17.26, 19.4 and Chapter 21.

So far, I have been able to repair the printer myself, sometimes after following useful advice from Facebook user groups.

The range and style of 3d printers has increased dramatically in recent years. Printing was called rapid prototyping, but now it is just as likely printed parts will be used rather than just evaluated. Printing is recognised as a production method. An example of this is some parts made for me by Markforged.

The parts help support a fibreglass seat on a Murray Tour-style trike. They are nylon with continuous strands of carbon fibre infill, mimicking more common composites such as glass-fibre-reinforced polyester or carbon-fibre-reinforced epoxy. Recently I installed the parts. They anchor the seat at the front, and at the back adapt frame material as a support.

19.4　Black continuous carbon fibre-reinforced nylon parts and home-made orange PLA test versions.

19.5　Reinforced nylon parts in use supporting a bike seat.

Arevo and Superstrata are currently making their first batch of complete bikes using similar printed carbon-fibre-reinforced plastics. They boast a total bike weight of 7.5kg. Their design involves little tooling and the material strength allows them to dispense with the standard structural seat tube.

19.6   2d CAD sketch of Superstrata E bicycle with printed frame, forks and wheels.

Markforged advertise that their continuous carbon-fibre-reinforced nylon has a strength similar to aluminium. Their printers are currently expensive with the Mark Two retailing for US$20,000. When other competing printers start doing the same job, prices are certain to fall. Meanwhile some Mark Two printers are installed at universities and could be used for student and other projects.

Some carbon fibre printing technologies are more accessible, and they involve printing using filament doped with short lengths of carbon fibre. This material can be used in some home 3d printers but parts are not as strong as those made with continuous filaments.

3d printed metal parts will also play an increasing role in bike production. Bastion cycles already 3d print titanium lugs for their bicycles, which are sold worldwide and use filament wound carbon fibre. Atherton Cycles in the UK was founded by mountain biking champions and siblings Dan, Gee and Rachel Atherton. They make and sell custom-sized mountain bikes using carbon fibre tubes and printed lugs.

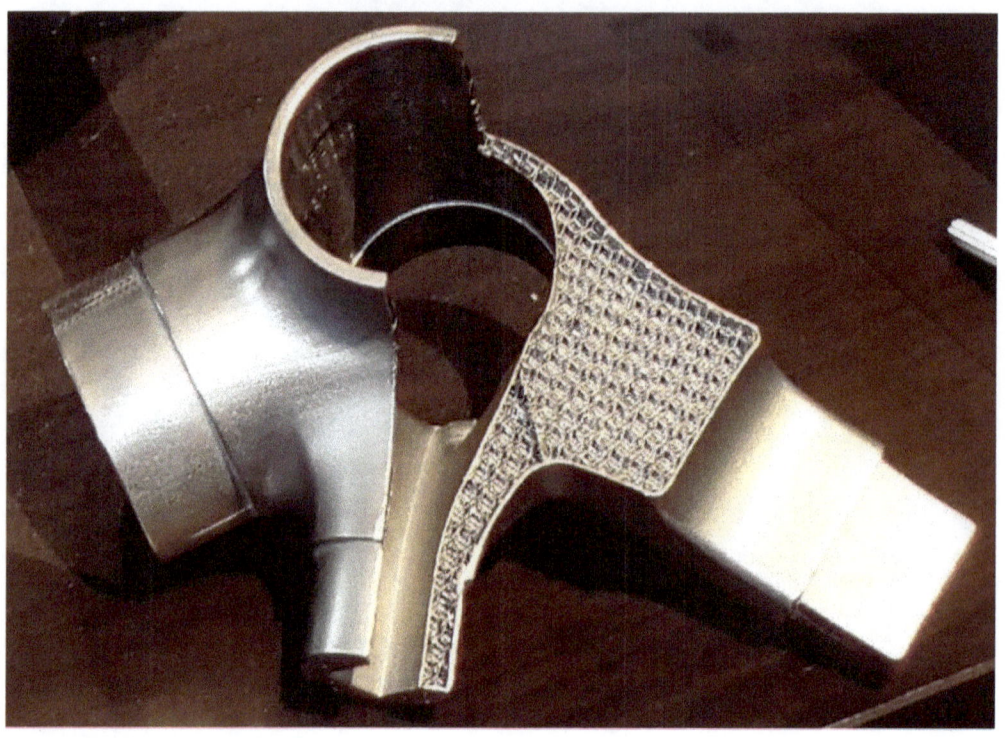

19.7   Bastion cycles printed titanium bottom bracket.

19.8   Printed rear dropout.

19.9   Bastion bike.

CAD and CAD-enabled manufacturing are here to stay in cycle design. There are now tools for routing timber for bespoke frames, printing parts in homes, factories and repair shops, or printing entire frames. These tools will become cheaper, more widely available and do more things in the future. It's possible that soon velomobile shells and internals will be printed and customised to riders' shapes and weights, reducing velomobile weights and wind resistances. Customising involving printing is already available for bikes, and as described in Chapter 8, body scanning is in use for streamliner design.

References

Atherton Bikes https://www.athertonbikes.com/technology

Bastion Cycles https://www.bastioncycles.com/experience/

Deakin University Carbon Fibre Printing https://www.carbonnexus.com.au/facilities/carbon-fibre-3d-printing

Nurse, S. *Context and methods for improved velomobiles* https://www.australasiantransportresearchforum.org.au/sites/default/files/papers/ATRF2019_resubmission_31.pdf

Nurse, S. *Numerically Controlled Routing* https://hupi.org/HPeJ/0004/0004.htm

Puckett, G, *Tubemitre and sprocket programs.* https://gilesp1729.github.io/

Superstrata bicycles https://superstrata.bike

20 Materials for Cycle Building

Bike sales exceed car sales in Australia, but this doesn't mean bikes dominate personal transport. Bikes are sold as toys, for racing and recreation as well as for transport, and they are subject to fashion. Some people don't know how to value, use, repair, maintain or even assemble bikes they buy — and their kids outgrow them and they are left outside and start to look tacky and unwanted. Inevitably they are given away, discarded or sold cheaply through garage sales, school fetes, recycling centres or op shops. But cycle builders can rescue and rework discarded cycles and other exercise equipment.

If you are interested in building a new style of cycle, it may be impossible to build a light version right from the start. To begin, build what you can from inexpensive or on-hand materials and try making it lighter and better later. An existing bike provides a physical model, and you will learn its advantages and deficiencies better than any theorising will. It's then simple to plan the next improved version by copying dimensions from the existing bike.

Here is a guide to articles and materials for use in home-made cycles.

Folding bikes

Folding bikes can be good material or reference designs for home cycle builders.
- They can be split at the hinge and an insert put between the two halves, forming a long bike or tandem.
- Older, single-fold types have steel frames, which are easy to work on.
- They are useful and make good restoration or improvement projects.
- They are sometimes available in electric-assist form.
- They fold, and bikes made from them can maintain the portability of the original folding bike.

Scooters, skateboards and other rolling things

- Small scooters have 100mm wheels, which make ideal pulleys for front-wheel-drive bikes.
- Front fork and handlebar assemblies make good adjustable steering assemblies for above-seat-steering bikes.
- Early folding scooters and stunt scooters are likely to have heavy, durable steel parts. Later scooters not designed for stunts have lighter aluminium parts, and most have fold mechanisms.
- Pneumatic tyre scooters can be converted to trailers.
- Skateboard wheels can be used as pulleys, and decks make simple seats for recumbent bikes or trikes.
- Prams, wheelchairs, exercise bikes and recumbent exercise bikes can include cantilever wheels, long seatposts, handlebars and large padded seats.

Fabric, foams and poles

Discarded sports or camping equipment and beach shelters often include light tubing, fabrics and poles that can be incorporated into cycles. A beach shelter cover I found was perfect as a bike wheel cover. Windsurfer parts I've used include the universal joint as a suspension block and the boom as a frame to support my recumbent bike on the car roof.

Yoga and camping mats from 10mm soft foam can be used to make aerodynamic wheel covers. More details are under 'soft materials' heading.

Steel tube

In Australia, round steel tube comes in sizes based on outside diameters (ODs) and thicknesses. Although dimensions are often quoted in millimetres, sizes are converted inch dimensions: ODs go up in increments of ½" or 3.2mm. Steel merchants often offer a complete range of mild steel tubes from ½" to 2" OD in 1/8" steps and 1.6mm wall, with whole inch sizes more likely to be available in non-standard thicknesses like 1.2 or 2mm.

Round steel tubes of 1.6mm (1/10") thickness fit tightly outside the next smaller size tube. Tubes of 2mm thickness have an interference fit and tubes of

1.2mm or 0.9mm thickness have a sloppy fit. If a tube has a sloppy fit and tubes are to be clamped together, a thin strip of mylar or aluminium can be used to take up the space.

Common tubes for small-scale bike construction include mild steel and chrome-molybdenum (cro-mo) steel. Cro-mo steel has better strength characteristics than mild steel, and comes in light, thin wall thicknesses such as 0.9mm. Some steels are heat treated to achieve high strength and can lose strength with weld induced heating but regular cro-mo can be brazed and welded without problem.

Steel tube used in recumbent bikes and trikes is usually general purpose and is also used in race cars and aeroplanes. Steel tubes for bicycles are much more likely to be special purpose and sold cut-to-length for a specific frame size and set of lugs/braze in sockets. As well as being made from special types of steel, racing-cycle framesets are from butted steels that vary in wall thickness. They are thicker on the ends where there are welds and high stresses, and thinner in the middle. This material disposition keeps stresses low while minimising weight.

Aluminium

Aluminium is a light metal commonly used for cycle frames, forks, rims, cranks, stems and handlebars. Aluminium tube and bike parts can be sawed, glued, turned and tapped at home but bending, welding and heat treating aluminium is best left to specialised tradespeople. Custom aluminium extrusions are used for bicycle rims and frames. Slotted extrusions allow for simple bike manufacture because seats, wheel frames and cranks can all be bolted on (see 17.20. 17.22. 17.23, 17.24).

Square and rectangular tube

For the homebuilder with limited access to tools, square and rectangular tube can be easier to work with than round. It offers the following advantages:
- Joins using nested rectangular tube do not allow the inner tube to rotate as happens with round tube.
- Complete bikes can be made with a minimum of welding: hacksaw,

drillpress, angle grinder, bench vice, file and a bit of sweat are the main tools required.
- Easier to drill accurately than round tube (always has a face at right angles to a drill press).
- Supports seats better than round tube: a timber seat sits on the face of a square tube but only on the top of a round tube.
- Square tubes can be set diagonally (45° rotated) giving alternate arrangements for placing seats and joining tubes.
- The N55 Node system is documented on the net and can be used to make rigid corners without welding.

The Greenspeed 20RS is an aluminium trike using square tube for the boom and was recently reviewed by Larry Varney for Bentrideronline.

Stress concentration

Often, tubes in home-made bikes fail not because of strength but because drilling, cutting or other metalworking leaves stress concentrations. Stress concentrators include cracks, sharp corners or small drilled holes. Crack propagation causes failure, and this can be prevented by keeping holes away from stressed areas and ensuring hole edges are smooth and reinforced by welds or plates (1.3).

Plastic types

Thermoplastic materials are formed into shape as liquids and solidify into their useful forms. They can be remelted and recycled at the end of their useful life. Thermoplastics include nylon and polypropylene and these materials are often used for injection moulded bike parts like bells, seat bases, wheels on kids' bikes, drink-bottle-holders and brake lever parts. The Trisled Rotovelo velomobile shell is rotomoulded thermoplastic. Rotomoulding is a process more often used to make large storage containers and water tanks.

Thermoset plastics are formed by mixing fluid chemicals that react together exothermically to form solids. They are often reinforced by glass or carbon fibres forming composite materials, and can be more brittle and less recyclable than thermoplastics.

Carbon fibre plastics often use epoxy resins and have a high strength-to-weight ratio. They are used extensively in aircraft manufacture. Carbon fibre can be elastic and act as suspension. It is used to make bicycle, recumbent tricycle and recumbent bike frames, as well as rims, wheels, forks, pedals, cranks, handlebars, wheel covers, seatstays, tailboxes and velomobile shells. DIY building with carbon fibre is mostly for the skilled craftsperson.

Fibreglass composite plastic most commonly combines glass fibre for tensile strength with catalyst-curing polyester resin. It is used to make surfboards, sailboats, canoes and windsurfers and in the HPV world makes recumbent bike seats, fairings and tailboxes. It can be used to reinforce and waterproof plywood and is readily available as kits from canoe shops, surf shops and hardware stores. Care must be taken when handling glass fibre string or cloth, which splinters. Generally, small fibreglassing jobs are simple and safe to do at home.

Corrugated plastic board

This material is the plastic equivalent of corrugated cardboard and is an extruded thermoplastic. It comes in large sheets and is light, inexpensive, tough and long-lasting. It is often called by registered trade names including Corflute and Fluteboard. It is manufactured in Australia by Corex. On bicycles and HPVs it can be used to make mudguards, aerodynamic fairings, spoke covers, tailboxes and luggage-carrying panniers. Just about anyone can make useful vehicle add-ons with plastic board.

Plastic board can be bought new from signwriter's suppliers or found in the form of discarded packaging for steel sheets or election posters. It is available in a variety of thicknesses and weights, and sooner or later you may want to buy new stocks of the right thickness and colour to suit your application.

To start work with plastic board you will need tough scissors, a large Phillips head screwdriver, a texta, a straight edge and some (preferably reusable) cable ties. For more detailed work, a soldering iron and heat gun are useful. To make a sharp bend at any angle, the structure of the board should be weakened by running a screwdriver along a straight edge before creasing. The board will bend more easily along the line of the flutes but creasing is always needed for accuracy. A creased line in plastic board can form a hinge, for example for the lid of a tailbox. Plastic board can be punctured with a screwdriver to make holes for cable ties. This requires considerable force, but an easier way to hole plastic board is with a heated soldering iron. The iron melts the board, and if two layers are holed at the same, the boards fuse together. This process smells and is best done outside, and the soldering iron becomes soiled with molten plastic. It's best to spare any iron used for delicate soldering and get an iron just for working with plastic board.

Tailboxes made from plastic board can be relatively simple and easy to remove from the bike. More complex tailboxes can have better weather protection for luggage and a better aerodynamic shape but become harder to make and remove.

More advanced techniques with plastic board include threading cable ties through one side of the board only for better aerodynamics, and using a heat gun. The heat gun brings the plastic close to its melting point and temporarily relieves its strength allowing shaping around a curve. The curved board can become structural and stronger than flat board. Peter Heal and Andrew Stewart documented manufacture of a tailbox from scratch and their photos are on the web. Matt Heal is on one of Pete's lowracers-with-Corflute-tailbox in the foreground of 17.9.

My building with plastic board has been ad hoc and on the fly. However, with the aid of computer-aided design, plastic board structures can be planned accurately. An example is the 'globe' design (for cutting a flat board to make it cover a sphere) shown in 20.1, which is a layout for a front HPV fairing.

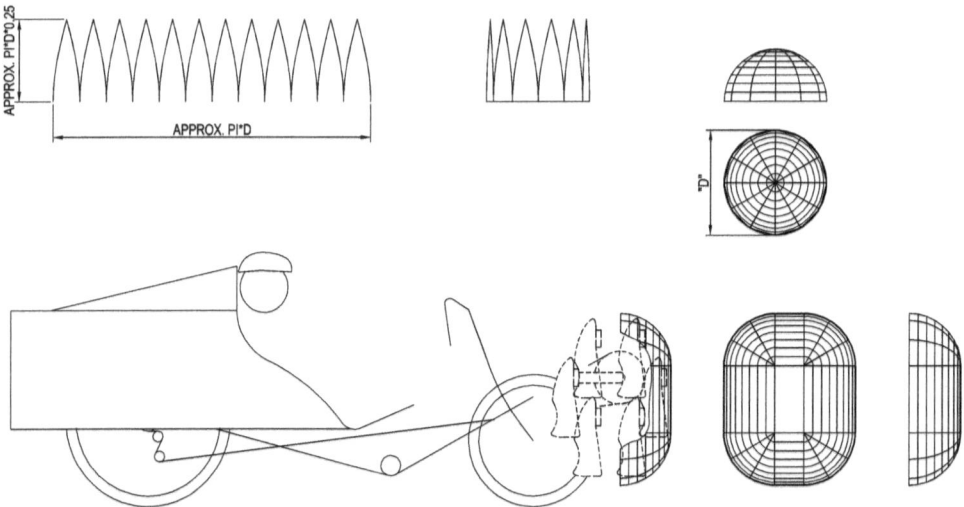

20.1   Layouts for front fairing from Corflute.

Once a folded flat fairing design is in the form of a CAD file, it can be transferred to plastic board using 1:1 prints. For production or greater accuracy CNC laser cutting can be used. MR Components sell a laser-cut Corflute fairing kit for DIY assembly by schools called the Nighthawk.

It's possible that plastic board fairings could be made on demand for customers using manufacturer's or third-party CAD files anywhere there's a water-jet cutter and a stock of board. This would save on shipping.

Timber, grasses and plywood

Timber is a useful, inexpensive and practical material for making cycles and cycle parts. Like metals, it comes in a variety of types, densities and strengths. Increased density usually means increased strength, and the Timber Species and Properties reference provides a guide.

Softwood is usually light in colour and weight but not particularly strong. Hardwood is darker, heavier and stronger. A combination of hard and softwoods can be used to make up a bike with the hardwoods reserved for highly stressed areas like chainstays, forks and bearing seats. Laser-cut steel can reinforce bearing seats on wooden bikes. The larger the laser-cut part the more evenly stresses are distributed into the timber frame.

A knot in a piece of timber is a source of stress concentration like a small hole in a steel tube, and timber with knots should be avoided. If unavoidable, knots should be in frame areas normally in compression.

Timber is available from scrap crates and pallets but is generally cheap enough to buy new. Tools available in Australian homes are more likely to be for woodworking than metalworking. Standard spade drill bits can bore large holes through timber using a standard electric drill.

Bamboo is a rapid-growing grass. It is used directly in bicycle manufacture and in kits for bicycles. Bamboobee make both, and their kits include routed jigs to help frame manufacture. Although bamboo grows naturally as tubes, even the best crops vary in size and shape. This makes it hard to make bamboo bikes in lugged construction. Alexander Vittouris has published work on the Ajiro prototype bamboo velomobile. He shaped bamboo as it grew to be ready for velomobile production.

Plywood is a worked form of timber or bamboo. It is made by peeling thin slices from logs — just like peeling potatoes — and gluing these veneers together in alternate grain directions. The resulting board is trimmed to size and is easier to work than raw timber. With grains in both directions, plywood splits less than timber, which lets cracks propagate in the grain direction. Most plywood has an odd number of layers and is stronger — less bendy — in the visible grain direction. This means that for many cycle parts cut from ply, grain direction is critical and should be specified on drawings. 20.2 shows some plywood parts for the self-jigging tailbox shown in 17.18.

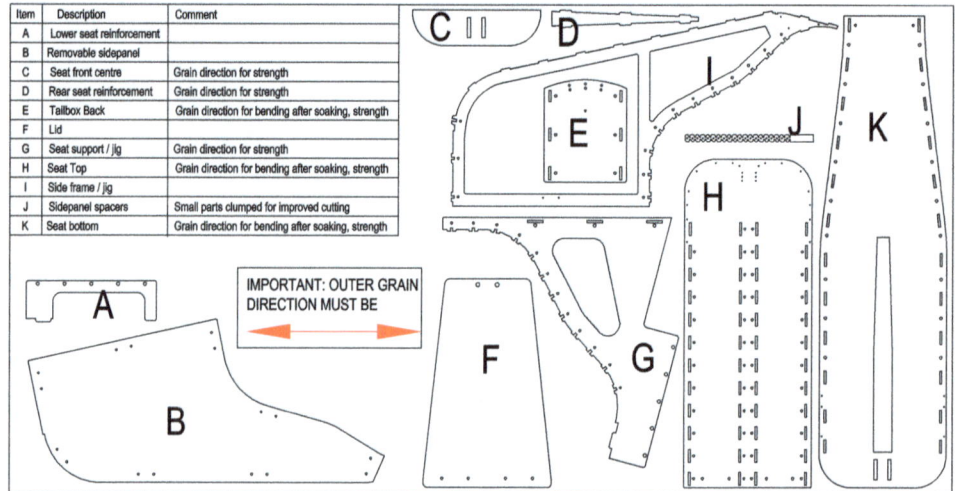

20.2 CNC routed plywood tailbox parts, and notes on grain direction.

Plywood is used as a structural material in boats and can make boxes for load carriers and seats for human powered vehicles. Plywood can be steamed or custom-formed with curves for additional strength. Modern skateboard decks are examples of strong, curved, structural plywood.

Soft materials

Soft foam of the type used to make camping mats make good cushioning on recumbent seats and can cover spokes to make wheels more aerodynamic. This material is often about 10mm thick and is called Zote foam or polyethylene foam sheet. The late John Tetz from the USA was a master Zote foam crafter and used it to make velomobile shells. He documented his work extensively and it is available on the web

Foams with open mesh such as Ventisit/ACS10 breathe and allow air to reach your back on a recumbent seat. It can also provide a shock-absorbing base layer for load-carrying boxes and panniers. Ventisit is sold either as sheets or preformed for specific recumbent seat types.

Lastly, fabrics can be used to make load-carrying panniers. Other uses include fairings and aerodynamic tailboxes for recumbents and velomobiles, or simply for decoration as shown in 17.19. Body socks and tail socks are light and relatively simple to make. One version I made is shown in the background of 17.9.

A large range of materials is available for making cycles. This includes new materials such as steel tube or upcycled materials such as old bike parts.

References

Bamboobee kits https://bamboobee.net/product-category/shop/build-it-

Corex fluteboard http://www.corex.net.au

Foam sheet https://www.par-group.co.uk/sealing-and-jointing/sponge-sheeting/polyethylene-foam-sheet-zote-foam

Tetz J. *Zote foam projects* http://www.recumbents.com/mars/pages/proj/tetz/projtetzmain.html

Morse, L *Tail Sock and Bodysock* https://lonniemorse.wordpress.com/2011/11/30/tail-frame-faq

MR Components *Nighthawk fairing* https://mrrecumbenttrikes.com/racingtrikes/nighthawk-fairing

National Association of Forest Species: *Timber Species and Properties* http://www.tocact.org.au/wp-content/uploads/2016/09/Timberspeciesandproperties.pdf

Heal, P and Stewart, *tailbox building* http://users.tpg.com.au/pheal/Tailbox/Tail_Box.htm

Plywood manufacture by F. A. Mitchell Ltd. https://www.famitchell.com.au/how-is-plywood-made

Recumbent Cycle fibreglass seat https://www.performercycles.com/seat-sd-02

Varney, L. *Greenspeed* GT20 RS review http://www.bentrideronline.com/?p=12828#more-12828

Vittouris, A. Bamboo Velomobile https://www.australasiantransportresearchforum.org.au/sites/default/files/2011_Vittouris_Richardson.pdf

Ventisit/ACS10 https://www.empind.com.au/shop/item/air-circulation-mesh-acs10 and https://www.ventisit.nl/en/applications/recumbents

XYZ trike https://www.n55.dk/MANUALS/SPACEFRAMEVEHICLES/spaceframevehicles.html

21 A boardgame with Alyson McDonald

21.1   Alyson McDonald with Stephen Nurse, December 2019.

21.2   Alyson with boardgame and tokens.

AM: It's early in the morning and because it's going to be 44°C in Melbourne today, we decided to get this interview over before we bake in the heat and Steve has to go home. We're at my dining room table in Richmond, the temperature's alright so we can start.

SN: So I rode over here and it wasn't too hot, but maybe on the way home, I'll break into a sweat.

AM: So what temperature does it have to be for that to happen?

SN: Oh. (laughs) I'm not really a gizmo person. I just go, 'Oh well, it's hot!' you know.

AM: You have to get up the Lennox Street hill, that's already hard core by my standards: I don't like hills! But anyway, Steve, we're going to talk about some boardgames today that you invented, designed, what's the correct terminology?

SN: Well, I guess it's both, and I started working on them 10 years ago and I've added bits and pieces to it in chunks.

AM: So it's ever-evolving, or do you think it's finished now?

SN: Oh, I think it's finished, but what you can see in front of you there, they're little models and bits and pieces, so people can actually add to them and make whatever they like as their game token as in Monopoly tokens. So in that sense it's not ever really finished.

AM: So you mean that other people could design some different ones at some point?

SN: Yes that's right, like none of the little models here are like my bike out the front, and I'm tempted to go, oh, I'll just add another model so people can use that. But there's no reason why you can't use it as a basis for design and make a little 3d print, or make a little 2d cutout that you can use.

21.3 Alyson's Rans Crank Forward bike. Photo Jeremy Lawrence.

AM: So I was going to say it wasn't finished because you haven't made my bike but now you're saying I have to do that for myself! How did you start with the whole boardgames thing anyway?

SN: I saw an article about a Spanish Cycling boardgame website (https://www.cyclingboardgames.net/index.htm) in a magazine called Velovision. They had lots of different boardgames on the site, but focused on the Tour de France or Giro d'Italia, so there's cards of all the famous riders, but they're all riding the same racing bikes.

AM: Right

SN: And I looked at the website and decided to make my own game. Even at that time 10 years ago, people had made up their own games and put them on this cyclingboardgames site.

AM: You were partly inspired by that, but you wanted to make it representative of another type of bike riding, is that right?

SN: Yes. It was sort of to normalise some of the bike culture I'm involved with so the tokens are recumbent trikes and velomobiles, and bikes with front fairings, and things like that, and not excluding racing bikes or town bikes. So yeah, I decided to do that and did it.

AM: Fair enough. But your original version of the game had 2d cut-out-and-fold tokens — oh, including a penny farthing, I didn't know you had that — and I think they've got a bit of a cool vintage vibe that was maybe inspired by that website too.

SN: I probably modelled it on a little tin model bike that was on the site and traced over an image of that to make those pictures.

AM: Yes, and some of them are wearing their bike shorts and their little racing caps, and there's one, he looks like he's just got his normal clothes on. So that's a pretty upright bike.

SN: Yes, that's right, it's sort of more about your experience of cycling, you're not going to win the Tour de France in my boardgame

AM: Oh really.

SN: Yes, if you want to do that you will have to go to the website and find one of the other games.

AM: Oh, right, but I also found, and I don't know whether this was conscious or not but an interesting difference between the previous cutout tokens and the 3d ones is that the 3d ones don't actually have riders on them, and you can sort of imagine yourself being on the bike maybe?

SN: That's right, I guess. It wasn't conscious decision, just what the medium lends itself to. And then once again there's nothing to stop you 3d printing or making a little cutout of you and putting it on the bike, you know that's the next step.

21.4   Dice and boardgame tokens.

AM: Personalisation.

SN: Personalisation, it's what you make of it. So that's an interesting comment, I haven't really thought of it in those terms. But there is one, there's a little person in the velomobile.

21.5   Velomobile part on screen and complete velomobile models.

AM: The person's actually attached and stuck to the wheel.

SN: So not very viable out of the velomobile.

AM: Sort of a velo-beast. And did you, like the models to me look quite realistic, how did they actually start, were they just drawn out of your head, or were you like looking at pictures or actually measuring real bikes or....

SN: Pretty much. In 2d CAD you can get a picture, and you put it in the drawing, and then you just trace over the top of it.

AM: Oh right. So you found photos of bikes viewed from the side, and then you can effectively get the measurements of everything just from that.

SN: Yeah, and then some features are scaled up because you can only print something about 2mm thick.

AM: Ah, because some of the tiny things would end up going into nothing.

SN: Yes, right, (pointing to a model's chain), like that bit's the chain, and it's scaled up. But that's okay, you get the impression of them rather than it actually being them. Another trick I use is to have 1: 25 scale. That's very close to 1mm is 1 inch (1 inch = 25.4mm) and so if you've got a 26" wheel, then you go oh, well in the model that's going to be 26mm and that gets the scaling done. If you can think of the inch size you put it on your model straight away in mm. That's sort of my trick, anyway it works okay.

AM: Yes, they come across as realistic to me. And it's interesting to compare the different bikes from the point of view of them being to scale as well. To change topic a bit, I read the blog post (https://modularbikes.blogspot.com/2010/08/ozhpv-challenge-board-game.html)about your original game concept (Now online, see https://www.thingiverse.com/thing:4068462 SN). That sounded like a real cool game and I was intrigued by the loaded dice. So can you explain that and how it changed when you came out with your later version?

SN: Well if you want to start something, and make, say, the world's greatest cabinet, even if you're not going to make it with your first attempt, you need to make at least one cabinet and then improve,

AM: Sure

SN: And so I wanted to make a boardgame, and I had a go, and it was more or less what I know, which was the OzHPV Challenge, which you've been to. The idea was that one bike type might be better in some events than in others, so one of these speedy velomobiles would be good in a long race where aerodynamics counted, but maybe not so good in the shopping race.

AM: Yes

SN: So the idea was to have a loaded dice to favour a velomobile in the long race. So that you would go round the board in the long-distance race, and so the velomobile dice would have, say two sixes on it.

AM: Right, so each player would have a different dice for each race as well, and you'd end up with lots of different dices.

SN: Yes, you would swap dice for different races, so you would have the dice with two sixes if you were the velomobile in the long-distance race, but you would have the dice with two ones and no sixes if you were in the shopping race with the velomobile. That dice would be a different colour. So I made the dice and a board but abandoned that initially and changed things round a bit and came up with this other concept.

AM: That sounds realistic to show what sort of outcomes you might expect from the different bikes. It could be a really good way to teach probability and so on.

SN: I think the same board as I've got now, or similar, with a hundred steps would be good for kids to play at school. And I think a good way to teach is not to let kids realise that they're actually learning something. Because if you said oh, we're going to learn about probability today, and you know you break out your formulas and they just go 'Oh no'. But then if you say we're going to play with dice, and we've got these little plastic bikes it might be different.

AM: It'd be interesting to see how long it took them to work out they were weird dice and they'd say, 'Oh, I know why it's not fair,' and then they would work out 'I know why it's not fair, because that dice has got two sixes, it's not a proper one.'

SN: I think that's actually the way to go, you don't put everything in front of someone because discovering is what makes learning fun, like being taught is not really all that much fun but if you're discovering along the way then that's a better thing.

AM: You're covering it by experience

SN: Yes and then I really wanted to show all these different bike types.

AM: But anyway, we should probably get back on the current version (https://www.thingiverse.com/thing:3359741). So I guess, even though it was originally based on a race or a competitive event you also wanted to make it relate to real life so can you explain some examples of how you did that?

SN: Well, the game I did later simulates a week in a country town, and you've got a few friends round, and you're spending the night at a pub but you are going for rides during the day and progress round the board and random events happen. So a bit like Monopoly, there are cards with chance items on them, you can pick up shopping or things happen to you. So they are mildly amusing things, you miss a turn, or move forward three places, and some of them are related to the bikes, so there's 'Schoolkids say cool bike' or something like that.

AM: And I take it this is something that's happened to you?

SN: Oh yes, this is my cycling world, and people who ride a standard bike all the time, that might not happen to them. And people yell at you to say, like, 'Your bike's a piece of rubbish, what are you doing on the road?'

AM: Yeah.

SN: And so actually, you ride a slightly different bike, so do you get that?

AM: I do, and actually one of the things I found annoying at first got was how many people would stop and talk because I wasn't into socialising with strangers necessarily. So at the beginning I was thinking, that's a bit weird, why would they want to talk to me, so I got a bit used to it, and maybe it's not so strange a bike anymore, and there's a bit more variety of bikes seen around Melbourne these days. And so generally, there's a lot of people asking where I got it and it's become a pretty standard conversation and it doesn't bother me so much now, but at the beginning I did find it weird! But definitely to translate that experience to when you are touring in country towns especially when there's usually a group, it's an even stranger phenomenon, and you see like, 5 or 10 people on weird bikes, or we've done trips where we've had 3 or 4 bikes with the kids trailers on the back and that sort of stuff and in a group it looks quite spectacular, and you get some sort of reaction from the locals in that case. Yes.

SN: Yes. I've got to say I don't know of any other bikes like yours in Melbourne, but there's no reason why there shouldn't be. I mean, they work for you, and that's your main form of transport, or one of them.

AM: The only reason why you don't see more is that you can't buy them in Australia. So we imported them ourselves, and at one point were considering doing that as a side-business. I'm not sure if you'd actually be making money, and you know, we're busy doing other stuff. If anybody ever asks me about it, I tell them the company you order them from, so if you want one it has to be from America (http://www.ransbikes.com). I like some of the other things that can happen to you on this game. I like the fact that some of the food and drink events are considered positive such as tea and a muffin, whereas others like stopping for a liquid boozy lunch and falling asleep are not positive and I can sort of relate to both of those.

SN: It's not meant to be terribly serious. So I am not sure what age it's designed for but I hope that kids would like it.

AM: Yes and there's a magpie swoop. That's a pretty classic one. What else is there?

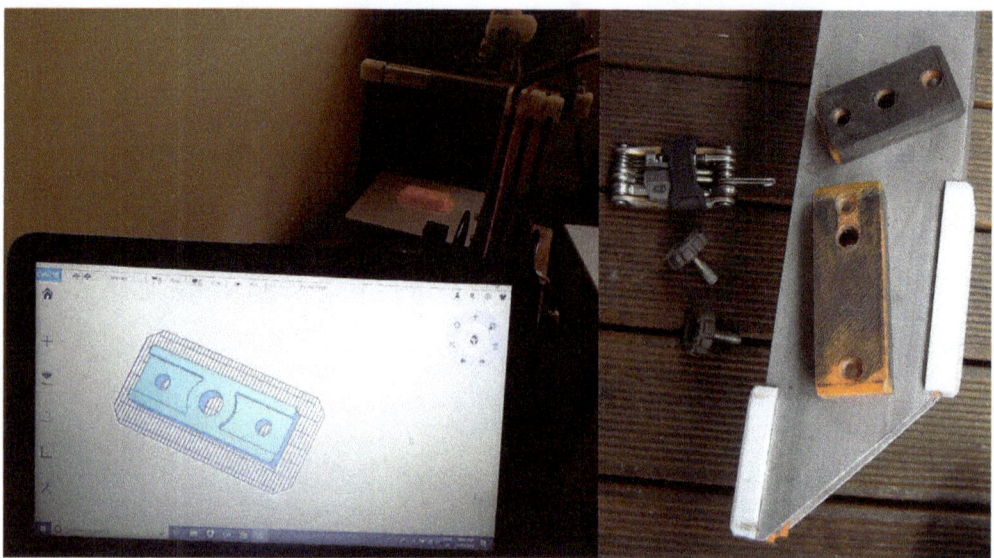

21.6 3d printing equipment, printed bike parts

SN: Well I guess the 3d printing is worth talking about. Up till now the printed boardgame tokens we've discussed have been toys, but I also make 3d printed-at-home parts that do proper jobs on bikes. And it's not just holding a light or something like that, it's almost a structural bike part. So I'm very impressed by what you can do and that people who want to do it don't need much training. Recently I helped some friends who just got a 3d printer get started. And they're making stuff and I showed them my Thingiverse page (https://www.thingiverse.com/stevenurseau/designs) where my models can be uploaded. So I don't know if they'll print these little models but they might.

AM: There were some comments on the boardgames website talking about 3d printing and CAD being difficult, but on the other hand, kids are learning it in schools these days. I'm pretty sure my daughter's school has a 3d printer and presumably they have programs to design and print with, and that's going to become more common. Kids are used to playing computer games and in a way it's just a bit of an extension of that.

SN: Yes, well I see this as interaction with computers but it's positive. It's much more positive than say, an addictive game where you have online purchases. You're relating to the real world.

AM: Yes it's doing something in real life

SN: I'm an engineer, and I've used 2d CAD (computer-aided design) most of my working life, but it was only in the later years that 3d CAD reached engineers like me in smaller industries. But now the bar's much lower. There's free 3d CAD and printing software, and my friends who live round the corner, the son's 16 or 17 and he got one of the software apps and learnt to use it himself, he didn't have industry experience, he just went for it so …

AM: And they have a lot more user friendly interfaces in these free programs, I haven't actually looked at any of them myself because I remember when I learnt it that it was hard to get into. It wasn't obvious when you open up the program how you even started.

SN: Yes the change in computers has been huge, so I'm old enough that when I was at uni we used punched cards to work with computers and like whoa, in 40 years there's been this tremendous change and nobody's foreseen it coming so quickly.

21.7 Enjoying cycling. Photos Jeremy Lawrence

AM: So back to 3d CAD, you can see the object you're designing and turn it around and it's only one small step past that when you actually print it out and say oh, that's what it looks like, that thing that I drew. That must still be exciting though, you actually get the thing out and say it actually looks like what it was supposed to.

SN: Well the old versions of CAD were all 2d and you could only make side or top representations of a bike or something, and then you would have to infer what the whole thing was in 3d. The 2d CAD is just lines and circles and variations on them and you had to construct it yourself and it was quite a skill. But now 3d CAD programs have drawing intelligence and lots of other things built in. They work out component strengths, and how you would change designs to make things stronger. That's big throughout CAD, and has always been one of the advantages and why 3d CAD has been around in car making and aerospace for so long.

AM: Yeah, so they use the program to work out how thick a certain component has to be so it doesn't break and all that sort of stuff.

SN: Yes, and with cars, say, that sort of intelligence built in to an early prototype saves you several months of making things and breaking them.

AM: I think we're done now, thank you.

SN: Thank You!

Appendix: Calculations of rise of rear pivot in Vuong Trikes. A=180, 135, 90 is achievable by mixing diamond and square cranks

FLAT GROUND — R=250, Q0=200, 170=P, 22.5°, 135°=A, 314.1, 184.9 =H0

TYPICAL TILTING — 212.8=Q, S=20°, 36.4, 72.8, 9.1°=RA, 5.6°, 223.1=H, 13.4°=B

MAX. TILT — 200, 55.4°, 135°=A, 120.2=P*sin(A-90)

Diamond, square, octagonal, spline cranks

GEOMETRY

Wheel Radius R	Nominal Track Q0	Pedal radius P	Pedal Angle A	Tilt Angle S	Pedal Drop Angle PDA	H0
mm	mm	mm	degree	degree	(180-A)/2	P×(sin((180-A)/2))
250	200	170	135	20	22.5	184.9

CALCULATED

Rise Angle RA	Rise H	S(MAX)	Actual Track Q0	Scrub Distance Q-Q0
degree	mm	degree	mm	mm
180 - SIN(RA)	R-(P × 0.5 × tan(S))			H-H0
9.1	223.1	55.4	212.8	12.8

Rise of Rear Pivot / Scrub Distance vs Tilt Angle S

R	Q0	P	A	S	H0	0	1	2	3	4	5	10	15	20	30	40	45 max	S(MAX)
250	200	180	180	0	250.0	0.0	0.0	0.0	0.0	0.0	0.0	0.0	0.0	0.0	0.0	0.0	0.0	59.5
250	200	135	135	22.5	184.9	0.0	0.1	0.1	0.1	0.1	0.1	0.4	1.0	1.8	4.6	10.1	14.9	55.4
250	200	90	90	45	129.8	0.0	0.0	0.1	0.1	0.1	0.2	1.3	3.0	5.6	14.8	34.1	–	40.4
250	200	180	180	0	250.0	0.0	0.0	0.0	0.0	0.0	0.0	0.0	0.0	0.0	0.0	0.0	0.0	35.0
250	200	135	135	22.5	223.2	0.0	0.1	0.1	0.1	0.2	0.2	1.0	2.4	4.6	14.7	–	–	30.9
250	200	90	90	45	200.5	0.0	0.1	0.1	0.3	0.3	0.5	0.8	3.2	7.9	16.0	–	–	19.3

Glossary

This book explains a variety of cycles so some jargon is needed. As well I use words like bicycle and cycle particular ways. To help, here is a glossary of some commonly used terms.

Audax: Worldwide, not for profit organisation promoting long distance cycling and awarding cyclists for completing time-limited rides from 50 to 1200km.

bicycle: A 2 wheel human powered vehicle with common styles including folding, diamond frame, step through, mountain, racing. On a bicycle, the line between the seat and the pedal axis is angled close to 70 degrees from horizontal.

bike / cycle: These are casual words for bicycle and bring in a larger range of vehicles such as trikes, ebikes, exercise bikes and recumbent bikes. In the sentence "I forgot to lock my bike", the bike could be any sort of human powered vehicle. Riders might not want or need to specify type.

bikelike: Engineered in a way to suit bicycles and cycling. Cycle weight is the sum of weights of all cycle parts, and cycles are serviced on the road and are out in the weather, so all cycle parts should be designed in a bikelike way for low weight, long wear, corrosion resistance and servicing with common tools.

BMX: Abbreviation for Bicycle Motocross. A style of bike available since the mid 1970's, usually in 20" wheel size. BMX styling is often used on children's bikes. Tyres and other parts originally designed for BMX are used on recumbents.

Butcher's bike: Bike with a small front wheel and large rear wheel designed for carrying loads above the front wheel. Often equipped with large 2-pronged stand for stability when loading.

CAD: Abbreviation for Computer Aided Design / Drafting.

2d CAD: Computer program for creating lines and arcs to build up two dimensional images for sketches, drawings, and file transfer to parts-making-machines.

3d CAD: Computer program for creating, adding and subtracting 3 dimensional solid shapes to build up three dimensional images and models. It is used to make drawings, assess designs, and control parts-making-machines including 3d printers.

3d printer: Machine using input from 3d cad to create parts directly. Sometimes 3d printing is called additive manufacturing, contrasting with manufacturing where material is removed from a blank to make parts.

captain: The rider with the dominant role in steering a tandem cycle. See also stoker

city bike: Bicycle with stepthrough frame, with seat further behind the pedal axis than standard. Allows riders to relax with feet flat on the ground when stopped.

CNC: Abbreviation for Computer Numerical Control, usually describing a manufacturing machine such as a lathe, router, laser cutter or 3d printer.

Corflute: A commercial name for extruded plastic in a two layer sheet form. It is sometimes called fluteboard.

cycle: see bike

delta trike: three wheeler with a single wheel at the front and two at the back.

derailleurs: Cycle parts which derail and control a bicycle chain in the most common, external gearbox type of cycle gearing. When a front derailleur is used, it switches chain between 2 or 3 front chainrings. A rear derailleur provides tension, is always required and switches chain between 5 to 13 rear cogs. See also 1 x drivetrain.

DIY: Abbreviation for Do It Yourself, usually related to making objects.

drivetrain: The set of cycle components for converting human or electric power to forward motion on a cycle.

1 x drivetrain: Derailleur gearing system relying on a single front chainring and multiple rear cogs. 1 x systems using generic chains have up to 8 rear cogs and ranges up to 11 to 42 teeth. 1 x drivetrains with 9 or more cogs use proprietary chains and parts and can have wider ranges.

dropout: Plate or lug that wheel bolts attach to.

DXF: Abbreviation for Document Exchange Format. An editable type of CAD file used to transmit information between 2d CAD programs and CNC machines.

ebike: Electrically assisted bike. They're part of a broader class of ecycles (E-cycles or Ecycles or e-cycles, take you pick) which include electric mountain bikes (emtb) and electric trikes (etrikes) and others.

electric bike: see ebike.

faired: Describing cycles including one or more fairings or aerodynamic aids. Velomobiles are usually completely faired with an aerodynamic shell surrounding the rider.

freight bike / load bike / cargo bike: Cycle with frame, wheel size or other significant features making it more suitable for load carrying.

FBB: FWD bike with the pedal axis fixed to the frame and not moving with steering. Zox bikes make an extensive range and the Raptobike is also FBB.

FWD: Abbreviation for front wheel drive. Recumbent bikes are often FWD machines.

groupset: Set of parts from a single supplier including most parts required for a cycle, ie cranks, pedals, derailleurs, brakes, brake levers, gear change levers, rear sprockets, bottom bracket and sometimes wheels.

highracer: Recumbent bicycle with groupset parts including 700C wheels, chainring, derailleurs, bottom bracket bearing, brakes and gearchangers. These parts are often interchangeable with racing bike parts.

HPV: Abbreviation for Human Powered Vehicle including vehicles travelling on land, sea and air.

longbike: Bicycles extended for load or passenger carrying including longtail and longjohn designs.

longjohn: Bicycle for load or passenger carrying with long or extended frame and steering link in front of the rider.

longtail: Bicycle for load and passenger carrying with long or extended chain and frame behind the rider.

lowracer: Recumbent bicycle with minimal height. Lowracers are designed for high speed through reduced frontal area. On lowracers, riders stay stable when stopped by using their hands as props.

MBB: FWD bike with the pedal axis moving with the steered front wheel. Cruzbikes are a well known example.

MTB: Abbreviation for Mountain Bike. A bicycle style originally designed for off-road use, built rugged with knobbly tyres and wide-range gearing. The style has influenced all cycling. Parts designed for MTB's include disc brakes, thru axles, flat handlebars and 1 x drivetrains.

OzHPV inc. : Abbreviation for Australian Human Powered Vehicles, an organisation promoting open – design Human Powered Vehicles including racing and touring. Sister organisations include BHPC / British Human Power Club and Trampkraft in Sweden. More details http://www.whpva.org/organisation.html

Pedal Prix: Australian velomobile racing for school and community groups. Races usually last from 6 to 24 hours, and riders take turns pedalling. Vehicles comply and are checked to a set of rules – for example riders must wear seatbelts – that ensure safety.

PLA: Abbreviation for Polylactic Acid. It is a corn-derived biodegradable plastic, and a material commonly used for home 3d printing.

quad / quadracycle: Lightweight 4 wheeled vehicle. They can be relatively heavy and complex but have good static and dynamic stability.

recumbent: Adjective describing a cycle where the line between the seat base and the pedal axis is close to horizontal. It's used as a noun as well, meaning a cycle where the line between the seat base and the pedal axis is close to horizontal.

recumbent bike / recumbent bicycle: Recumbent 2 wheeled human powered vehicle.

recumbent trike / recumbent tricycle: Recumbent 3 wheeled human powered vehicle.

RWD: Abbreviation for rear wheel drive. The default for most cycles.

speedbike: Fully faired recumbent cycle – usually a 2 wheeled lowracer – designed for ultimate outright speed.

stoker: Rider who contributes to a cycle's power but does not steer.

STL: A file format for communicating shape information from 3d CAD programs. From an STL file an object can be made using a 3d printer.

tadpole trike: Three wheeler with two wheels at the front and one at the back.

tandem: Cycle with two riders, one behind the other. Tandems can be fast because they have motive force of two riders without undue extra weight or wind resistance.

thru axle: Lightweight wheel shaft used to properly secure disc brake wheels. Thru is rarely spelt fully (through) in bicycle or engineering use.

tilting trike / leaning trike / tilter: A three wheel cycle with a mechanism allowing tilting during cornering.

trike / tricycle: Three wheeled human powered vehicle

tube mitreing: Cycle frame building method: cutting a round tube in preparation for attaching another round tube. Accurate mitreing is important when brazing because close contact between surfaces is needed for high weld strength.

upright bike: Bicycle

velomobile: Recumbent trike with a near-complete surrounding shell, mainly for aerodynamics but also for weather protection.

Picture Credits

Picture not credited in main text are by Stephen Nurse or from Wikimedia Commons. Thanks to all these Wikimedia Commons photographers for contributing under Creative Commons and other Licences. Credits and links to files and their licences are below.

Files licensed under Creative Commons Attribution-Share Alike 4.0 International .

9.5   2016 Gomier Trike by Solomon203
      https://commons.wikimedia.org/wiki/File:Gomier_Manufacturing_tricycle_of_Taiwan_Yakurt_20160422.jpg

9.6   Windcheetah trike by Erik Wannee
      https://commons.wikimedia.org/wiki/File:Windcheetah.jpg

9.23 Varna Handcycle by Erik Wannee
      https://commons.wikimedia.org/wiki/File:Varna_handbike.jpg

10.16 Flevobike_rug-aan-rug by Erik Wannee
      https://commons.wikimedia.org/wiki/File:Flevobike_rug-aan-rug.jpg

10.24 Van Raam Double Rider by Erik Wannee
      https://commons.wikimedia.org/wiki/File:Van_Raam_Double_rider.jpg

16.8 Jouta VX lean to steer trike by Erik Wannee
      https://commons.wikimedia.org/wiki/File:Jouta_VX.jpg

10.25 4 wheeled sociable surrey by Pacopac
      https://commons.wikimedia.org/wiki/File:2019-12-26_Quadricicle_espentat_per_turismes_al_Jard%C3%AD_del_T%C3%BAria_a_Val%C3%A8ncia_01.jpg

11.10 Bikepacking in Oregon, USA by KBryan0409
      https://commons.wikimedia.org/wiki/File:Bikepacking_on_a_fatbike_in_Eastern_Oregon.jpg

11.28 Electric cargo recumbent quad by Leonhard Lenz
      https://commons.wikimedia.org/wiki/File:Cargo_Bike_Spring_Race_at_the_International_Cargo_Bike_Festival_Berlin_2018_07.jpg

13.3 Wooden balance bike by brumbrumbikes
      https://commons.wikimedia.org/wiki/File:Brum_Brum_Wooden_Balance_Bike_for_Kids.jpg

16.3 Pushing a skateboard by Wil540

https://commons.wikimedia.org/wiki/File:A_hard_push_-_Far_Rockaway_Skatepark_-_September_-_2019.jpg

16.24 Yamaha Niken motorbike. Yamaha Niken by Wikimedia Commons user Thesupermat.

https://commons.wikimedia.org/wiki/File:Yamaha_Niken_-_Mondial_de_l%27Automobile_de_Paris_2018_-_003.jpg

Files licensed under Creative Commons Attribution-Share Alike 3.0 Unported .

9.10 Alleweder Velomobile by kapege.de

https://commons.wikimedia.org/wiki/File:Alleweder.jpg

10.5 IGo trailerbike by Weehoo

https://commons.wikimedia.org/wiki/File:IGo_by_Weehoo_Inc2.jpg

Released into public Domain

10.26 Pedalled Cafe in Wierden by HandigeHarry

https://commons.wikimedia.org/wiki/File:Fietscaf%C3%A9.JPG

Files licensed under GNU Free Documentation License.

16.13 Tripendo tadpole leaning trike by Drahkrub

https://commons.wikimedia.org/wiki/File:TripendoTilted.jpg

www.ingramcontent.com/pod-product-compliance
Lightning Source LLC
Chambersburg PA
CBHW061131010526
44107CB00068B/2906